"Pam Douglas takes on the complicated business of episodic television and makes great, grand sense of it. For years she's been a star of USC's School of Cinematic Arts, imparting these secrets to her students. Now these secrets have been written down. A textbook, a how-to, a resource, an inspiration, this book has knowledge, has wisdom, is a joy to read."
Howard A. Rodman, Artistic Director, Sundance Screenwriting Labs

"Solid career advice and industry insights. Provides crucial foundational guidance for the aspiring television drama writer."
David Trueman, reviewer, *Script Magazine*

"*Writing the TV Drama Series* sheds much-needed light onto the befuddled, and oft overlooked subject of television programming development — invaluable to teachers, students, or anyone else interested in the world of television."
Brian Johns, Eastman Kodak Scholarship Program Director

"Written by a television insider, this well-written text takes one, step by step, through the maze on why and how television programs make it from pitch to script to pilot to series. Pam Douglas' style is fun to read; she packs in information and the definite how-to's of making it as a series television writer."
Jule Selbo has been a series writer/producer on *Life Goes On, Young Indiana Jones Chronicles, Melrose Place, Undressed, Maya and Miguel* and many others

"Remarkably comprehensive and up-to-date, *Writing the TV Drama Series* is a candid, enthusiastic introduction to the craft and culture of dramatic television."
Jeff Melvoin, Executive Producer, *Alias, Northern Exposure*

"Pamela Douglas provides valuable insights and insider tips in this essential guide to writing the television drama. Her step-by-step instruction to jumpstarting and surviving a career in the television business is packed with current industry information and practical advice from renowned industry pros. Chapter Five, which highlights working on staff, is dead-on. It took me years to learn what Pam has so artfully and honestly laid out. A must-read for any aspiring television writer."
Toni Graphia, Writer-Producer, *Roswell, Carnivale, Battlestar Galactica*

"This book covers the waterfront in writing for dramatic television."
Peter Lefcourt, Writer-Producer, *Beggars & Choosers, Karen Sisco, Cagney & Lacey*

"A knowledgeable insight to writing TV drama. A book that is a delight to read."
Amy Taylor, Cedar Grove Entertainment

"Right now is the golden age of TV drama, and this book is far and away the best resource I know of for any writer wishing to work in this tremendously challenging and rewarding field."
Daniel Petrie, Jr., President, Writers Guild of America, West; *The Big Easy, Beverly Hills Cop*

"Pamela Douglas demystifies the entire process of writing one of the most intimidating and challenging formats — the television drama series. This comprehensive book takes the reader on a step-by-step journey from the birth of a series concept to what happens long after the final scene has been shot. Suddenly, the impossible seems possible, thanks to *Writing the TV Drama Series*."

Marie Jones, book reviewer, absolutewrite.com

"The breadth and depth of practical advice on real-world writing should enlighten and inspire any aspiring TV drama writer. It should enlighten because it is clear, free of jargon, and explains the business and the design of television dramas. It should inspire because it cuts to the chase — a writer gets an outline of the drama life cycle and knows what is required from pitch to pilot to longevity of a series. The interviews with successful writers makes this book valuable all by themselves, but there's so much more."

Diane Carson, Ph.D., Editorial Vice President, University Film & Video Association

"*Writing the TV Drama Series* is an invaluable resource for anyone aspiring to be a television writer. Having worked with beginning writers for years, the information in Pamela's book is exactly what they need to know: how to write excellent scripts and how to become savvy enough about the business to break in and get their first job writing for television. I recommend it to every new writer I work with."

Carole Kirschner, Head of the CBS Diversity Institute Writers Mentoring Program; Program Director, WGA Showrunner Training Program

"Pamela Douglas has written 'the' book on writing hour episodic drama. She breaks the process down into simple-to-understand steps, while carefully weaving the inseparable elements of craft and business. This is a must read for any screenwriter who wants to get in — and stay in — the television series loop. In the rapidly changing landscape of hour episodic television, Pamela Douglas is on top of the trends and thinking one step ahead of them. Essentially, she has created the gold standard for any book on this topic."

Catherine Clinch, Contributing Editor, *Creative Screenwriting Magazine*; Publisher, MomsMediaWorld.com

"*Writing the TV Drama Series* is both practical and enjoyable; I repeatedly recommend this guide to series writing to aspiring television writers. Douglas keeps it easy to follow, and every page is loaded with valuable information that will help writers navigate those challenging first years."

Erika Kennair, Entertainment Diversity Representative, NBC Entertainment Strategy Dept.

"Through her experiences as a writer on well-known series, Pamela Douglas teaches you to write from the heart while being conscious of all of the details that accompany working in the fast-paced world of television: writing within budget, analyzing and breaking down scenes, working with a staff of writers, the drafting process from outline to shooting script, and breaking into the business. As a production assistant working on a serial program, *Writing the TV Drama Series* helped me to understand how a concept is developed into a full story that airs over months. I know it will help you too."

Joshua Friedman, author: *Getting It Done*

"Think of Pamela Douglas as a Sorcerer and that you're lucky enough to be her apprentice. The 3rd Edition of *Writing The TV Drama Series* delivers on many levels."
> D.B. Gilles, author: *The Screenwriter Within* and *You're Funny! Turn Your Sense of Humor Into a Lucrative New Career*

"*Writing the TV Drama Series* remains the best of book of its kind, a must-have not only for aspiring (or working) drama writers, but for producers, execs, agents, and anyone who needs to understand — or think critically about — the inner workings of TV dramas."
> Chad Gervich, writer/producer: *After Lately, Cupcake Wars, Wipeout*; author: *Small Screen, Big Picture: A Writer's Guide to the TV Business*

"For the past decade or so, TV drama has been the most interesting and successful form of storytelling in our culture. And I can't imagine a better one-volume guide to writing TV drama than Pamela Douglas' book."
> Michael Cassutt, writer/producer: *Max Headroom, Beverly Hills 90201, The Dead Zone*

"I took Professor Douglas' class as a graduate student at USC — it was her guidance that led me into a career in television. This book is a brilliant distillation of that semester with the added bonus that I can refer back to the juicy bits when I'm in a bind. I keep my copy at work so I can review her practical advice on how to structure a script, what makes a character compelling, and how to make a scene sing. And her chapter on how to behave on a writing staff is invaluable — commit it to memory!"
> Janet Lin, writer/producer: *Bones*

"The definitive work on dramatic TV writing just got more definitive. Pamela Douglas' brilliant 3rd Edition is a must-have for anyone seriously considering writing television. This is not a how-to book, but rather a manifesto for great television writing."
> Jack Epps, Jr., Chair of the Writing Division, School of Cinematic Arts, University of Southern California; screenwriter: *Top Gun, Dick Tracy, The Secret of My Success*

"From fan of television to the aspiring writer to the established professional, Pamela Douglas' *Writing the TV Drama Series* (3rd edition) deserves to be read, studied, and embraced. Easily digestible with end of the chapter summaries, teleplay excerpts, and analysis and interviews with some of the most talented and important writers in the business, her book is not only an excellent read, but more importantly, inspiring. If television is considered to be the writer's medium, *Writing the TV Drama Series* is the best resource that I've ever come across."
> Stefan Blitz, editor-in-chief, ForcesOfGeek.com

"The book is wise and wonderful, better than any book on writing TV series that I've read. I'm depressed because I wish I had read it before I had written the last two series proposals. Chapters Two and Three are essential for anyone wanting to write a series. Highly recommended!"
> Christopher Keane, author: *Romancing the A List*; writer/co-producer: *The Huntress*

"In all my years working as a writer and a teacher of screenwriting, *Writing the TV Drama Series* is the most comprehensive and user-friendly book that I have come across on how to construct a drama series from the idea stage through the finished pilot script. It's focused, precise, and above all, entertaining. I plan on recommending it to anyone with a mind toward writing for the small screen."

Maria Jackquemetton, writer/executive producer: *Mad Men*

"Fascinating, informative, and thoughtful. Pamela Douglas' new edition of her book deconstructs the television drama in a way that makes it an accessible and invaluable tool for both beginners and professionals alike. I wish I'd had a book like this when I was starting out in the TV business!"

Nicole Yorkin, co-executive producer: *The Killing*, writer-producer: *Flash-Forward*, *The Riches*, *Carnivale*, *Judging Amy*

"As many are beginning to realize, we are living in the Golden Age of Television. Shows such as *The Sopranos*, *The Wire*, *Mad Men*, and *Breaking Bad* demonstrate that continuing storylines enable TV series to tell epic tales that follow the triumphs, pratfalls, heartbreaks, and false epiphanies of ensembles of characters over the course of years and even decades. It is the kind of storytelling that Tolstoy and Dickens explored and the best TV series today display the same texture, nuance, and eye for detail as those masters of the epic novel. Yet there are few books that help aspiring television writers gain a fundamental understanding of crafting a teleplay. This book by Pamela Douglas is one such volume. The author's professional savvy comes through on every page. This is an excellent source for anyone interested in writing for the most dynamic art form of our time."

David Weddle, writer/supervising producer for *Battlestar Galactica*, writer/co-executive producer for *CSI* and *Falling Skies*, author of *"If They Move Kill 'Em!" The Life and Times of Sam Peckinpah*

"There are few people who so innately understand story as Pamela Douglas. Her explanation of the narrative process is concise and inspiring. However, this book is not simply a tutorial in structure and character. Douglas clearly details the political realities of collaborating with people throughout the television industry, providing essential lessons for anyone hoping to succeed in the business in any creative capacity."

Bear McCreary, Emmy-nominated composer of *Battlestar Galactica*, *The Walking Dead*, *Eureka*, and *Terminator: The Sarah Connor Chronicles*

WRITING THE TV DRAMA SERIES
HOW TO SUCCEED AS A PROFESSIONAL WRITER IN TV

3RD EDITION

BY
PAMELA DOUGLAS

MICHAEL WIESE PRODUCTIONS

Published by Michael Wiese Productions
12400 Ventura Blvd. #1111
Studio City, CA 91604
(818) 379-8799, (818) 986-3408 (FAX)
mw@mwp.com
www.mwp.com

Cover design by MWP
Interior design by William Morosi
Printed by McNaughton & Gunn

Manufactured in the United States of America

Library of Congress Cataloging-in-Publication Data

Douglas, Pamela
 Writing the TV drama series / Pamela Douglas. -- 3rd ed.
    p. cm.
 Includes bibliographical references.
 ISBN 978-1-61593-058-6
 1. Television authorship. 2. Television series--Authorship. I. Title.
 PN1992.7.D68 2011
 808.2'25--dc22
                                    2011017715

To Raya Yarbrough and John Spencer
with love

Table Of Contents

Chapter One

Chapter Two

Chapter Three

Chapter Four

Chapter Five

Chapter Six

Chapter Seven

Chapter Eight

Preface to the Third Edition

In times of great change, the question is: *what remains?*

In 2005, when the First Edition of *Writing the TV Drama Series* was published, the rules of TV were knowable and clear. Hour dramas had four acts with commercial breaks every 13 minutes or so. A network TV season was usually 22 episodes that ran from September to May. And viewers sat on living room couches to watch their TV sets, tuning in to their favorite programs at the times when the programs were scheduled for broadcast.

Back then, I wanted to tell you how to get into this field and do good work once you're here. That much remains.

By the Second Edition in 2007, many of the rules had changed — but the rules were still clear. On broadcast TV, hour drama shows went to five or six acts; basic cable was offering scripted series that followed traditional paradigms; on premium cable, HBO and Showtime always won the critical awards, and their commercial-free model had become a distinct form of its own. Pilot opportunities for new writers had blown open, but the pilots themselves were written and made the same way they'd always been.

Back then, I wanted to tell you how to use the new rules to write well and succeed. That remains also.

For the Third Edition, I initially thought I'd update the major shows, add a few fresh interviews, and reflect more of what's happening in alternative forms and on the Internet. But as I researched this edition, I discovered that almost everyone — from showrunners to struggling writers to industry executives to new media creators — were no longer merely adjusting the rules. Now they were asking basic questions: What is television? What is drama? What is a series? What are the delivery options? What are our obligations to the audience? Does a mass audience exist? Even what is reality?

And yet, after the smoke clears, more remains than appeared at first. No matter whom I asked about the future of television, the name of Aristotle, the ancient Greek philosopher, kept being invoked, not only by writers of great drama series, but by someone doing Webisodes and someone else making "Unscripted" shows. Though Aristotle set out the principles of drama thousands of years ago to describe archetypal tragedies in the plays of his time, those essential dramatic principles remain today.

The writer's skill at storytelling, understanding what drives human beings, the guts to touch the passions, fears and aspirations of viewers, and honestly portray the universal issues of our lives — that content still relies on the art, craft, and insight of people who write.

So this Third Edition will present it all: the traditional basis for writing TV drama juxtaposed with new forms, traditional delivery systems seen in the light of current technology, and interviews with "Guest Speakers" whose ideas diverge from each other more than in past editions. These range from deep social reality that concerns the creator of *The Wire*, to nuts-and-bolts from a producer of so-called "Reality" shows, and from working writers coping with a shifting marketplace to programming decisions by the President of AMC cable who is part of shifting that marketplace.

In the past I paraphrased *All About Eve*, advising readers to hold on to their seat belts. But in zero gravity, the challenge is instead to go with the flow as you explore an evolving landscape. In a world afloat, it turns out that the TV drama series is something that does remain.

Introduction

More than a thousand students have come through my classes in the two decades I've taught at the USC School of Cinematic Arts. At the same time, my professional career was growing to include story editor and producer credits on television dramas, the Humanitas Prize, and awards and nominations including Emmys, Writers Guild, and American Women in Radio and Television, and a position on the Board of Directors of the Writers Guild. Always, my screenwriting and teaching have complemented each other.

I bring my working life into the classroom: What is it like to be actively breaking stories, writing, rewriting, giving and getting notes, seeing how your scripts translate to screen? I clearly recall freelancing television episodes, but I also know how the other side of the desk reacts to pitches, because I've been in both chairs. I've written for both broadcast and cable, and for virtually every dramatic genre. In my class, students learn from someone who has been there.

Imagine you've stopped by a typical episodic drama class in the middle of a term. Ten students sit at a table, scripts and DVDs from our in-class library — *House, The Good Wife, Mad Men, Breaking Bad, Dexter, The Wire* — among others in the middle. The class has not begun, but people are returning scripts and discs, reaching for one they want next.

At the beginning of a term I used to ask if any students didn't have a television so I could pair them with someone who did. But when I asked in 2009, the whole class raised their hands. I started getting on their cases: How can you speculate episodes for shows you've never seen? Was it laziness? Arrogance? *No!*, they responded. They were watching — just not on a television set. Everyone was viewing on a computer, or even a cell phone. They knew even more shows than in previous years; they were ready.

In class, we operate like the writing staff of a TV series in which writers suggest improvements on each other's work, while I function as "showrunner," or final authority on revisions. The standard is professional quality, and our models are the most brilliant, incisive, daring scripts

1

on networks or cable. Since I hold the bar so high, no one brings in trivial subjects. Because television drama frequently reflects complex and wrenching problems in contemporary society — such as racism, sexism, violence, spirituality, and sexual identity — the writers must confront these issues with honesty at the same time as they learn their craft.

On other occasions, I come to class in the midst of my writing, full of some creative problem, and let the class in on my process. Or I might screen a clip and deconstruct its elements and how it fits within the total structure of a show. All this leads to finished scripts that aim to be competitive with the best drama written for screen.

That's my goal for you too as you work with this book. My students are sophisticated, smart, dedicated, and some are wonderfully talented. Still, I was initially surprised at what they didn't know. When I add my summer seminars, which are open to the public, I discovered strange misconceptions about television, the art and craft of TV drama, and the life of a working writer. That's one of my reasons for creating this book, since I'm uniquely aware of what beginning writers want and need to learn.

My approach is practical: The better you write, the more work you'll get. Give 'em better than they deserve because you deserve the best, even if your first assignment is on something you leave off your resume years later.

As you go through this book, imagine that you're in my classroom. I'll be talking to you, even asking you questions. Though I can't hear your answers, I suggest you treat the chapters interactively anyway so that you'll be applying the principles.

Throughout, you'll find useful tools, a complete map of the TV series terrain, and lessons from those who have traveled it before. But, ultimately, the way to write better is to be true to what's real in your stories and to write more. You're not alone — I'll show you how.

What's New In This Edition

If you're familiar with the Second Edition, you'll notice how much has been updated. Though the chapters on craft present the same essential principles, small changes occur throughout, replacing older shows with current ones and considering the Internet and new platforms in all subjects.

Among the larger changes, the book has gone from seven chapters to eight. The final chapter that was a brief treatment of new outlets in the Second Edition is now a full chapter dealing with the future of TV drama on the Internet, the impact of new delivery potentials on writers, and an international perspective. Since the book has become global, I thought that expansion would be significant.

Entirely new "Spotlight" sections include one on "Dramedy" and one on "Unscripted/Reality TV." Also the "Procedurals" section is more comprehensive and now includes *House* and *The Good Wife* as well as *CSI*. The Pilot section has been amplified as well.

Among the fresh interviews, I'm especially proud of landing one with Charlie Collier, the President of AMC Cable TV. I never had a network president in the book before, but the rise of basic cable as a phenomenon made this relevant. Other new interviews include: David Isaacs (*M*A*S*H*, *Mad Men*), Michelle and Robert King (*The Good Wife*), David Simon (*The Wire*), and others. In the Reality segment I have a candid interview with a Reality producer, and other writer-producers have been quoted throughout.

I re-interviewed Steven Bochco, and edited his earlier interview to blend with this one. I also re-interviewed my former students, creating a unique longitudinal study of what happens to film students in the 14 years after they graduate.

To make room for all these enhancements, I had to edit out some interesting material from the Second Edition. Interviews with the producers of *Lost, Battlestar Galactica* and *Deadwood* are gone, as is the blogging chapter on *Grey's Anatomy*. Instead, I incorporated portions of those in other chapters. You can access the full deleted interviews in the Archives section of my website *www.PamDouglasBooks.com.*

My motivations for working so hard on this Third Edition are partly in response to how much television is evolving, and partly in response to the respect with which this book has been met, for which I'm grateful. Not only has it been recognized as the premiere book on the subject world-wide, but I've discovered that it has two distinct readerships. The main one, of course, is people who hope to become writers, both students and the general public. But we're gradually accruing a second audience: people reading for insights into contemporary media. For example, Critical Studies scholars and Communications analysts have been referring to this book, and my interviews (including those for the international translations) have asked more about the nature of dramatic television than about how to break in or how to write a scene. That's a little different from a few years ago. I wanted this new edition to be truly comprehensive in order to keep its mantle as THE book on this subject.

How to Use this Book

If You're a Writer...

The entire template is here. All you have to do is follow the chapters, step by step.

I recommend this process: First, read through the entire book for an overview. During this early read don't worry about taking notes or writing your script. Understand the terrain and the many options. Chapter One, Chapter Eight, and all the interviews are especially helpful for this kind of survey.

Second: Prepare to write your own scripts. It's a good idea to generate at least two — one spec episode for an existing show and one original pilot. It's even better to have more than one of each, but you have to start somewhere. Of course, some of you are more advanced and already have scripts. In that case, use this process for revisions.

If you begin with a spec episode, it's up to you to study your show on your own. That means watching every episode available and accessing all relevant websites. The systems in this book will work for any hour drama series, but some shows are better choices than others.

Rule One: Choose quality. Even the worst shows hire the best writers they can find, and by best I mean writers who deliver authentic characters and situations. Imitating weak or contrived writing will just make you look untalented. At the beginning of 2011, samples being widely read by agents and producers include *Breaking Bad, Dexter, House, The Good Wife,* and a few others. If you're reading this in future years, you can figure out what's worth speculating by following the most-current Writers Guild and Emmy award nominees for writing.

Rule Two: Choose a show in current production. This requires a bit of research because shows may be on the air but in a final season. So an excellent series like *Friday Night Lights,* which concluded production, would not be useful even though it's still running. The reason is purely practical: writing contests tend to require current samples. But that absolutely does not mean you should avoid learning from great classic shows like *The Sopranos*. In fact, you must! Just don't spec those shows.

Rule Three: Choose a show where you can bring a fresh insight or experience that fits its world. For example, if you don't know the culture of New Orleans, don't even think of writing for *Treme*; no matter how much research you might do, it will come out fake. On the other hand, you don't have to be a psychopathic killer to write for *Dexter* — although you do need to understand how he thinks.

Once you've chosen the show and learned it well, turn to the book. Re-read Chapter Three. See the analysis of the classic series? Now go to the show you've chosen and see if you can break it down into scenes like this, or into sequences. Define the "A," "B," and "C" (and maybe "D") stories. See if you can make a grid for an episode, even in very rough form. Then make a grid for your own episode.

Next, go on to Chapter Four and follow each step — Outline, First Draft, Second Draft, and Polish. While you're working, check in with the scripts (or DVDs) from the show. Have you caught the voices? The rhythm of the scenes?

If you're writing a pilot, start by re-reading the "Spotlight On Writing Your Pilot Script," which is between Chapter Four and Chapter Five. Then go back to Chapter Four and follow all the development steps — Outline, First Draft, Second Draft, and Polish.

While you're writing, be an artist and set aside your marketing head. After you're done, you'll be able to use Chapter Six on how to break in. And if you're fortunate, you'll be ready for Chapter Five about working on a staff. But take your mind off "*Ka-Ching!*" — at least until you have something worth offering. Pandering to a quick buck will sabotage your career. As I told you, even the worst shows try to hire the best writers.

If You're a Teacher...

This book follows a syllabus I've honed over the years and I'm consistently using, so I know it works. Each student is required to have a copy of this book, and I've found it helps to refer students to specific pages to see how to pitch and outline, and to read about scene structure, act structure, and all the aspects of storytelling. That doesn't eliminate the need to teach those subjects, but seeing examples makes life easier for everyone.

I teach the chapters in the same order they appear in the book, except that the class in writing spec episodes is separate from the class in writing pilots. My students spend a semester in the spec class to learn the essentials of writing for series, and at USC that class is a prerequisite to writing an original pilot. Both classes use this book, but I emphasize different chapters.

I also amplify the text by screening and analyzing episodes. The explications of two *NYPD Blue* segments in Chapter Three are examples of deconstructing scenes purely from a writing point of view. For the spec class I begin with a show they might write, and later in the term I screen clips from classic shows that demonstrate specific principles. I've found that students may learn better from a classic they're not attempting so the techniques stand out. For instance, selected scenes from *The Sopranos* and *The Wire* are especially revealing though the students wouldn't write those shows. For the pilot class I like to screen opening scenes from *Lost* and *The West Wing* because they demonstrate how to focus on character within a large ensemble. But you could choose clips from any drama series you admire. Your personal enthusiasm for the work will count.

One other difference between the book and the classroom is that I don't use guest speakers in real life. In the book they add dimension and inspiration. But in my classes I give personal, direct feedback on whatever each student is writing, so we function like a workshop or writers room. Assuming that you are a professional writer, you know this process of notes all too well. The class will feel like every show you've ever worked on.

I do not use and I disagree with "exercises." In my opinion, the practice of not-really-writing — doing some sort of literary calisthenics — trivializes the creative process and wastes time. Any principles that can be gleaned from some academic exercise are better absorbed when a student is motivated by building to a product. If the students are going to complete at least one (preferably two) drafts of a teleplay in a few short months, they need every writing moment to work on their scripts.

I hope that if you are teaching people to write, you are a writer your-self. But some of you who may offer workshops on TV series are from the business, marketing or administrative/executive sides instead, and I'd like to help you be successful too. In fact, this book might be even more vital to you because it includes voices and experiences of actual writers and reflects their process, which amplifies the different experience you bring. But I suggest that you vary your curriculum to present more about sales and careers and less involvement in the art of writing. The book can be adapted that way by emphasizing Chapters One, Two, Five, Six, and Eight, which place television drama in a socio-economic context and explain how the industry works.

In addition to teaching how to write for existing series and how to write a pilot, USC also offers a survey course in the history and analysis of television series, examining shows from the 1950s to the present from a screenwriting viewpoint. It's taught by one of my colleagues in the Screenwriting Division of the School of Cinematic Arts, and has become a popular part of a liberal arts education.

I mention that to give perspective to your role as a teacher. I believe that we, as teachers, have an obligation to help people become educated in the larger sense. Television has a literature as extensive as theatrical films. No teacher of feature screenplays would ignore all Oscar-winning movies from the past five years (not to mention *Casablanca, Chinatown, The Godfather*, or the Hitchcock legacy) when presenting the art of screen-writing and instead limit all examples and aspirations to whatever movies happen to be selling tickets this month. Yet in television, you may feel pressure to deal with only this season's fleeting hits. Resist.

Of course, you know to tell students to write for current shows and create sample scripts that will leverage their careers. But you also know that this season's shows are probably not the ones that will matter in five years, maybe not even next year when your students graduate. How can you reconcile that contradiction? The solution is to communicate the approaches that will last. You can start your students on a solid path, but they have to keep going beyond their time with you.

So, writers and teachers, hold on to this book. You may return to it again and again as you write new scripts and your careers evolve. In this Third Edition, I hope I've given you something that will last.

FROM JOHN WELLS

John Wells is Executive Producer of *Southland*, and previously ran *ER* and *The West Wing*. He is also past president of the Writers Guild of America West.

Pamela Douglas: If you could go back in time and talk to your own young self when you were a student in film school or college, what do you know now that you wish you'd known then about writing and producing television series?

John Wells: I wish I'd known how long it was going to take. You come out and you sort of assume it's going to be a couple-of-year process and you don't really start making any headway until you've wrtitten about a foot and a half of material, measured up off the floor. That's when you really start to think of yourself as a writer in the way you look at the world. It's a craft that takes a tremendous amount of time.

I wish I had more of a sense that it was much more like learning to play a musical instrument. After four or five years you start to not embarrass yourself. It takes ten years before you can even begin to call yourself proficient. And that's very difficult for students because they've been through twelve years of primary school, four years of college, and often a couple of years of graduate school and they think they've already done sixteen, eighteen years of education, so they want to go do it right now, though they've actually just started.

It looks deceptively easy from the outside. If you look at the lowest common denominator you think, "I can do that." The craft that's necessary — the time it takes to have enough trial and error and to keep going with it — that takes a very long time to develop. I'm very suspicious of writers who haven't been writing for ten years, I will often ask people for three or four or five pieces of material if I've read one thing of theirs that I like. I know they've given me the thing they're proudest of, and I'm looking to see the growth, and how much they've done and how much they've committed themselves to the long-term process of writing.

I've supervised well over 600 scripts, and personally written well over a hundred, and I still finish each one disappointed in my work. It's a life-long endeavor, never something you succeed at. I've been working professionally for twenty years and I'm always learning something new every day about writing.

PD: You could have chosen to write in any medium. Why TV?

JW: The feature world, which I remain involved in, is not a medium, generally, where you're able to write about character in the depth I like to write about character. There are characters now on *ER* whose growth I've been writing about for years. I don't mean to compare myself to Dickens, but I heard Steven Bochco talk about that years ago, when he explained that what he was trying to do on *Hill Street Blues* was like the way Dickens published a chapter a week.

And subject matter is different in television. The kinds of things we can write about seriously are more appealing than most of what you're offered to do in features.

Beyond that, it's much easier to be involved creatively in your work in television than in feature films. It happens a lot faster, so there's not time for as many cooks in the kitchen. But also you get to see your work and see it quickly. I've done work on features that haven't been produced for years, and [when asked for another draft] it becomes hard to remember what you had in mind when you first wrote it three years ago. In television, you'll finish a script and see dailies on it ten days later.

PD: People talk about how television is changing now with cable, the Internet, and the influence of DVR. What does the future hold for the art of television drama?

JW: The technology makes for short-term changes, but we're still doing what Chaucer was doing a thousand years ago. We're still writing stories. I think we are structured in such a way that we're interested in people, and we're interested in hearing their stories and metaphors for our own lives and going through cathartic experiences. That hasn't changed.

I actually think it's a more exciting time for a writer because there are many more ways for your material to get made. You can write something and make it on a digital videocam that you buy at a store. You have an opportunity to work on shows on cable which have content you can't do on broadcast television. The opportunities are limitless. There isn't as much money to be made doing it, but you have thoughts and impressions about the human experience you want to share with others. This is the way to share it, and now there are more opportunities than ever.

PD: Any final words of wisdom for a beginning writer?

JW: It's going to take a lot longer than you think, and don't give up. Just keep writing.

There was a guy I went to USC with who I used to see every year at a New Year's party. And every year I'd ask him what he was doing. He told me what he was working on, and I realized it was the same thing he was working on last year. That went on for three or four years. You need to be writing, at the minimum three or four specs a year, different shows. And you need to do that while you've got whatever day job you have to keep you alive. That's the sort of commitment you need to really succeed.

Even my friends who came out of school and immediately got jobs or sold screenplays — within three or four years they ended up having to do their period of four or five or six years slogging. I really don't know any talented writers who ended up being successful who haven't had a struggle. That's just what being an artist is all about.

CHAPTER 1

WHAT'S SO SPECIAL ABOUT TV DRAMA SERIES?

Imagine the power.

Picture the whole world dotted with hundreds of millions of screens glowing with the light from television images. Inside each TV set, computer monitor, and mobile screen — your own, for example — visitors tell stories about their dreams and problems, loves and rages, their thrills and their losses. You care about them, probably more than you admit, and even talk about them when they're not around — after all, they come as often as you invite them.

Sometimes they're broiling over issues in the news. Or sick and scared about that, or lying, or brave. At one time they were attacked and fought back and barely survived. But no matter what, they'll be back next time, your same friends, there with you in your most vulnerable places, at home after work and on weekends, on your phone while you wait alone for a plane, on your computer when you can't sleep at night. Intimate.

Maybe one of them is Tony Soprano, the mob boss, asking Uncle Junior, "I thought you loved me," and watching Junior's lip quiver, unable to answer. Or *Mad Men*'s Don Draper hurrying home for Thanksgiving with his family after all, imagining them happy, only to discover they're already gone. In *The Good Wife* pilot, you were reeled into the fraction of a second when Alicia, standing by her philandering husband, fixes on a bit of string on his jacket, as if removing it would put her life back in order. On *House*, you were drawn into a doctor's moral quandary when he must choose between allowing the tyrant in his care to perpetrate genocide or killing his patient. On *Treme*, just months after hurricane Katrina, amidst destroyed homes and near-empty streets, you rooted for Chief dressing in his Mardi Gras costume of immense yellow feathers, dancing and singing with enough heart to bring back the dead and New Orleans. Joy and tears, up close and personal.

Think about the impact. Once you understand the way viewers relate to their favorite shows, you'll get a feel for the kinds of stories that work and how to wield this awesome power.

Three Qualities of Episodic TV Series

Among the traits that distinguish primetime series (both dramas and comedies) from other kinds of screenwriting, three are especially significant for writers: endless character arcs, the "long narrative" for serials, and the collaborative process.

EPISODIC CHARACTERIZATION

In feature writing you were probably told to create an arc for your protagonist that takes him from one state to its opposite; the character struggles toward a goal, and once that is attained, your story ends. Someone who is unable to love is changed when a mate/child/friend appears and, through fighting the relationship, the character is finally able to love. Or someone who has been wronged seeks revenge and either achieves it or dies for the cause. All fine for movies that end. But series don't.

So how do you progress a narrative without an arc? Well, you create a different kind of arc. Remember what I said about series characters being more like people you know than figures in a plot. If your friend has an extreme experience, you continue knowing him after the event. You're invested in the process, not just the outcome.

But watch out — this does not mean the characters are flat. Your continuing cast should never be mere witnesses to the challenge of the week. On the contrary, characters who are not transformed by the plot need something instead: dimension. Think of it like this: instead of developing horizontally toward a goal, the character develops vertically, exploring internal conflicts that create tension. The character may be revealed incrementally within each episode and throughout the series, but viewers need to trust that Alicia Florrick and Walter White are the same people they knew last week. Does that mean those characters are without range or variation? Of course not, and neither are your friends.

THE "LONG NARRATIVE"

Episodic drama comes in three forms: anthologies, series with "closure," and "serials."

Anthologies are free-standing stories, like short movies, unconnected to other installments except by a frame. *The Twilight Zone* had a continuing host, style, and franchise, but the casts were different each week. As the precursor of today's episodic television, anthologies flourished in the 1950s when showcases like *Playhouse 90* presented literature more like stage plays. But anthologies are rare today, and we're not focusing on writing them.

Series with closure have continuing main casts but new situations that conclude at the end of each episode; they *close*. This is especially true of "procedurals" like *CSI, NCIS,* any version of *Law & Order,* and in fact the majority of fare on the traditional broadcast networks. Syndicators and cable channels that run repeats prefer this kind of show because they buy large packages (the first four seasons, or 88 episodes, is typical) and sell them to local and overseas stations who may rerun them in any order. If the episodes have no "memory," that is, no significant development of ongoing relationships, the order of the episodes isn't supposed to matter. Or so the thinking goes.

Most series have some closure, even if they continue other storylines. But when a series is well developed, the writers and fans follow the characters and find it hard to resist their history as it inevitably builds over time. In its early seasons, *The X-Files* had a new alien or paranormal event each week, and though the romantic tension between Mulder and Scully simmered, it didn't escalate. Then interest from viewers pushed more and more of a relationship and turned the partners into lovers by the end of the series. Most *X-Files* episodes can still be enjoyed in any order, but serial storytelling is beguiling.

Today, the best shows that close each episode also have ongoing dramatic stories. *House* and *The Good Wife,* for example, have built followings on their continuing characters. But from a writing point of view, they are constructed as procedurals (more about that term later).

Serials: Now, there's a dirty word in some minds because it also describes "soap operas." Daytime serials like *The Young and the Restless* and *General Hospital* used to have loyal viewers and succeeded according to their own aims. But primetime writers and producers don't like to be identified with them because of the heightened melodrama (which is needed to drive the story enough to run five days a week), and the speed with which episodes are produced too often results in stereotypical characters, dialogue that lacks subtlety, and unbelievable situations.

Current heirs to soapy melodrama flourish in teen relationship shows, on the CW network especially. In the future, the inheritance may well be the Internet, where inexpensive, quickly-produced fare without known stars or elaborate production values can be made by anyone with a digital camera and editing software. And those episodes can run throughout the day and night.

Meanwhile, what about primetime serials that run on premium cable, basic cable, and broadcast networks? Decades ago, shows like *Dallas* and *Knots Landing* were described as "nighttime soaps," and did have the overblown romanticism and hyperbole typical of their daytime cousins. But most primetime series aren't like that anymore. Recent serials include award-winning dramas on HBO, Showtime, AMC, and elsewhere: *Mad Men, Dexter, Breaking Bad, True Blood, The Wire, Treme, The Sopranos, Big Love, The Tudors, Boardwalk Empire, The Walking Dead*. And most of the acclaimed series on networks and other cable outlets use serialized storytelling along with closed stories.

A serial is any drama whose stories continue across many episodes in which the main cast develops over time. It's called the "long narrative," the epitome of what episodic television can offer: not one tale that ties up in an hour or two, but lives that play out over hundreds of hours. Think about it — as a writer you have the opportunity to tell a story that is so rich that it expands for years. At the conclusion of *NYPD Blue*'s twelve-year run, the series produced around 250 hours of story. That's not 250 police cases (actually two or three times that many because each episode included several cases); the significance is 250 hours of living with these detectives and their cares, 250 hours dealing with the consequences of twelve years of experiences.

As you watch television, look for the way closed stories mingle with the long narrative. Not only will that give you insight into the show's construction, but also a larger sense of what a story can be.

The Sopranos

COLLABORATION

If you go on to write for television, you'll never work alone. Series are like families, and even though each episode is written by one writer, the process is collaborative at every step. Writers sit around a table to "break" each story, then review the outline and all the drafts together. Sometimes a writer may be placing a long arc in many episodes rather than writing a single episode. On *House* and *Nurse Jackie*, medical consultants — some of whom are also writers — supply essential scenes. And sometimes one writer may do a revision or dialogue polish on another's script. The image of the isolated artist creating his precious screenplay secretly in the night isn't the reality of life on a series. (Though that's not to say staff members don't write their drafts privately, or that they aren't artists — some are brilliant!)

You may have heard the comment that happy families are all alike, but each unhappy family is unhappy in its own way. Television staffs are full of writers, so how normal can they be? Dysfunctional staff families abound, but so do creative mixes that are encouraging and inspiring. As a beginner, you'll learn tremendously on a staff. Read Chapter Six for how staffs function and tips for getting along and getting ahead.

But first, if you're going to write for TV, you need to dump some misconceptions.

FIVE MYTHS ABOUT TELEVISION

MYTH 1: TV IS SMALL MOVIES.

Not really, though that does seem to make sense on the surface. Both TV dramas and movies deliver stories played by actors who are filmed and shown on screens. And many filmmakers — writers, directors, actors, cinematographers, editors, and so forth — work in both theatricals and television. In fact, Michael Crichton and Steven Spielberg were involved with TV veteran John Wells at the inception of *ER*. Action movie producer Jerry Bruckheimer does *CSI*. Alan Ball, who wrote the movie *American Beauty*, became executive producer of *Six Feet Under* and *True Blood*. Melissa Rosenberg, an executive producer at *Dexter*, wrote the theatrical hit *Twilight*. And Frank Darabont, nominated for three Academy Awards, including for writing *The Shawshank Redemption,* is producing *The Walking Dead* on AMC.

A funny experience on a series brought home how connected film and TV writing can be. My agent told me that several writers had quit the staff of a show I admired. I couldn't figure out why — the series was winning awards, it was renewed, and the characters had

Dexter

plenty of potential. Not to mention the writers were making a bundle. Maybe the showrunner was a monster. But I met him, a bright guy, no crazier than anyone else in town. So I went to work.

First day in my new cubicle, I waited to be called to a story meeting, or given an assignment, or a script to rewrite. Nothing. I read all the magazines in the waiting room. Second day, I observed everyone else writing furiously on their office computers. Why was I left out? Had I offended someone? My mind fell to dark ruminations.

Finally, I popped into the cubicle next to me — "What are you writing?" The writer looked up, wide-eyed — didn't I know? Everyone was working on their features. "He wants to do it all himself," my fellow staffer said about the executive producer. "He keeps us around to bounce ideas and read his drafts. But he thinks it's quicker if he just writes the show." There I was on a TV staff and everyone was writing a movie. Pretty soon the studio pulled the plug on our feature scholarships, and that was the end of that job. But that illustrates an axiom: a writer is a writer, whether television or feature or for any new media.

Still, the more you know about features and television, the more unique each is. People go to movies to escape into a fantasy larger than life with spectacular stunts, effects, and locations. At $10+ per ticket, audiences demand lots of bang for their bucks. And teenage boys — a prime target for features — relish the vicarious action that big screens do so well. If you saw *Avatar* rerun on television, or rented a summer blockbuster, the giants of Pandora became toys, and armies of thousands were reduced to ants. Some bubbles are not meant to be burst.

From the beginning, theatrical features grew out of shared entertainment — think of crowds watching vaudeville. Television didn't intend that kind of experience. In fact, the parent of TV is more likely radio. A generation before television, families gathered around their radios for vital information, whether the farm report or the war. And radio dramas were character-driven; beloved familiar personalities scrapping and coping with each other, bringing someone (often women, hardly ever teen boys) to tears or laughter every day. Close, personal, at home.

And real. Before radio, people got their information about the world from newspapers. That lineage continues in what we expect of television. Television became fused with what people need to know and what they believe is fact. So it's not an escape, not fantasy, but the fabric of daily life.

Oh, you're saying what about *Star Trek* or *Smallville*, for just two examples — they're hardly real. Well, I did a brief turn on *Star Trek: The Next Generation*, and I can tell you the producers were interested in stories about people — people who lived in a distant environment with futuristic gadgets, yes, but the core was relationships among the crew, testing personal limits; and, at its best, the exploration wasn't distant galaxies but what it means to be human. As for *Smallville*, the young Clark Kent is a metaphor for every teenager who struggles with being different, figuring out who he is and how to be with his friends. This is heart stuff, not spectacle.

Which is not to say you should write without cinematic qualities. The pilot of *Lost* opened with visually tantalizing images that drew the viewer into the mood and quest of the series. But even there, the focus was personal jeopardy: It began on Jack's eyeball, then an odd sneaker on a tree, then a dog out of nowhere, and took its time placing us in a jungle before following Jack as he discovered were he was, moving without dialogue to the beach. Still tight in Jack's point of view, only gradually do we see the crashed plane, and the first word from a distance: "Help!" Immediate, direct, close.

Screenwriting students are taught to write visually and minimize talk — "Play it, don't say it." Generally, that's good advice, so I was writing that way when I started in television. Then a producer pointed to a chunk of description (which I'd thought was a clever way of replacing exposition) and said, "give me a line for this — they may not be watching." Not watching? That's my brilliant image up there!

But come back to the reality of the medium. It's at home, not a darkened theatre. No one is captured, and the viewers might be eating, painting toenails, doing homework — you know how it goes. As the creator, of course you want to make the screen so beguiling they won't turn their eyes away, but if the "viewers" have to get a point, put it in dialogue. People may be listening to the TV more than watching it. That's not such a bad thing. Whereas viewers are distanced from the screen in theatrical films, voyeurs to other people's stories, television drama has the effect of people talking to you, or at least talking to each other in your home. It's compelling in a different way.

When students ask whether I advise them to write for features or television, after I tell them to try both, I ask about their talent. Do they have an ear for the way people speak naturally? Are they able to convey the illusion of today's speech while actually writing tight, withheld lines? Can they write distinct voices for dissimilar characters? If they don't have the talent for effective dialogue, I nudge them away from TV because action would be easier for them.

As you contemplate the differences between gigantic theatrical entertainment and what works on a family-sized TV or personal computer screen, take the next step: what sort of storytelling and filmmaking is likely to be successful on a screen the size of a cell phone?

So, no, television is not a small version of movies; it's a different medium; and it's bigger. Yes, bigger. The most successful features are seen by millions of people in theatres, and more when the movies are downloaded from websites, rented as DVDs, and rerun on TV. But even a moderately successful series, if it continues for enough years to go into syndication, is seen by hundreds of millions — all those lights glowing from screens around the world.

MYTH 2: TV IS CHEAP.

Well, I don't think $5–$20 million to produce a single hour is all that cheap, or more than $100 million for a full season. Sure, when you compare that television hour to a two-hour feature whose budget is more than the GNP of several small countries, maybe it doesn't seem so much. But at the high-end no one's hurting in TV, and for writers, being on a series is a way to get rich (more about staff work in Chapter Six). Of course, not all series are on the high end, and the business side of television is more like a manufacturing company than an entrepreneurial venture. Pay scales (at least the floors) are set by guilds and unions, and a budget for the year is managed by the show's executives. It's a lot of money, but it's all allocated.

So toward the end of a season, some shows do tighten their belts. One showrunner gave me a single instruction as I joined his series: "It doesn't rain in this town." After he had sprung for high-profile guest stars, overtime shooting, and sweeps week specials, he couldn't afford to make rain on the set for the rest of the year. You may have noticed another sign of overrun: the "wrap-around" episode — the one where the main character relives his previous episodes. Chances are, those memories were triggered not by nostalgia, but by the need to use clips instead of spending on production.

That said, series budgets are ample for what you want dramatically within the world of the show. As a writer, your investment needs to be in the quality of the story and depth of feelings you can elicit rather than production dazzle, so avoid: distant or difficult locations, special effects, extreme stunts, large guest casts, crowd scenes, and CGI (computer-generated images) unless those are part of your series. If you write them, they'll probably be cut, and by tightening you gain focus on the main characters, which are the strength of television drama.

MYTH 3: YOU CAN'T DO THAT ON TV.

Come on, you can do anything on cable television — language, nudity, controversial subjects or lifestyles, experiments in ways of telling stories. However, broadcast stations are licensed by the FCC (Federal Communications Commission), which obligates them to operate in the public interest. So local stations are susceptible to pressure from groups which might threaten their licenses when they're up for renewal; and the networks, which also own stations, are sensitive to public mores — though those cultural standards change with time. Certainly, public norms have come a long way since the 1950s when married couples had to be shown fully dressed and sleeping in separate beds. Now even the least adventurous television is closer to real life. And none of this applies to HBO, Showtime, or other cable outlets.

The old days of censorship are past — but not entirely. In 2004, network censors stunned the creators of ER. It involved one episode where an 81-year-old woman is having a medical exam — an emotional moment in which the elderly woman learns about cancer, and some of her aged breast is visible. Essential for the dramatic impact of the scene, the show's producers argued, but the network pressured them to re-edit the scene so the breast could not be glimpsed.

A new level of accommodation was reached when HBO's bold drama *The Sopranos* was sold into syndication on A&E. Having planned ahead, HBO filmed alternate scenes and lines during the original production. While most of the "sanitized" episodes retain their power, some bizarre moments result, like Paulie (a tough gangster) cursing about the "freakin" snow while they go off to kill someone. That sort of thing drives some serious writers to cable where they can practice their art without interference… although, even there, Syfy Channel's *Battlestar Galactica* made do with "frack."

So, yes, on broadcast television some limits still exist. But here's my advice: Don't censor yourself as you write your first draft. Have your characters talk and behave the way people actually do today. Stay real. If a word or image has to be edited, fix it later, but keep the pipeline open to how people truly are, because that's the source of powerful writing.

MYTH 4: ALL TV SERIES ARE THE SAME.

I once heard that statement from a producer who'd been successful in the era before audiences had unlimited channels and websites to surf. Now, with competition for fresh programming, a show that rests on formulas and conventional prototypes risks going unnoticed, cancelled after four episodes.

But television series do follow rules, and you'll find a list of them at the end of this chapter.

MYTH 5: TELEVISION IS A WASTELAND.

In 1961, Newton Minnow, an FCC Commissioner, declared television a "vast wasteland," and the epithet stuck. Minnow was referring to shows such as *Bonanza*, *The Flintstones*, and *Mr. Ed* in an era when three networks, each smaller than now, shared airwaves that were considered a scarce commodity, dedicated to informing or elevating the public. The talking horse just didn't do it for him.

Well, half a century later, part of the wasteland has become a garbage dump strewn with fake jilted lovers beating up on each other on so-called "Unscripted" shows. The rest ranges from televangelists to pornography, political pundits to purveyors of snake oil, sports to scientific discoveries, wannabe singers to singing animals, and includes fiction of all kinds that may be funny, freaky, fascinating, or familiar. And some is brilliant literature, on a par with the greatest writing and filmmaking created anywhere.

Those are the shows I focus on when teaching hour drama, because I believe that you learn best if you learn from the best. As to the wasteland — with a thousand channels and sites, and access to programming from every era of television history and from all over the world, television is whatever you choose to watch.

Nor is television monolithic, even within American primetime. I've heard people disparage TV as aimed at 12-year-olds. I answer *Yes*, TV shows *are* aimed at 12-year-olds — if you watch certain stations at 8 PM. Pre-teen and teen programming fills the early evening shows on the CW, Fox, and some cable outlets, attracting viewers whom advertisers believe are especially susceptible to their commercials. Beyond sales of acne medications and cosmetics, some of those shows even link to websites where viewers can buy the clothing styles worn by the actors.

I don't recommend emulating those shows as you learn to write, but I do understand that very young writers may be more comfortable with characters close to their own age. If a student sincerely tells me that she hasn't had enough life experience to deal with adult issues or relationships, but wants to learn the craft, I direct her to a well-written show with a young cast. *Friday Night Lights* was a perfect case of honestly observed high school students written with insight. So if you'd like to write teen television, go ahead. If you choose truth as your guide, your script will ring true at any age.

Traditionally, the primetime evening, from 8 PM to 11 PM, was divided into components:

8:00 PM — family sitcoms featuring children, "Unscripted" game shows and contests, teen melodramas.

8:30 PM — more sitcoms, though not necessarily with children, "Unscripted/Reality," teen shows continue.

9:00 PM — sophisticated comedies, hour dramas that are thoughtful, romantic, inspirational, or teen.

10:00 PM — the most sophisticated hour dramas for adults; on cable, serious half-hour "dramedies;" historic miniseries.

At least that's how it used to line up. Of course, now you can view anything at any time on demand or by recording the show, and cable reruns its programming throughout the week. Most networks stream their programming on the Internet, and if for some reason you still haven't caught the show, you can buy or rent the DVD.

So you'd think that the traditional schedule is meaningless. Funny thing, though — despite all the alternate options, most people still watch shows at the time they're broadcast. Programmers at networks still vie to "counter-program" their rivals, and "appointment viewing" is still the goal — making people feel it's so important to catch the latest installment of *True Blood* that they will make plans to be in front of a screen at 9 PM on Sunday night, even though they could easily view it any day later.

Most talented writers want to work on the 9 PM or 10 PM shows, and in fact those are the ones I recommend learning. When you're out in the business, though, you may find more openings at 8 PM and in less lofty outlets at first. That's okay, you have to start somewhere, and in Chapter Six you'll read about breaking in.

True Blood

The Rules of Series TV

• AN HOUR SHOW HAS TO FIT IN AN HOUR.

Actually, a network or basic cable hour is more like 45 minutes, plus commercial breaks, although pay cable may take the entire time. Usually, scripts for drama series are between 50 and 60 pages, though a fast-talking show like *The West Wing* sometimes went to 70 pages. On networks that break shows into five acts plus a teaser, writers are stuck with reduced screen time, and find themselves with 8-page acts and scripts coming in around 48 pages. Each script is timed before production, and if it runs long (despite the page count), the writer needs to know what to trim in dialogue or which action to tighten; or if it runs short, where a new beat could add depth or a twist, not simply padding. And you need the craft to get it revised overnight, which leads to the next rule:

• SERIES DEADLINES ARE FOR REAL.

Your show is on every week, and that means there's no waiting for your muse, no honing the fine art of writing-avoidance, no allowing angst to delay handing in your draft. If you can't make the deadline, the show-runner has to turn over your work to another writer.

From the time your episode is assigned, you'll probably have one week to come in with an outline, a few days to revise it, two weeks to deliver the first-draft teleplay, a gap of a couple of days for notes, then one week to write your second draft — a total of around six weeks from pitch to second draft (although polishes and production revisions will add another couple of weeks or so). Maybe that sounds daunting, but once you're on a staff you're living the series, and the pace can be exhilarating. You'll hear your words spoken by the actors, watch the show put together, and see it on screen quickly too.

It's fun until the nightmare strikes. On a series, the nightmare is a script that "falls out" at the last minute. It may happen like this: The story seems to make sense when it's pitched. The outline comes in with holes, but the staff thinks it can be made to work. Then they read the first draft and see that the problems aren't solved. It's given to another writer to fix. Meanwhile, the clock is ticking. Preproduction, including sets, locations, casting have to go ahead if the script is going to shoot next week. Tick tock. Another draft, and the flaw — maybe an action the lead character really wouldn't do, or a plot element that contradicts the episode just before or after, or a forced resolution that's not credible — now glares out at everyone around the table. Yet another draft, this time by the supervising producer. Tick tock. Or maybe it's not the writer's fault: the exact fictional crisis depicted has suddenly occurred in real life, so the episode can't be aired. The script has to be abandoned — it "falls out." Meanwhile, the production manager is waiting to prep, and publicity has gone out.

I once heard a panel discussion where a respected showrunner told this very nightmare. The cast and crew were literally on the set and absolutely had to start shooting that day for the episode to make the air date. But they had no script. In desperation, the showrunner, renowned as a great writer, commenced dictating as a secretary transcribed and runners dashed to the set bringing one page at a time. A hand shot up from an admirer in the panel audience, "Was it the best thing you ever wrote?" "No," he laughed, "it didn't make sense."

• DRAMA SERIES HAVE AN ACT STRUCTURE.

Put away your books on three-act structure. Television dramas on networks have for decades been written in four acts, though many broadcast shows now use five acts, and a few are broken into six. You'll learn more about that in Chapter Four, where a teleplay is analyzed. For now, think about what happens every 13 to 15 minutes on a traditional network show. You know: a commercial break. These breaks aren't random; they provide a grid for constructing the episode in which action rises to a cliffhanger or twist ("plot point" may be a familiar term if you've studied feature structure). Each of the four segments are "acts" in the same sense as plays have real acts rather than the theoretical acts described in analyzing features. At a stage play, at the end of an act the curtain comes down, theatre lights come up, and the audience heads for refreshments or the restrooms. That's the kind of hard act break that occurs in television. Writers plan toward those breaks and use them to build tension.

Once you get the hang of it, you'll discover that act breaks don't hamper your creativity; they free you to be inventive within a rhythmic grid. And once you work with that 10- to 15-minute block, you may want to use it off-network and in movies. In fact, next time you're in a movie theatre, notice the audience every 15 minutes. You may see them shifting in their seats. I don't know whether 15-minute chunks have been carved into contemporary consciousness by the media, or if they're aspects of human psychology which somehow evolved with us, but the 15-minute span existed before television. In the early 20th century motion pictures were distributed on reels that projectionists had to change every 15 minutes. Then, building on that historical pattern, some screenwriting theorists began interpreting features as eight 15-minute sequences. Whatever the origin, four acts became the original template for drama series on the networks.

But as the value of advertising segments declined on traditional networks, more commercials began to be inserted to make up for the loss, leading to series written in five acts. These may also have a teaser (explained in Chapter Three) which is sometimes almost as long as an act, giving an impression of six acts, each around eight to ten pages long. On the other side of the spectrum, premium cable series like those on HBO and Showtime have no act breaks, and may be structured more like movies.

Despite the push to crowd more advertising into shows, the effort is doomed. Viewers recording on TiVo and other devices easily skip the commercials. Downloaded versions have ads, but not in a way that interrupts the story. So after several years swinging from four-act structure to five and six acts — between 2006 and 2011 — and an aversion to act break structure on premium cable, a surprising reversal has occurred. If you look at the writer's first drafts of many hour dramas, ranging from *House* (which airs in five acts plus a teaser) to *Breaking Bad* to *The Wire*, you'll see the four-act structure back again. From a construction viewpoint, it just plain works, even if it is adjusted in the final drafts later.

• EACH SERIES FITS A FRANCHISE.

Not Starbucks, although enough caffeine is downed on late rewrites to earn that franchise too. Some typical television franchises include police/detective, legal, medical, sci-fi, action-adventure, and family. Each brings expectations from the audience that you should know, even if you challenge them. For series creators, franchises are both boundaries and opportunities. You'll find more about how shows are created in Chapters Two and Five, and in "Spotlight On Writing Your Pilot Script," but you can get a clue why franchises are useful if you ask how hundreds of stories can derive from a single premise.

The solution is to find "springboards" that propel dramatic conflicts or adventures each episode. Those catalysts occur naturally in most of the franchises: a crime sets the cop on a quest for the perp; someone in trouble beseeches lawyers who must mount a case; a patient is brought for a doctor to save. The hook for each episode is rooted in a specific world in which sympathetic main characters must take immediate action. In other franchises — family, workplace, high school and romantic dramas, for example — springboards are less obvious, relying on conflicts between characters rather than outside provocations. In these, a personal inciting incident (even if it's internal) sets each episode in motion.

Decades ago, audiences expected the franchises to deliver predictable storytelling where any problem could be resolved within the hour, as many procedural shows still do. Take westerns, for example. The template was the frontier town threatened by bad guys (black hats). The good guy marshal (white hat) wrangles with weak or corrupt townspeople, gets a few on his side (room for one exceptional guest role), defends the town against the black hats, and rides off into the sunset.

With that old formula in mind, think about HBO's *Deadwood*. Yup, there's the bad frontier town of rough nasties. And it has an ex-marshal, a lead character who left his badge in Montana to forge a future on the edge of the abyss. But similarities to the franchise are superficial. Everyone in *Deadwood* is surviving any way they can in a world without an outside redeemer, struggling to make sense of life in a moral wilderness.

Clearly *House*, *Grey's Anatomy*, and *Nurse Jackie* all use the medical franchise, where doctors (and nurses) must deal with new cases each week. But if you compare them to older examples, such as *Marcus Welby, M.D.*, you'll see how far *House* and the others have to stretch to reflect contemporary life. Welby, the kindly doctor, free of deep introspection, worked alone in his nice little office. But real doctors and nurses face ethical and legal issues as they treat both the victim of a gunshot and the man who shot him, and they cope with their own humanity — guilt, exhaustion, ambition, and the competing pulls of the job and the rest of life, including romance and self-doubt on *Grey's*, addiction on *Nurse Jackie*, and a doctor's deep psychological issues on *House*. To express today's medical whirlwind, the form itself needed to change. *ER* developed "vignette" techniques in which multiple short stories flit by, some on top of each other, and *Grey's* continued that layering.

From the moment ABC slotted *Grey's Anatomy* to follow *Desperate Housewives*, the network mandated the tone: "Sex and the Surgery." Executive Producer Shonda Rhimes responded in *Los Angeles Magazine*, "I don't think of it as a medical drama. It's a relationship show with some surgery thrown in. That's how I've always seen it."

Meanwhile, the family drama franchise is flourishing — like *Big Love*, *The Sopranos*, and *Breaking Bad*. Some families. I suppose you could call *True Blood* a family drama too, because episodes emanate from relationships among the continuing cast (some of whom are related or "living" together) as much as external events. Not exactly *Leave It To Beaver*. Take a closer look and see if you can identify the elements that update the franchises on your favorite shows. Think about how you'd compare *Mad Men* to *The Wonder Years* — both character-driven shows of an era gone by. What has changed?

In the detective franchise, a light show like *Monk* on USA played out the traditional form: one detective gets one new crime mystery each week and, after investigating red herrings that fall mostly at the act breaks, cleverly solves it by the end of the hour. Though *Monk*'s obsessive-compulsive characterization was a fresh, entertaining element, structurally this was a basic "A" story series (more about A–B–C storytelling in Chapter Three). Check out the shows this basic cable channel mounted after the end of *Monk* to ride that popularity: quirky main characters in predictable plots.

This kind of imitation is hardly creative, but from a programmer's viewpoint it's safe, and if you find yourself in one of those formulaic shows, here's my advice: use the formula, but inhabit it with people and their true feelings set amidst honest social concerns. If you fulfill the minimum expectations, executives may never notice how much further you've gone, and you'll have a better writing sample for yourself (not to mention doing your soul some good).

On higher profile police/detective series, on both broadcast and cable, you'll see mostly ensemble casts and complex intertwining plots that are propelled by issues in the news or social concerns. Some use cutting-edge forensic technology, as in *CSI*, *Fringe*, and several others, where the real star is science that engages the intellect. Detectives have always solved puzzles, of course, but the show's audience seems fascinated with futuristic tools that try the bounds of human capability.

Series that rely on stories that are solved by investigative procedures are called "procedurals" and include forensics (*CSI*), detective work (*Law & Order*), and medical diagnoses (*House*) that follow clues to wrap up a new case each week. Procedurals will be discussed in depth in a Spotlight between Chapter Three and Chapter Four, including hybrid shows like *The Good Wife*.

Along with the many casually watched procedurals, viewers are following densely plotted novelized series with the kind of passion studio executives crave. Dana Walden, president of the 20th Century Fox Television studio, told *The New York Times* in October, 2006, "We were all having conversations about event drama, and an event drama *is* a serialized drama."

But how many hours will people devote every week to intense serialized dramas? And if you miss the first few episodes, it's like reading a novel beginning in the middle. Would audiences become commitment-phobic?

CSI

Several solutions exist: catch-up marathons (as all serialized shows on cable run), replays and streaming available on many Internet sites, and DVDs. In fact, sales of *Lost* after its first year validated the whole business of selling DVDs of entire seasons of series, which was just emerging at that time. On Showtime, *Dexter*, a character-driven psychological thriller, offers an interactive clues game on the Showtime website to hold its fans. Webisodes, going as far as parallel series produced solely for Internet distribution as were made by *Lost* and *Battlestar Galactica*, are now the norm.

Monumental history-based series such as *Rome* and *The Tudors* proved the staying power of dense storytelling, not just as "limited series" (which used to be called "miniseries"), but also across seasons similar to regular programs. Though history is necessarily book-ended by lives — Marc Antony and Cleopatra died, and so did King Henry, not to mention all those queens — and their long narrative is less than infinite, these shows are examples of developing depth of character in a societal context. After considering them, take a look at *Treme*, for a more recent, brilliant exploration of how to work stories through an extreme historic place and time.

Still, the broadcast networks find it prudent to fill their schedules with reliable procedural franchises. And yet, those are volatile too. For example, the action-adventure franchise that thrived in the days of easy bad guys

The Walking Dead

like *The A-Team* and *Starsky & Hutch* has transformed to shows like *The Closer*, in which a character said "I'm in America observing an empire on its deathbed, a tourist doing charitable work among the addicted and sexually diseased." In this context, Showtime's *Sleeper Cell* was an ambitious attempt to dramatize a range of characters and motives that are unfamiliar to most Americans. The action and adventure in shows like those emanate from the terrain, rather than having the franchise itself control the story.

Nor could great drama like *The Wire* be defined by its franchise, though it obviously had cops and robbers. And obviously a family drama built on personal relationships among the ensemble. And obviously a spiritual quest built on confronting mortality and the will to survive, even in hell. It was all of those and more, which is part of what happens when creative possibilities are allowed to expand.

That's evident in the range of science fiction — now there's a genre that has boldly gone where science fiction hadn't gone before on TV. While the Syfy Channel (owned by NBC-Universal) continues a predictable roll-out of fantasy adventures like *Stargate SGI*, *Eureka*, and any number of fright movies (*Mansquito*, anyone?), which serve its niche audience without extending it, the channel also lucked into the critically-acclaimed *Battlestar Galactica*, which was sometimes a more searing political allegory than even *West Wing* was, while venturing into contemporary relationships on the level of premium cable dramas. At the same time, *Fringe*, using a traditional science-fiction genre, became a network hit, attracting viewers who are not traditional sci-fi fans, and the adventurous programming on AMC is bringing not only *Mad Men* and *Breaking Bad* but also *The Walking Dead* — a quality drama about zombies.

If I had to guess the frontier of science fiction writing on television, I would look toward the characters. In 20th century sci-fi series, the leading edge was technology as used by fantasy heroes, usually "perfect," in action-heavy battles between good and evil, which tended to play to children and adolescents. Though contemporary sci-fi/fantasy shows are as different as *Lost* is from *Fringe* or *Battlestar Galactica* or *The Walking Dead*, they all follow flawed human beings, and the questions they explore involve both relationships and serious issues about what it is to be a citizen of this planet; and they're watched by wide demographics. With so much range in this franchise, if you're interested in trying it, I suggest reaching up toward real dramatic writing, and leave cartoon-like thinking to the movies.

The vitality of 21st century television drama has re-interpreted traditional franchises. But that doesn't mean they'll disappear. When I was a beginner freelancing any show that would give me a break, I landed an assignment on *Mike Hammer*, a network detective series. At my first meeting, the producer handed me two pages of guidelines. The first was titled "Mike Hammer Formulaic Structure." On the second were rules for writing Mike, for example, "Mike speaks only in declarative sentences." To be a strong man, he could never ask questions, you see.

The formula went something like this: At the top of the show, a sympathetic character approaches Mike for help. At the end of Act One the sympathetic character is found dead. In Act Two Mike is on the trail of the killer, only to find him dead at the Act break, and yet someone else has been killed (proving there's a different killer). In Act Three the real bad guy goes after Mike, and at the Act Three break, Mike is in mortal jeopardy. Act Four is entirely resolution, one-to-one, Mike against the killer. And guess who wins. As I started, I thought such a rigid form would be stultifying, but I discovered it was fun. Relieved of certain structure choices, I felt free to be inventive with the guest cast and the kinds of situations that could lead to the turns and twists.

Years later, an executive of the Children's Television Workshop (makers of *Sesame Street*) asked me to develop and write a pilot for a children's series, later named *Ghostwriter*, that would be structured like primetime network dramas, complete with long character arcs, parallel stories, complex relationships, among a diverse ensemble cast, and even references to controversial issues. I'd never written for kids, but I was intrigued. In forming the series with the CTW team, we began by identifying a general franchise — in this case detectives, because solving mysteries was a way to involve the whole cast and incite each episode's quest. Beyond that, we stayed close to what human beings truly care about, how they reveal themselves, and what makes people laugh, cry, be scared, and fall in love — people of any age.

Ghostwriter was originally intended for kids around eight years old to encourage them to read. But CTW was astounded when research reported that the audience age range went from four years to sixteen. That's not even a demographic. I think the show exceeded anyone's expectations because the realistic characters rested on a franchise that was so robust it could carry not only a very young cast but also some educational content while moving the stories forward with high tension.

But when is a franchise not a franchise? Dick Wolf, creator of *Law & Order*, told *Entertainment Weekly*, "*Law & Order* is a brand, not a franchise. It's the Mercedes of television. The cars are very different, but if you buy a Mercedes, you're still getting a good car. *CSI* is a franchise — like certain restaurants. *CSI* is the same show set in different cities, while the *Law & Order* shows are all very different from each other." No doubt *CSI*, which still competes head to head with *Law & Order*, which is in perpetual reruns, would describe itself as an even bigger car.

Large as *CSI* and *Law & Order* may be, the stretch-limousines of franchise enhancement belong to HBO. With the 2011 arrival of *Game of Thrones*, based on a quasi-medieval imaginary world, the question is if this show will do for fantasy what *Deadwood* did for Westerns and *The Sopranos* did for gangsters. Like *Deadwood*, *The Sopranos*, *Rome*, and *Boardwalk Empire*, *Game of Thrones* uses history and screen tradition only as a starting point to develop unsentimental relationships observed with such honesty they transcend the prototype. Bluntly realistic, *Thrones* can be seen as a reaction against fantasy clichés such as the struggle between absolute good and evil. Villains wrestle with scruples, heroes compromise, and moral rigidity will get you killed. It's a complex narrative that continues expanding the possibilities of writing for TV.

When you're ready to plan a script as your showpiece for a series, ask yourself what the underlying franchise is. Even if the show is innovative and evolved beyond the tradition, the franchise may give you tips for constructing your outline (more on this in Chapter Four).

READY, SET, GO!

Writing primetime TV drama series is an adventure into an expanding universe. If you rise above outdated ideas about television, and have pride in your talent so that you never write down, you can create for the most powerful medium in the world. In the next chapters you'll find the tools you'll need, so get ready to jump on a moving rocket!

Summary Points

TV drama series have unique qualities:

• Characters continue over many episodes instead of concluding a dramatic arc as in a two-hour movie. Focus on depth of characters rather than looking for characters to change.

• Storylines may evolve over many episodes, especially in serials. Emphasize increments or installments of a series-long quest rather than tying up a plot. However, most shows have some stories that "close" (resolve) within an episode while other dramatic arcs continue.

• Network and basic cable drama series are written in acts marked by cliffhangers at commercial breaks, though premium cable shows may not have formal act breaks.

• Certain franchises offer springboards that suggest hundreds of stories from a show's premise.

What's New?

Adventurous cable programming, new markets, and new delivery options have spurred growth and change in television, and provide fresh opportunities for writers. Examples from current shows and re-interpreted franchises demonstrate some of the possibilities.

Spotlight on Writing "Dramedy"

The best thing I can say about the term "dramedy," which conflates the words drama and comedy, is that it's better than the alternate: "coma," although that might actually be a closer fit considering how unconsciously the label is applied to nearly everything on television.

The techniques of balancing serious subjects and humor go back as long as humans have told stories. I can imagine a cave person sitting before a fire relaying how Moog-The-Brave chased a rabbit around a tree until he fell down dizzy; I see the wise storyteller waiting artfully for the laugh from his audience, exactly before the reveal that while Moog was on the ground, the rabbit turned back, leapt for his neck and killed him. Humor set up the listeners to be shocked by the serious turn. Shakespeare was pretty good at that, I hear — creating a comic foil immediately before the most tragic scenes. All the great Shakespearean tragedies have some comedy. But do you really want to belittle them with the label "dramedy"?

The effort to define types of stories began with ancient Greek philosophers, who divided literature into tragedy, which ended with the death or destruction of a hero, while comedy focused on ordinary people and ended with their success. In later centuries the division was simplified into tragedy describing plays where people died at the end, and comedy where they didn't. The word "drama" referred to all the action in the middle, funny or not.

Then came commercial American television with a need for promotional categories. By the 1960s, the system was codified by the networks: half-hours were situation comedies ("sitcoms"), and hours were dramas. The sitcoms usually had a live audience or laugh track so no one could miss the point that it was funny. Hours were unfunny genres dealing with police or doctors or western gunfighters, and later serialized soap operas. Even today, if you visit a network headquarters — and also many production companies and even talent agencies — you will see the architecture split. Often one side of the reception desk leads to the comedy offices with their own executives and staffs, and the other side are the drama people.

You might pitch to the Vice President for Drama Development or the Vice President for Comedy Development, but not both.

Problem is, it doesn't make sense any more, and hasn't for a long time. The best half-hour comedies have emotional storylines and sometimes comment sharply on contemporary issues. Very few are filmed before live audiences, and no one would be caught with a 1970s type of laugh track. Meanwhile, both the Emmy Awards and the Writers Guild place various dramas in the comedy category even though they are an hour long because they are so light or because their intentions are comedic. It's a slippery slope on both sides.

The idea of half-hours having to be funny has been ingrained in the public even if creators want to stretch. As a young writer in the late 1980s, I was on the staff of *Frank's Place*, a half-hour in which the showrunner wanted to handle serious subjects. It was set in a funeral parlor in New Orleans and had a predominantly African-American cast (rare then and now) who dealt with stories that involved mortality, ethnicity, class distinctions, and regionalism. From the outset, it wasn't going to fly.

The creator, gifted writer-producer Hugh Wilson, had a comedy background with success on the hilarious *WKRP In Cincinnati* and the *Police Academy* movies. How dare he attempt drama, the critics thought. And then there was the audience, who wrote letters — yes, actual letters because it was the 20th century — telling us the show wasn't funny enough. Well, the episode when the old man died wasn't intended to be funny. Heartbreaking, insightful, amazing, suspenseful, whatever, but it wasn't supposed to be funny. Finally, the battle was lost. The series became a half-hour comedy. I'm not a comedy writer, and I was long gone before it ended. But to me it was an education in expectations.

So we're free of all that in the 21st century, right? Uhhhh... well, currently there's *Nurse Jackie, Hung, United States of Tara, The Big C, Weeds, Secret Diary of a Call Girl, Entourage*, and previously *Sex and the City* among half-hours that are borderline comedy/dramas. Looking at the hours, *Desperate Housewives, Grey's Anatomy, Glee*, and previously *Ugly Betty, Boston Legal, Ally McBeal*, and *Gilmore Girls* are among hour shows considered comedies by the TV Academy and Guilds. Very little on either list is laugh-out-loud funny.

Generally the attributes of "dramedies" are these: continuity of character and storylines, including serialized episodes, depth of backstories, and development of dramatic arcs, as opposed to the setup/joke paradigm where laughs are expected at specified intervals. "Dramedies" may be light, but if they have laughs at all, they would be of a wry or ironic sort. As to why they are not pure dramas, on the other hand, the characters might be less deep — closer to caricatures — and might tend to zaniness, as in *Weeds* or *The Big C*, or focus on clever or jokey dialogue quips, as in *Gilmore Girls*.

So what? Parsing these definitions matters to you because you are entering a field where the boundaries are dissolving. A term like "dramedy" makes a show harder to write because it causes you to think of all shows flowing into an amorphous funny/serious heap. It helps to have something to hold onto — benchmarks in history and in previous shows and in expectations.

If you are writing the hour drama series, you will find yourself bringing some comedy to the table some of the time, especially in episodes where you're building to tragedy. If you are writing something that intends to be funny, you must have a strong hold on the underlying dramatic elements. No one can get away with joke-to-joke writing in any form longer than three-minute webisodes. And outside of children's adventures, no one can get away with unrelieved "dramatic" action that lacks a perspective of humor at times. In writing today's TV drama series, you have to do it all. Hey, Shakespeare did okay.

GUEST SPEAKER: DAVID ISAACS

David Isaacs has multiple Emmy nominations for his writing on shows ranging from *M*A*S*H* to *Mad Men*. Having written a full spectrum of sitcoms before arriving at a drama series, I asked for his wisdom on the difference.

Pamela Douglas: What is it that makes something a comedy? What makes something a drama?

David Isaacs: Not to be glib, but the easy definition would be comedy is more situational. We're watching the moment-to-moment foibles of regular folks as they stumble through their lives. Comedies tend to be structured around an identifiable premise like *Everybody Loves Raymond*, which is about a guy who is trying to strike a balance between the family he grew up in and the family his marriage has created. We laugh at that because we see ourselves in it — that's my family or somebody's family we know. That's traditional.

The comedies we have now tend to be ironic, or snarky, such as *30 Rock* or *The Office*, which poke fun at an institution. So it's looking for the vulnerability of people and how we all laugh at each other's mistakes and pain from a distance.

Drama, to me anyway, deals with human conflict on a much deeper level. Life, death, illness, malice, personal and family dysfunction. The stakes are profound. It's no wonder that most of our filmed drama revolves around police work, hospitals, and the judicial system. They deal in humanity.

PD: Yet we can point to shows that have both, some that are a half-hour long and are awfully dramatic and hours that aren't weighty.

DI: I think that has a great deal to do with the proliferation of networks. There's just more room to experiment and cross over. USA Network has a whole set of series, *Burn Notice* and *Royal Pains,* for example, that are tongue-in-cheek dramas. On ABC, *Desperate Housewives* is a drama that satirizes drama. The HBO half-hours seem to be situational, but portray more inappropriate heroes, as in *Hung, Entourage,* or *Eastbound & Down.* The half-hours on Showtime seem to be darker, delving into traditionally dramatic topics: *Weeds, Nurse Jackie, United States of Tara, The Big C.*

PD: All of those are heavily character-driven more than situational and they tackle serious issues. How do they call themselves comedy?

DI: Well I'd have to give them their own category: Dark Comedies. I was thinking about *M*A*S*H* in comparison to those shows and I don't think you could find something as dramatic, as filled with humanity, than war. What's worse than young people destroyed for a cause that was tenuous at best? But *M*A*S*H* was so much part of its time. You'd call it edgy in 1975, but you wouldn't call it edgy now. You'd have to do it in a more graphic way.

These cable half-hours are in that tradition. In my opinion *Nurse Jackie* is a progeny of *M*A*S*H,* but *Jackie* can go so much further in depicting

Mad Men

some really grim stuff. She deals with the day-to-day madness in somewhat the same fashion as the characters in *M*A*S*H*. There is a steady stream of wounded and dying, it's soul-wrenching work, and the healthiest people — Hawkeye, Trapper — realize that if they can't poke fun at it, if they can't laugh, they will go insane, they will lose it. Jackie's not away in Korea, she has a husband and family, but she's just as dedicated to saving lives. The steady glimpse into tragedy, though, takes its toll in any hospital, and so she's starting to fall apart inside, using drugs, having an affair. You couldn't have done that thirty years ago. So the edge is further out there.

PD: For years you wrote comedy and then you wrote for *Mad Men*. How is that different for a writer to change from comedy to drama?

DI: If you do television comedy like *Cheers* or *Frasier*, in front of an audience, it was very much about attitudinal conflict. So as a writer of comedies you're writing in a world where there are no unexpressed thoughts.

Writing for *Mad Men* was suddenly about the subtext. It was about insular action, almost novelistic. That was a big adjustment. I had written movies and I understood we're telling it a different way. However in traditional TV comedy, where I grew up, we were writing argument to argument until we hit the real conflict and hopefully the funny. With *Mad Men* there was very little reaching a flashpoint.

I'll give you an example. In the midst of the second season of *Mad Men* we were dealing with the character of Pete, our entitled account exec. The build-up had been Pete and his wife trying to get pregnant, and failing that, adopting a child. And his wife was constantly pressuring him. There was the conflict too of Pete being in love with Peggy. None of it was being expressed, but the audience is certainly aware of what's going on with Pete and the pressure he's brought on himself. There was a scene where Pete arrived home and his wife was going to confront him about moving ahead with the adoption and it was going to blow up. We were all struggling with what should happen. Then I remembered something my father had done when I was little. He came home one night and was upset about something at work. My mother had cooked him something he didn't want. We lived in a second floor apartment. My father took the food and threw it out the window. It was a shocking thing. No argument up to it, just all that unspoken backstory pouring out in this incongruous act — this uptight patrician couple acting so working class. And Matt [Weiner] said that's great; that's exactly what we should do.

PD: If beginning writers think they're comedy writers but they want to write drama, what do they do with their talent? Can you do both in an hour drama? Clearly there are some hour dramas that are branded as comedies. The Television Academy and the Writers Guild didn't know what to call *Boston Legal* — half the time it was judged in the comedy category for Emmy Awards and half the time as a drama. There are a lot of hybrids out there now.

DI: The short answer is you can do both. Matt Weiner, who created *Mad Men*, did only half-hours until he switched gears and wrote the *Mad Men* pilot as a spec. That script got him on *The Sopranos*, where he learned a whole different approach under David Chase. After *The Sopranos* ended, Matt got to make *Mad Men* as he had written it.

The key in all of this is character. It really is about character. Drama or comedy, or both, that's what drives you through a story. Even in a procedural like *CSI*, you're still invested in writing three-dimensional characters, characters with desires and personal flaws getting in the way of their work. You really have to approach a script through the characters, no matter how far flung the idea, no matter how high concept it is as comedy — something like *3rd Rock from the Sun* — as wild and crazy as that was, the writers created a very definitive group of characters. They were from another planet, but there was a real family dynamic between them.

There's no difference in that from watching *The Wire*, which may be the greatest television show I've ever seen. There you have a group of cops who are working together to counter the most base, despicable behavior by a group of people who themselves are being exploited by another group of people who are just downright evil. And these cops are thrown together and they all have their own problems. And yet somehow, they're like family to the viewer. You're wondering how this force they're fighting against is going to affect their lives. What will be the fate? And plenty of funny things go on in that, humor on a level that is again very dark, but you're laughing because it lightens the moment; it relieves tension.

New writers have to understand what creates character and how it guides you to tell a story. Real drama and real comedy are about some condition that people are afflicted by, or an obstacle in their lives, and you eventually find some way for them to deal with that dilemma.

CHAPTER 2

How Shows Get on TV and the TV Season

Fasten your seatbelt — here comes a heady two-year ride, from the first glimmer of a new series, twisting through one year of development, and then barreling through a full season on the air. We'll be touring the traditional network cycle, though you already know from Chapter One that TV is changing. Currently, many cable outlets (both basic and pay services) premiere series in winter and spring, and don't compete with the network season, and some networks are testing year-round production so that they stay competitive with cable, especially during the summer. I'll discuss those variations at the end. But now, take a look at the chart (Chart 2.1).

"Year One" represents the months of forming and selling a new series. See the dividing line before May? That's when a new show first gets picked up by a network. In "Year Two," we'll follow a series that's in production. Month by month, you'll experience the process as if watching your own project grow up.

Let's begin by making believe you have a great idea for a television series. Screech! That was the sound of brakes. You're not likely to get your original show made if you're a beginner. At least, you're not going to do it by yourself. For decades, the custom has been to climb the ladder: You'd join a staff and go up the ranks until a network invites you to propose a series of your own. By then, the reasoning goes, you'd understand the way things work so you could reliably deliver an episode every week. No novice could have enough experience. Simply, no one would listen to you no matter how interesting your idea might be.

Chart 2.1 Traditional Two-Year Development and Production of a New Show

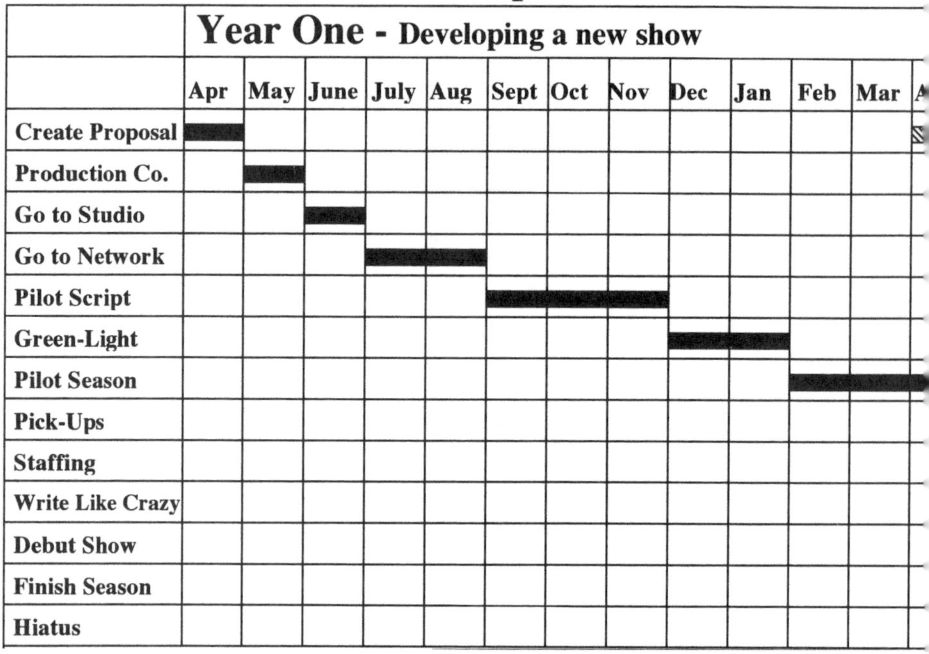
Year One - Developing a new show
Apr
May
June
July
Aug
Sept
Oct
Nov
Dec
Jan
Feb
Mar
Create Proposal
Production Co.
Go to Studio
Go to Network
Pilot Script
Green-Light
Pilot Season
Pick-Ups
Staffing
Write Like Crazy
Debut Show
Finish Season
Hiatus

So let's back up and understand why beginners don't create new series. (I know, we haven't even gotten to the first month, but hold on, you will get on the track.) Consider what a drama series does: It manufactures hour-long films that air every week and continue (the producers hope) for years. Your ability to come up with a pilot (the first episode) doesn't prove you can write episode 7, or 20, or the 88th episode at the end of four years. It doesn't necessarily demonstrate that the series has the "legs" for anyone else to derive a full season, either. (Having "legs" means a show has the potential to generate enough stories to last a long time.) And it surely doesn't guarantee that you would know how to run a multimillion-dollar business with hundreds of specialized employees (actors, set builders, editors, office staff, directors, truckers, camera operators, electricians, composers... without even counting writers).

Television series aren't bought or sold on ideas, but the ability to deliver on those ideas.

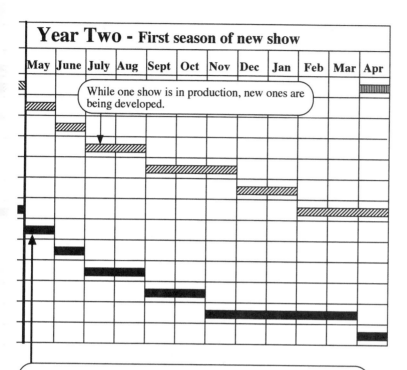

Year Two - First season of new show

May	June	July	Aug	Sept	Oct	Nov	Dec	Jan	Feb	Mar	Apr

While one show is in production, new ones are being developed.

In May networks announce which pilots are picked up for next season. If "yes" go to second year-- production. If "no" start over with another proposal.

Now, don't freak. There are ways. The closed loop of staff writers becoming showrunners who hire staff writers who will one day be showrunners is loosening. Sometimes feature filmmakers who have clout but no television experience are paired with TV veterans. A second infusion of outsiders is the twenty-something producers, often with a track record in small Internet series or credits in independent films, journalism, or published fiction, including graphic novels (comics). Since some outlets pursue teen audiences, they tend to prefer writers under 30. But could they have the experience to run a show? Here's how it worked at *The O.C.*.

At 27 years old, Josh Schwartz, creator of *The O.C.*, became the youngest person in network history to produce his own one-hour series. He was a junior at the USC School of Cinematic Arts when he sold a feature script for half a million dollars. A few months later, he sold his first TV pilot. And suddenly he was a TV producer, though he never spent a day on the staff of a series. Fox supplemented him with *Sex and the City* writer

Allan Heinberg, who helped structure stories for the first 13 episodes, and Bob DeLaurentiis, who'd spent two decades running shows. DeLaurentiis oversaw all aspects of production while Heinberg ran the writing staff. As for Schwartz, he wrote or rewrote episodes. In an article in *The New York Times*, Schwartz commented, "It's not like writing a movie — you still have to learn how to map out a season, how to track characters. It's not something I could've done by myself for the first time. You need people ... who've been through it. Who know how to build to sweeps, or this is how a teaser works. I had to get educated."

That brings us to your starting point on:

YEAR ONE
APRIL

CREATE YOUR PROPOSAL

So, here you are with your fresh idea — though I hope you have more going for you than that, even if you've never worked in television. The genesis of new shows ranges from the sublime to the ridiculous. On the high end, fifteen years of journalism covering Baltimore's police department led to a fact-based book titled *Homicide*, which was bought by experienced television producers and turned into the series *Homicide: Life on the Street*. And a decade later, that journalist, David Simon, created *The Wire* and *Treme*. On the other end of the spectrum, the comedy show *$#*! My Father Says* originated in a series of Tweets. You might not have years of journalism or an audience following you on Twitter, but do arm yourself with something, at least accomplishment as a screenwriter.

One of my former students (described in Chapter Seven), parlayed his credit on a quirky independent film *But I'm a Cheerleader* into several steps that led to writing a pilot for the WB (with his writing partner), and then the team joined the writing staff of *Smallville*, and nine years later they became the showrunners. Leverage whatever is special about you.

In this early stage, you're not aiming to shoot a series, only to land a meeting with a production company that has a track record. So your first goal is to be "adopted." For this, you'll need the same tool that will carry you all the way to the network, so everything else rests on square one, when you're on your own. Let's assume your idea has been percolating all winter, and now in April you're ready to form it into a presentation of some kind. But what kind? Actually, this stage doesn't offer the clear guidelines you'll find in the other steps. You'll need to discover the most compelling way to put across your unique concept. With that in mind, here are six possibilities:

(1) Write a TV Format

That term "format" can be confusing because it's used in different ways throughout filmmaking. "Format" may refer to a film stock or camera lens, to the way a script is laid out on a page, or even a genre or franchise. In this context it means a series proposal. Though a format isn't an exact process, certain components are advisable because you'll be asked about them in meetings anyway. In reality, most formats aren't even written except as notes for a network pitch. But I suggest you write everything, for now, to clarify your show for yourself and a production company. Lay it out this way:

Cover page: Find a title that grabs attention and suggests the tone of the show (funny, scary, dramatic, provocative, comforting, whatever). The title will probably change; think of it as a toe in a doorway. Underneath, identify the franchise or general category (e.g., teen drama, comedy-drama, political thriller, sci-fi...). If it's based on something (book, play, movie, cartoon) you'd better say so, but make sure you have clear rights to the underlying work. Your credit is "Written By" or "Created By" and that goes on a separate line. Place your contact information at the bottom of the page. If you're represented by an agent or manager, of course, the cover is done by their office and your agent will be the contact.

Do register the completed format with the Writers Guild (specifics on that are in the Appendix). But do not put your WGA registration number on the cover — it's tacky. Also don't include any dates or draft numbers. Every draft you deliver is the first, untrammeled and never before revealed to human eyes — or that's what you'd like the producer to think. (No one wants something that's been rejected or gathering dust.)

On the top of Page One, write a "Log Line." You've encountered that term in screenwriting classes, but did you know it originated in television? For decades, television station owners have been required by the FCC to keep a log of everything they broadcast. These had to fit on a line, like

"Lassie finds lost boy." Then *TV Guide* and newspapers began printing short episode summaries like this one from *Joan of Arcadia*: "Joan learns the downside of vanity when God asks her to take a cosmetics class."

Soon the promotional tag found its way to movie posters, as in: "Tom Cruise stars as Nathan Algren, a heroic American military officer hired by the Emperor of Japan to train the country's first army. After being captured by his Samurai enemies, Algren becomes unexpectedly inspired by their way of life and fights to defend what he has come to love." Or, for a simpler example: "The women of Stepford have a secret." Before long, either full log lines (like the one from *The Last Samurai*) or "hooks" (like the one from *The Stepford Wives*) became necessary to pitch films, episodes, and series, not merely to log them or advertise.

A log line for a series may be less specific than the story summaries you'll use for individual episodes. The goal is to orient a listener (yes, listener, not reader) to your project, to catch an executive's attention. "MTV Cops" is a famous log line for *Miami Vice* from an era when MTV was new and hot. *Grey's Anatomy*, on the heels of the success of *Sex and the City*, was described as "Sex and the Surgery." When he was first presenting *The O.C.*, Josh Schwartz knew the Fox network was looking for an updated *Beverly Hills 90210*, so he pitched his show as "90210 on the beach in Orange County," and later admitted that was a Trojan horse to set up a far more nuanced show.

Once your log line sizzles, take the first couple of pages of your format for an Overview. This is not a summary of the pilot (a common mistake), but an introduction to the world and the quest of the whole series, including location, style, tone, context, and, most of all, characters. Though full characterizations come later, the main cast must be mentioned up front. Use brief tags like "a single, middle-aged probation officer who adopts a child from one of her cases" (from Allison Anders' series proposal *In the Echo*); "a 29-year-old Congressional aide running against her boss" (from Rod Lurie's proposed *The Capital City*).

Within this Overview, suggest springboards for future episodes so decision-makers believe the series has legs. That is, state the source of future episodes, for example: Each week the character must balance the tension of her marriage with the intrigue and politics of a legal case; each week the detectives pursue three cases, walking a thin line between vigilante justice and the job; each week we fall in love with the vampire, only to discover we're bitten again. As in any fiction writing, make 'em laugh, cry, be scared or angry or fall in love. The overview may be as far as you get in a pitch, so make it soar.

Follow the Overview with the centerpiece of any series: characters. If viewers don't root for your main cast, if they're not compelled to find out how the people are coping or loving or fighting back each week, you don't have anything. Remember, TV drama isn't really about the concept; it runs on the emotional fuel of endless character arcs, as discussed in Chapter One.

Take one page each for the few leading roles. I said few. Yes, you've seen excellent ensemble shows with casts in double-digits, but in a proposal, the listener's eyes will glaze over after you get past your third or fourth character. So focus on one fascinating, eminently castable character and engage us in her spirit and goals. You can do that again with roles for antagonists or partners, providing their connections to the protagonist are gripping. Beyond those few, summarize the secondary cast with only a tag for each, even if those parts will grow later.

After the characters, you need to tell some stories. You might summarize a potential pilot in a couple of pages. (More about pilot writing in a moment.) But networks really need the sense of a mid-season episode because that's a window to how the show functions every week. Some proposals focus on episode seven. Some list log lines for five to ten potential episodes. Some describe the long arc and the end of the quest after five years on the air. Whichever method suits your series best, be sure that you communicate an arena so rich that its possibilities seem endless.

That's it for standard components, but that's not it for a proposal. People refer to series pitches as dog-and-pony shows, and so far I haven't suggested any special enticements, furry or otherwise. Try photos, artwork, clippings, endorsements, biographies — come up with something fun. But don't do the baked goods angle; it's been tried, and readers get annoyed. You know, placing your proposal in a cake so the executive is sure to notice it. However, if your show is set in a bakery, maybe you should get cooking!

(2) Write a Pilot

Pilot scripts are assigned by networks in the course of development, and I'll tell you how that works when we get to September on the chart. (We're still only in April.) Normally, producers proposing a new series don't go in with a pilot already written because it's too expensive for something not likely to succeed (most proposals die, and so do most pilots). Also, network reactions might change the series. Why spend $30,000 or more for a script about a hermaphrodite in a beauty pageant when the network will only buy if the contestant is a poodle? But if your writing is not known, and you're passionate that a sample would convince readers, then speculating a pilot could be smart strategy.

Matt Weiner, creator of *Mad Men*, wrote the pilot while he was toiling away on sitcoms. At the time no one would buy it, but the quality of the writing landed him on the writing staff of *The Sopranos*. Years honing his skills on that great show and winning awards finally made it possible for him to film the *Mad Men* pilot made exactly as he'd envisioned it long before.

J. Michael Straczynski, creator of *Babylon 5*, is said to have written all five years of his series while he was on the staff of a *Star Trek*, so *Babylon 5* was finished before he ever proposed it. But don't try that at home, folks.

Short of writing 100 episodes, the worst you risk is another unsold script. If it's written well, a pilot can serve as a writing sample along with any other screenplays or episodes. And as soon as you have clout (or know someone who does), you can take it off your shelf.

For more about writing a pilot, see the "Spotlight On Writing Your Pilot Script" between Chapters Four and Five.

(3) Write a "Backdoor Pilot"

A backdoor pilot is a two-hour movie, and might be a clever way to propel a series. The game involves writing a pilot that masquerades as a movie, and, in fact, works as a closed story. But the seeds of subsequent tales and promising character developments are embedded in a situation that could easily spring many episodes.

You could offer it as a screenplay and be thunderstruck when someone else observes that it could lead to a series. Or you could come clean with your intentions up front. Depends on who you're dealing with, but you certainly should tell an agent what you have in mind. Another compromise is the "limited series" (which used to be called "miniseries"). That's longer than a movie but less of a commitment than a full season, usually running six to eight hours over several weeks. If the movie (or limited series) does well, you have a great shot at the series. Either the backdoor pilot or the "partial order" gives a network a chance to hedge the bet. And if it doesn't go to series, you still have a movie script.

(4) Create a Presentation Reel

A showrunner once invited me to his office to discuss a series that had suddenly landed in his lap. He didn't have a clue about it, he said uneasily; it was loosely based on a hit movie and had been sold as a series on the basis of a 15-minute reel made by one of the movie's producers who didn't have time to do the show. So the newly anointed executive producer was hastily interviewing writers to find the series. The problem was that 15 minutes of "possible scenes" using the movie producer's actor friends (who would not be in the actual series either) didn't add up. Not that the 15 minutes weren't cinematic — they were beautifully atmospheric — but the group in the office were TV writers looking for the kinds of elements I've told you about: a) springboards suggesting where stories would come from; b) characters with potential for long arcs; c) some sort of quest or motor for the star. The reel turned out to be sort of a Rorschach test: everyone came up with a different show... which meant no show at all, finally.

Even if you're not a Hollywood movie producer who can sell a series off a few scenes, a reel might be helpful if used cleverly. Think of the dog-and-pony show, and imagine an executive in his office. It's 4 PM and he's been taking pitches every 20 minutes since his breakfast meeting at 8 AM. You walk in with a DVD. He might wake up for that.

If you want to try, here are some tips:

Be careful it doesn't scream student film. You know: the long zoom toward the doorknob, which is ever so beautifully lit, and the reflective moments laden with symbolism. Often, student films aim at film festivals where their art is appreciated. In television, which moves faster, those same qualities may come off as indulgent. So make sure your reel looks professional and suits the medium.

Keep it short enough so you have time to pitch before or after the film, including the set-up time. You may have only 15 minutes, total, in the meeting.

Do pitch the show. The reel is only eye-candy. Unlike the movie producer, you're not going to get away with not knowing how the series is going to work.

Have fun. Creative, original filmmaking can be an exciting calling card as long as the series would be able to sustain your approach.

(5) Attach a "Package"

A "package" consists of "elements" that enhance your project's profile. Later, the package may include writers who are more credited than you, directors, main cast, possibly some special perks (for example, location, animation or an underlying source if those are relevant), and maybe even a sponsor. Certain "packaging agencies" pride themselves in assembling all the creative talent from within their own shop. But for you, at this stage, it comes down to nabbing a star audiences find interesting; someone they'll tune in to see. These concerns belong to studios and networks, usually not writers, but if you're trying to load the dice, you might see who you can "attach."

Ah, there's another bit of jargon. When a writer, director or actor is "attached," he has committed to work on your project. It's more than an expression of interest, and must be confirmed in a letter or even a contract. Be careful who you attach, though. Say you've courted your idol and finally convinced him to come aboard. Then you learn the network is looking for a vehicle for their hot new thing, and will "greenlight" your series only if Hottie is the star. But now you're stuck with your idol. That's one of many reasons talent is rarely packaged at this point.

(6) Get a Web Following

A friend of mine was thrilled the day a major studio said they wanted to buy her original series. They had read her pilot and a short series bible she had attached, she was represented by a respected agent, and she even had a few credits. This would be the Big Break, she believed, as she went to the first meeting with her expected new creative home. And then they dropped the question: "What is your YouTube number?" Huh? They were interested in her project all right, but they wanted assurance that an audience would be interested. So they expected her — a writer — to somehow assemble enough of a film crew to post samples of what she was proposing online and gather "heat" before they would go forward.

My friend didn't go for it, but the approach might work for someone else. If you have the equipment and skills and if the nature of your show lends itself to Web-based storytelling (which tends to be comedic and able to be broken into short segments), that's an example of a potential end-run around the established process. The famous attempt was *Quarterlife* by multi-credited film and television producers Marshall Herskovitz and Edward Zwick. They posted 10- to 15-minute segments online, each mimicking a television act. When a network came calling, they packaged the individual acts into a perfect hour. It didn't work, but that may have been as much a factor of that particular property rather than a comment on future possibilities.

Go ahead and try them all — one through six — if you have the time and money. But that would take another year. So to stay on our cycle, let's make believe you've created a terrific format, and backed it up with impressive writing samples. Now you move ahead to square two:

MAY

THE PRODUCTION COMPANY

You're on the hunt for a production company with your new series as bait. In May, you might get a producer's attention because the previous season has ended and work for the new one not quite begun. If your proposal is ready sooner, you could also "put out feelers" in April during "hiatus." (You'll hear about the hiatus in Year Two.) Now, you need a company that can get you into both a studio and a network. Better yet, try to meet a showrunner who has an "open commitment" or "blind overall deal," which means a network is obligated to buy a show from him. Who knows, he just might be searching for something new.

But how are you going to find him? Through your agent; like it or not, that's how this industry works. Any competent agent knows who's willing to take series pitches, who is between shows, who might spark to your idea, who is willing to deal with a beginner, and who has relationships at the kinds of outlets that fit your show. The agent can put you in the room. So if you already have an agent you can skip this section. NOT! Don't ever lie back and think an agent is going to do it all for you. To paraphrase: Agents help those who help themselves. If you don't have one, see Chapter Six, "How To Break In."

But what if you're determined to plow ahead on your own? It's not impossible to get to production companies, and in some cases they may be more accessible than agents. Comb websites and read *Daily Variety* to scope out who's interested in developing new series. If you have the magic bullet for a company who needs to get with the times and climb back to the top, or if you're young, talented, have some awards or credits, and an aggressive personality, you may well get past the receptionist. Part of the technique is finding the perfect match to your sensibility and your project. And part of it, quite frankly, is age.

I'll be candid with you about this issue. I'm sure you've heard about age discrimination in Hollywood. Some networks tend to chase young demographics, though not all are the same; in fact the top cable outlets and sophisticated network dramas prefer talent that has been honed. Still, the youth bias has created an opportunity for young writers. Very young. I know of a high school student whose homemade pilot was seriously considered, though it never sold.

At USC, my graduate screenwriting students range in age from mid-20s to mid-30s, so one year I joked to a class that they'd better not turn 30, just keep turning 29. Well, in the fall I got a call from Jennifer, a good writer who'd graduated the previous spring. She was upset because she applied for a writing job and the secretary asked her age. (That's illegal, by the way.) Jennifer, who had just celebrated her 30th birthday, remembered my joke and quickly answered "29." "Oooh, I'm sorry," the secretary cooed, "our ceiling is 26."

You may have heard about the writer who was hired on *Felicity* on the basis of being 18, and fired when she was discovered to be (gasp!) over 30. But the point for you is being young might help you get a meeting. After that, you'll have to wrangle not to lose your project to more seasoned writers, but right now we're talking about first steps.

Whatever your tactic, start by researching television production companies that do projects like yours. At the tail of each episode you'll see a list of producing entities. Sometimes several logos appear because an expensive series may spread the cost among various backers, so to find out who is actually developing series, try phoning the show or the network and asking. Other resources include websites, *The Hollywood Creative Directory*, the library of the Writers Guild of America, and the Academy of Television Arts and Sciences. Information on all those is in the Appendix.

Once you have your targets, write to them and follow with a call asking to pitch your series idea. Don't mail the format, but if you can catch the reader with a beguiling few sentences, you may flush out someone curious enough to take a brief meeting. You don't need to wait for a response from your first choice before hitting up a second place. Contact them all at once.

At the meeting, you need to hook the listener quickly. Of course, you hope that listener is an executive producer or head of the production company. But if you're shunted off to an assistant, go ahead anyway. Make an ally so you'll have a chance to repeat the pitch to the decision-maker another day.

What are they looking for? Energy. That's amorphous, I know, but it covers the sense that the series has possibilities. Remember, a series pitch is not the same as telling a movie story where the plot beats need to be in place. This is the first step in a long development process, and if this company becomes involved, they'll probably steer you toward revisions so the project will sell, or so it fits in a specific time slot, or competes with other series coming down the pike. They'll be watching how flexible you are, wondering if they'd be comfortable working with you for years, kind of a blind date. If you're defensive or reluctant to revise your precious property, they'll wish you luck trying to do it all by yourself — elsewhere.

They'll be checking whether the concept is viable; that is, whether they can physically produce it each week within a likely budget. But they won't ask that question unless you satisfy two other qualifications: (1) The show is completely new and unique, and (2) the show is exactly like what has succeeded before. Yes, it's a paradox. The solution is to be original within a franchise, even if that franchise is re-interpreted, as I discussed in the first chapter.

And, of course, you know what every TV series needs above all. Come on, you know the answer: Characters. The heart of your pitch is how fully you engage the buyer in the people you have created. But you already know that from your format, because you're well prepared.

So let's imagine you've pitched to a few executive producers and settled on one company that has everything: a studio deal, the juice to take you to a network, the ability to deliver the show, the willingness to keep you in the loop even though you're a beginner; and, most of all, they "get" your idea. You've found a creative home.

Maybe.

JUNE

THE STUDIO

Most production companies can't go to the networks by themselves. That's because network series are "deficit financed." Networks pay a fee to broadcast each program, around 75% of the cost of making it. For an hour-long drama that costs five million, the shortfall is around a million dollars per week. Every week. Companies don't have that.

Studios do. Think of the studio as the bank. From the point of view of a "suit," every time a studio endorses a series with one of the production companies on their lot they're taking a calculated risk. Four years may go by before they see any return on their investment, if they ever do, and most shows are cancelled before that. But, oh, when a show finishes the 88th episode, they hit what they call "the mother lode," "the jackpot," "Valhalla." Now they can sell the shows at a profit to cable channels, syndication and foreign markets. A single hit underwrites years of failures. Will yours be that hit?

That brings us back to you. Probably, you have no agreement in writing with the production company. They're waiting to see if the studio will get behind this project. While you're away, the producer is talking to the Vice President for Dramatic Series Development of the studio where he has a deal. If the producer loves your show, he's pre-pitching it, maybe touting you as the next great thing.

Or not. He may be testing the waters to see if you're approvable before he sticks in his own toe. That might involve sending your writing samples to the studio executive, or even, quietly, to a contact at one of the networks. He may also test the general "arena" of the show, without specifically pitching it: "Any interest in a drama about house plants; I have a great fern." Prepare yourself, because if weak signals start coming back from the studio, he might drop the project; or he might keep the project but begin nudging you aside. You'll know you're being dumped if his conversation includes the term "participating," if he floats names of possible writers who aren't you, and if he talks up the title "associate producer." Sometimes that indicates an actual job, but it might be honorary, a way to shift you off the writing staff. Remember, you do have the right to say no and take your project elsewhere.

Let's imagine someone up there thinks you're interesting, at least enough to let you audition. So back you go to the studio lot. But this time, you and the producer will refine and rehearse your pitch, and together, you'll go to the VP.

If your producer is powerful, and he has an open commitment or overall deal, the studio may let him make network appointments on his word alone. If he's not that strong, or he's not so confident of your show, he'll ask you to pitch your heart out again. Though your original format has been revised, you're essentially presenting what you developed in April. But now the producer is sitting next to you, and you're talking to a big desk.

Let's say you pass "Go." You advance to the next squares:

JULY AND AUGUST

THE NETWORK

Traditional network television operates on the lemming model: All the creatures rush to the precipice at the same time, and most fall off. You'll observe this behavior in most of the following stages.

All the networks "open" for new series pitches during the summer. They announce an exact opening date to agencies, and sometimes it's in the "trades." Depending on their needs — that is, how many series are returning, how many slots they have to fill for the fall — some might begin meetings in June, and some might be hearing proposals as late as October. You want to get in there as soon as possible, before they're filled, though they're inundated no matter when you go. And the playing field isn't level. The big shots (companies with successful shows on the air) will have scarfed up prime broadcast real estate before your meeting is even scheduled.

The process is well established and organized, though it looks like a shell game to an outsider. Each network may hear around 500 pitches during their open season. Out of those, each chooses 50 to 100 to become pilot scripts. Of those, 10 to 20 might be made into pilot films. Out of those, a few become series. Those numbers vary each year, but here's a simplified example from just one of the four broadcast networks: Take 20% at each cut — 500 pitches yield 100 pilot scripts yield 20 pilots which yield five series (see Chart 2.2). That's a ten percent overall chance of making a sale, if all else was equal, which, of course, it isn't.

Chart 2.2   New Series Development at One Network (a hypothetical example)

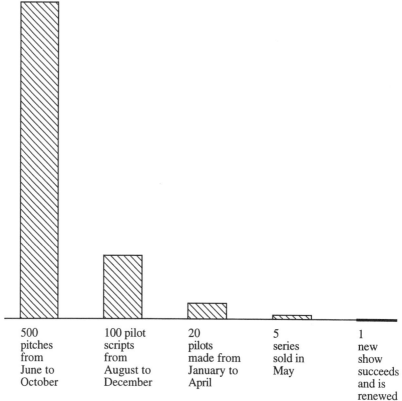

| 500 pitches from June to October | 100 pilot scripts from August to December | 20 pilots made from January to April | 5 series sold in May | 1 new show succeeds and is renewed |

Instead of dwelling on the odds, let's stay focused on your own opportunity. First, understand the human side of what you're walking into at a network. The Vice President for new dramatic programs, and the Director of new dramatic programs (along with a lesser title, Manager of new dramatic programs) are taking meetings all day, every day, for three or four months. A parade of showrunners come in and out of that office every 20 minutes or so. In fact, your own producer may be fielding other shows besides yours, which means they're in competition with you.

On the day of the meeting, everyone is dressed up. You'll gather in the lobby with your executive producer and possibly someone representing the studio, an agent from a major packaging agency (likely, the producer's agent), and other components of your package. That might mean a network-approved high-power writer who would guarantee the pilot script, or a television star.

I once went to a network pitch on a show where the lead actor was essential. When the day came, the actor was called to a dubbing session. And we couldn't change the appointment. So we went in with a blow-up of his headshot and set it on a chair.

You'll have a cheering section in your meeting, and the first little while will seem like friendly greetings. Then the moment comes when the producer says, "You're on," the room falls silent, and all eyes are on you. Now, pitching to a network executive is a craft unto itself. Some execs nod, smile, and act interested. With others, it's like talking to Mount Rushmore. Regardless, keep your energy high. With the nice guy, you skip out of the meeting sure you just sold a series. With the mountain, you believe you failed. Neither might be true.

If you haven't heard in a week or two, the studio (or your producer, depending on the network relationship) phones the network. They're usually pretty quick about saying no, and in that case, the studio will set up a meeting at the next network on the list. This can go on several times, but after four networks, and a surreptitious call to basic cable, if you're not getting a nibble, they'll probably drop your project. Remember, the property is still yours at this point, and no one owes anybody anything.

But let's say you were funny and intriguing and fresh and unique — and the network thinks your show is just like another one that's a hit — so you pass Go again. Of course, you're not greenlighted to make a series — you know better than that by now. The assignment is only to write the pilot. That's the next group of squares:

September to November

THE PILOT SCRIPT

Whoever writes the pilot will have at least a "developed by" credit, and may even receive "created by" credit on the series. That will generate a royalty on every episode, and his name will appear on screen forever, even if the pilot-writer is long gone. Don't assume that's you unless your writing proves that only you can capture the style and world you've proposed.

Or have you already written the pilot? If you took a chance on it, the producer will wonder if it's going to hurt or help your prospects. That's a sticky situation because asking you to set aside your pilot in favor of someone else's draft is emotionally wrenching. But if you lose the whole deal because your pilot is less than mind-blowing, that's just as wrenching.

Some professional writers have built careers doing pilots for other people's shows. They're savvy about the ingredients any pilot needs, they bring a pedigree of successful series, and they know how to win over network readers. It's an oddity because these special pilot writers, who may earn up to half a million dollars for a one-hour script, usually are not the ones who will write the episodes each week, so network decision-makers are evaluating a hyped-up version of the show. It's kind of a bait-and-switch, where they're buying one writer's voice, but another will write the series.

Let's say they love your project because they love something about you — your hip writing style, insight into a subculture, your humor, your passion. Or maybe you're just less expensive — $30,000 for the pilot script instead of half a million. Now the network calls the studio who calls the producer who calls your agent who calls you and you get a contract to write.

So, how do you do this thing? Pilots come in two flavors: **premise** and **ongoing**. A premise pilot begins with a "before" and propels the quest or situation the central character will tackle throughout the series. For example, *The Good Wife* opened with a life-changing event when Alicia Florrick's husband, the D.A., is accused of a crime, and within the pilot loses his position and ultimately goes to jail. On her own with children to raise, Alicia returns to her career as a lawyer. At the law firm, she meets the characters who will become her new relationships while she continues to cope with the new roles within her family. And thus begins both the procedural and serial elements that roll out from the premise pilot.

Northern Exposure opened in New York City, where the lead character, Joel Fleischman, learns that his medical school scholarship requires him to work as a doctor in Cicely, Alaska. Joel fights to get out of this commitment but soon finds himself staring out a train window until he arrives at a frozen place where he's greeted by a moose. As we're drawn into his new world, we meet the characters who will become Joel's new relationships, and their arcs are set in motion.

In an ongoing pilot, the world of the show is in place and many of the characters are entrenched in their dramatic missions. The challenge is to reveal these characters and relationships without the aid of an outsider's introduction, which we had with both Alicia and Joel. An example of an ongoing pilot was *ER*: a day in the life of an emergency room at a Chicago hospital in full swing. New characters arrived — Nurse Carol Hathaway on a stretcher, and Dr. John Carter as a young intern — but the elements of the show were already in play. The same can be said of *Big Love, The Wire, Mad Men,* and many other serials.

Boardwalk Empire, which opened with a celebration among bootleggers in Atlantic City the day prohibition became law in 1920, and *Breaking Bad,* in which the lead character is diagnosed with terminal cancer, both took an external incident to push forward characters whose relationships were ongoing, using both ways of piloting a show.

Whichever type of pilot you choose, you'll need the same ingredients. In addition to terrific writing, which includes building tension toward cliff-hangers at act breaks and creating rich and provocative characters, just as you would in any episode (see Chapter Three for more about this), pilots have a special burden of exposition. Without the audience feeling they're being informed, you need to establish the rules of your world, the engine for future stories (springboards), and enough "backstory" (history) on the characters so their current situation is understandable. You want viewers riveted by the characters. Simply, your pilot has to make people tune in to episode two.

Some techniques are similar to beginning a feature, where audiences don't yet know the characters either. But features are easier because once people have bought tickets and are sitting in the dark, they'll give a movie time to unveil itself. Television has to grab people in the first minutes or they're clicking the remote. So, sure, use everything you know from theatrical screenplays in terms of presenting a new character, but start the story faster. Also, use everything you've learned about avoiding clunky exposition (bury it in an argument, play it in a scene instead of explaining, use visual evidence, parse it out in bits, reveal it as part of the plot instead of for its own sake, and so forth). If you're "living" your writing, instead of manipulating it, some of these problems may solve themselves. And if those central characters and your idea are as vibrant as the format you pitched, the pilot might come naturally.

Easy or difficult, approximately 50 pages are going to be due at the network around Thanksgiving. From a network's point of view it will be the first draft. Of course, it won't. You will have gone through every step with your producer, and the studio may have read drafts as well. No one wants to take a chance that this won't work, so if your drafts aren't delivering the spirit that landed this assignment, they'll bring in another writer, who will share the writing credit. So all through October and November you're rewriting like crazy — you and everyone else who's doing a pilot. And, true to the lemmings, everyone else's pilot is due at all the networks the same time as yours. All over town everyone is anticipating:

December and January

THE GREENLIGHT

Several possibilities: The network may send notes for a second draft of the pilot. If so, you'll gnash your teeth: What do they mean they don't like the central character — that's exactly who I pitched and that's who they bought! They wait until now to tell me they have another pilot too close to this, so we have to change everything! What am I supposed to do with a note like "not funny enough" when this drama was never supposed to be funny at all! No, I can't turn this drama about men in prison into a vehicle for Lady Gaga! Huh???

After the gnashing, you'll sit with the producer and maybe your studio development person and figure out what you can fix, and what, if anything, may be left alone or argued. If they believe your situation is precarious, the studio may ask for a major rewrite. In any case, your finished script is due by Christmas — the same as everyone else.

And like everyone else, you're hoping your pilot script will be plucked out as one of the twenty or thirty percent that get "greenlighted." That means the network gives the production company the go-ahead to produce the pilot. These greenlights may be announced anytime from December through January. They lead to:

FEBRUARY TO APRIL

PILOT SEASON

Instead of snow, a climate of anxiety hangs in the sunny skies of Los Angeles in winter. It's accompanied by a giant sound of vacuuming, inhaling all unclaimed film crews down to the last grip and gaffer, all the sound stages, every available television director, and all the actors who cycle through pilots year after year in "holding deals" (contracts which hold an actor exclusive to a potential series). George Clooney was cast in fifteen failed pilots before *ER*. Welcome to pilot season.

Though it begins with your script, the produced pilot is enhanced by "production values" (locations, techniques, or personnel) that make it more expensive than a normal episode. For example, Disney spent a remarkable $12 million on the two-hour pilot for its 2004 series *Lost*.

When fully edited, a typical pilot will be 44 minutes long, the length of a network hour without ads. But once in a while a network asks for a 20- or 25-minute "presentation" instead, like a demo for a record company. That's bad news for you as the writer, because your finely honed 50-page script must be slashed to 30 pages, losing secondary story lines, nuance, and sometimes risking the sense of the show. Networks order these presentations anyway because they cost around two million, which is roughly half the cost of a pilot. If this befalls you, just sit down and cut the pages. You really don't have a choice.

Except for production revisions (for casting, location, timing, and so forth), the writer's work is essentially finished by February. Still, I advise you to stick as close as you can to the production. If the producers will let you, be on the set, see the "dailies," go to meetings. Of course, you know better than to breathe down the director's neck or stand in the way of rolling cameras. Just don't fade out after you've written "fade out."

By April, all the pilots in all genres at all the networks are edited and tested at the same time. This testing, incidentally, is a tribal ritual in itself. Unwitting tourists in Las Vegas (chosen because Vegas attracts visitors from all over the country) are given $10 gift certificates in exchange for registering their reactions on an electronic dial while viewing a pilot. If something scores poorly, it may be re-edited; way too late to rewrite, though. With the pilots done, it's time for:

MAY

PICK-UPS

All the lemmings arrive at the edge of the precipice at once — and off they go to New York by May. Isn't it strange that shows are (usually) produced in Los Angeles, and network and studio executives are based here, and the entire creation of the pilot happens on the West Coast, yet the verdict is rendered 3,000 miles away? That's because the decision is corporate, involving huge investments that impact parent companies and involve advertisers who (they hope) offset those costs. It's Big Brother time.

Once the pilots have gone, no one can do anything but wait. That doesn't stop studio executives from checking into top New York hotels and haunting lobbies where screenings are in progress upstairs. They can't really influence the outcome, can't attend screenings or discussions, so what do they hope to gain? Gossip — leaks, hints, a raised eyebrow that their show may go. Or die.

I once wrote a pilot for a company whose glory days were memorialized in posters of hit series lining the corridors. But the rooms off the corridors were empty. Every one of their series had concluded or been cancelled the season before. They fielded a number of possibilities, but only one went to pilot — mine. It was early May, and only one light was on in one office — the executive producer's. He went there every day and sat at the phone. He ate lunch at the phone. Waiting. Waiting for the call from New York. He sent his secretary to the city to listen for rumors, but she hadn't heard anything. I brought him lunch one day, but we didn't have much to talk about, staring at the phone.

Finally, in mid-May the call came: "We're not going to pick you up." There was no explanation — there never is — but post-game analysis guessed that too many similar shows were offered, or too many competing shops had early commitments, or too few slots were open, or none of the above.

But let's make believe your phone call is some version of "Pack your bags — we'll see you in New York." Your order will probably be in one of four categories:

• Full season

A traditional network season is 22 episodes, though some shows do 24 or even 26. In reality, even an order for a full season is hedged: The pick-up (commitment to air) is "13 plus the back 9." That means 13 episodes will be broadcast, with the decision on the final 9 contingent on their performance.

• Short order

This is common and might be bad news for show creators. It means the network agrees to air only six episodes — or only four! If those hook an audience quickly, more episodes are ordered. But how many shows find their audience in three weeks? With so many options, viewers might not even visit the newborn until week three. And some series take a while to get their legs. Historically, icons like the original *Star Trek*, *All in the Family*, and other famously successful series, took months before word of mouth alerted viewers to check them out.

Now, the heap of dead series, killed before people hardly knew they were on, casts a stench over creativity at the networks. Bottom-line network executives tend to avoid risks, but that policy backfires because fear-based decisions send some of the most creative producers and writers to cable where longer orders are customary, or where seasons are conceived as 12 episodes long (or even as few as 8 episodes in certain "full" seasons) but you are fairly secure you'll be back for season two. It's similar to having a full season with a hiatus, and some creators like that pace.

• Midseason

Midseason pickups may be the best news, some showrunners think. Though a late debut denies the show a spot on the fall schedule, and probably limits the number of episodes that would air the first year, some producers like it: Their show is removed from the crowd of September premieres and saved from the insistent pressure to be on the air in a few months. Networks also like midseason shows because they create an illusion of year-round programming, which helps the network compete with year-round cable. And midseason replacements are a cushion against inevitable cancellations. If the network lets the show go ahead and produce a few episodes, pending a slot, you'll have the time to write as well as you did in the pilot.

That said, as the writer, you'll feel disappointed. You have to wait until late fall or early winter to find out when you're on the air. And it's hard not to wonder if you'll ever be given a place at all.

• Back-up scripts

Back-ups are the smallest pick-up, accompanied by a better-than-nothing sigh. It means the network won't let you produce any episodes but would like to see additional scripts. They're holding on to the show because the concept interests them, but something in the pilot didn't work. It might be casting, tone, location, or something at the core — the direction of the stories themselves. This is a second opportunity to prove the series can work by actually writing up to five episodes, sometimes called "back-up pilots." You, the writer, are in the spotlight, and assuming they haven't held back because the writing is weak, this can be your chance to shine.

Let's make believe you got a pick-up for 13 on the air. See the chute from May on the outer circle in Chart 2.1? Well, hold on because you're about to be swept down it to:

YEAR TWO
JUNE

STAFFING

Hurtled out of the development chute, still tumbling, you land in June with three months to put an hour series on the air every week. That doesn't mean producing the first hour. It means scripts for the first five to seven episodes, plus three "in the can" (ready to air). But you have next to nothing. The sets have been struck and need to be re-built. You have no crew, no office, no production facility, and only your personal cell phone. And you urgently need a writing staff right now.

Shows that are ongoing or announced early aren't in this fix (and neither are cable series, but more about that at the end). Optimistic showrunners started reading sample scripts and speaking with agents as far back as February, especially if the pilot was attracting an industry "buzz." But without an actual order, they couldn't staff. And some producers are taken by surprise.

I was once hired on a staff in June and we didn't gather until the first week in July, although we were scheduled to premiere the first week of September. The executive producer, a highly-regarded writer-producer, had written a personal pilot that didn't fit neatly into a usual franchise (sometimes called a "passion project") and everyone thought it was a long shot. I think he was actually out of town on vacation when the pick-ups were announced; that's how unlikely he thought this would be. So there we sat in a temporary office lent by the studio — four adrift writers and the surprised showrunner. He opened with "Anyone have ideas for stories?"

But that's rare. With months to imagine winning this lottery, most show-runners are ready, and the instant the series goes, negotiations commence with writers. If you were in the mix from the beginning (if the concept was yours or you wrote the pilot), your deal is already in place. If you're trying to join a staff, June is when those jobs open and fill quickly, so your agent should have been pitching you in the months before.

The next chapter tells how a writing staff works, so we'll skip over that and assume by the end of June everyone is in place and writing has begun. It continues:

JULY AND AUGUST

WRITE LIKE CRAZY

Ditch the idea that summer is vacation time if you're writing for network television. July and August are the crazy-making months when the staff is turning out scripts as fast as they can. Though each show has its own rhythm, if you're in any writers' room, you'll be "breaking stories" around the table, dissecting outlines as they come in, and discussing early drafts by the other writers every week at the same time as you write your own. (In Chapter Four, I explain the steps of writing.)

Probably, the first episode exists: It's the pilot. But the audience might not discover your series the first week, or even the second. So in a way, the first three episodes will function as pilots. Episodes Two and Three have to reach a balance between orienting first-time viewers by reprising the overall "mission" and identifying the cast, while progressing the stories to hold people who watched before. If the pilot was a premise that deposited a character in a new environment or quest, then Episode Two is expected to deliver what happens there. It may be the most difficult and least rewarding episode on a show.

Think about it — the audience doesn't know the characters, so viewers are not yet emotionally invested. But neither do you have the benefit of the inciting situation or curiosity that sets the series in motion, since that happened the first week. Nevertheless, this "development" episode must sizzle with the tension and anticipation of the pilot. That calls for one of the more experienced writers — not you. Your earliest assignment might be Episode Four or Five, depending on the size of the staff.

While the staff is writing, production is rolling out shows. Probably, you'll be invited to sit in on casting guest stars in your own episode. Once shooting starts, "dailies" (unedited scenes) are screened almost every day. Go to the screenings, no matter how hard you're writing. After you hear how the dialogue plays, you might want to rework the cadence of a scene you're writing. Dailies also reveal the strengths of the actors. If chemistry between actors burns through the screen, you'll want to use it.

But don't get beguiled by stars. You've probably heard the joke about the starlet who was so stupid she slept with the writer. Well, that doesn't make sense in television where writers do have power, and smart actors know it. They'll want to have lunch with you to pitch stories for their character. I was on one show where an actor researched each writer's birthday and sent exquisite hand-made cards; on another, an actor distributed coffee mugs personalized with each writer's name. Some showrunners warn new writers not to hang out with the actors, fearing they'll be too easily influenced. I say, go for it — talented actors contemplate their characters, and that can inspire you.

As the series evolves, the head writer must decide whether to let characters develop in a way he didn't foresee, or stick to the original plan. Some showrunners begin with a chart of story arcs for the whole season. In fact, many established series invite their large staff to a retreat in early June (or whichever month precedes their season). On a whiteboard, they might assign each character a color-coded marker and track the five-or-so main roles from Episode 1 to 22 in a stack of horizontal lines. After all arcs are complete, they slice vertically, showing how the stories intersect (see Chart 2.3). If you work for that executive producer, no one can abscond with the series.

Chart 2.3 Sample Character Arcs for a Season on One Series

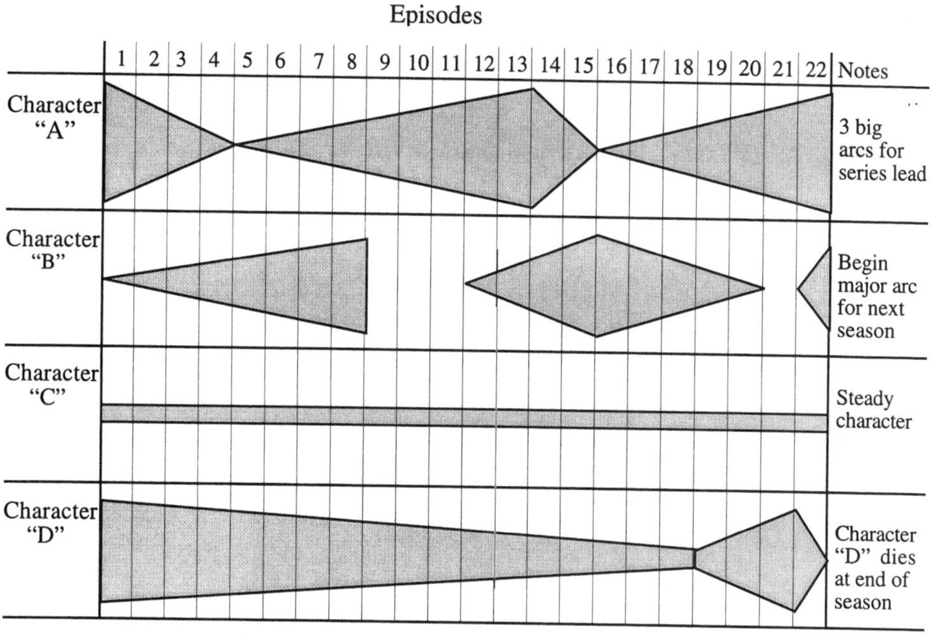

Episodes

Character	Notes
Character "A"	3 big arcs for series lead
Character "B"	Begin major arc for next season
Character "C"	Steady character
Character "D"	Character "D" dies at end of season

But other showrunners have a freer approach. The team that headed *Northern Exposure* used to build their series "bible" as each script came along. In one episode, a writer would invent a brother for a character, or a secret past, or a private fear. These were listed as "facts to wax" and distributed to the staff. After years, they accumulated a compendium of what various writers created — quite a different approach to a bible.

I used the term "bible" — no religious connotation (unless you worship the show). A TV bible is a document intended to help new writers and directors understand the rules of a series. Complete bibles contain elements similar to a "format" — a log line, franchise, an overview of springboards, tone, style, and the quest of the series, followed by character sketches and story guidelines.

The king of all series bibles was made for *Star Trek: The Next Generation*. At around 100 pages, it included intricate diagrams of the Enterprise, details on how the ship's bridge operates, definitions of technical terms, characterizations that not only summarized every crew member, but also analyzed the relationship and history of each one with every other, an admonition of what to write and not write for the series; and it was accompanied by summaries of every story the show had ever aired, as well as every idea in the mill. *Trek* had to go this far because it was open to non-professional submissions. I think it was kind of self-defense against repeated questions from its many fans.

But that's extreme. Some bibles are just a few pages including the premise, character bios, and the kinds of stories they intend to tell. Others, like *Northern Exposure*, are amassed rather than generated.

And, frankly, most shows don't bother with bibles at all. They take too much time when everyone is busy making the airdate. Websites, even blogs, from many sources — the network, the showrunner, sometimes other writers on the show, even fan-sites — have replaced formal bibles as a source for information. But if one will be composed, now is the time.

While the staff writes and rewrites through the summer, network notes trickle down. Each episode is read by the network — Legal, and Standards and Practices, on top of the executive assigned to your show. Those notes go to the showrunner, so if you're a beginning writer he'll filter and interpret them; you won't interface directly with the network. Your boss is choosing when to fight the network brass and when to accommodate the notes. It's just part of the network landscape.

All this work leads to:

SEPTEMBER AND OCTOBER

THE DEBUT

If it was a stage play, you'd have flowers and a party opening night. But in television, you're doing postproduction on a later episode by the time the pilot airs. ("Postproduction" means everything after filming, like editing and scoring.) And that pilot was written a year ago, before the series was a glimmer in the eye of any of the current staff. Still, send up the fireworks in the parking lot after you watch it on TV like it was new.

At AMC, *The Walking Dead*, a dramatic series about zombies, was showcased on Halloween after a week-long festival of the best feature films in the genre. For the staff involved in making it (writer/director Frank Darabont to the crew and everyone in between) it was a full-blown Halloween party, costumes and all.

So even though the show is no longer new to the people who worked on it for months, it seems new anyway because once the show is broadcast, it becomes public property, out of the creative cocoon. "Overnights," which are quick national ratings, are on the showrunner's desk the next morning. He'll tell the staff to pay no attention to the numbers, just keep writing; and, indeed, lower-level writers are shielded from marketplace pressures, temporarily. But how can you not feel buoyant if the show is liked, or disappointed if you played to an empty house? Just remember, it's not going to do any good to blame the network (look what they put us up against — of course we have no numbers), or blame viewers (they don't appreciate us because they're all... insert adjective), or blame your producer (he should've known the title sequence/opening scene/music/actor/whatever wouldn't work), or blame yourself (I have no talent). Hey, probably none of those are true. It takes time for a series to catch on. Assuming you really have 13 guaranteed on the air, and a few critics recommend the show in reviews, and the marketing people do their thing, and the audience does join you in Episode Two or Three, and they become involved in the characters — then:

At Halloween — the end of October — the showrunner gets the call from the network: You've been picked up for the "back nine." You'll have an entire first season for the series to grow and stake its turf. Breathe out now.

November through March

COMPLETING THE SEASON

When I used to work as a freelancer, I often made my whole year's salary between October and February. By then enough of the season is in place so that some of the early tension is eased. Under an agreement with the Writers Guild, shows with full-season orders must give out two freelance assignments. These not only extend opportunities to new writers and those in "protected categories" (under-represented minorities or disabled, for example), but freelance scripts can also be auditions for the staff. They bring relief and fresh perspectives and stories to an exhausted staff. Or so the theory goes.

In reality, most shows are written entirely by the staff and the few outsiders tend to be friends or writers coming off cancelled shows. Still, go ahead and pitch a freelance episode in the fall or winter. It's a good way to meet producers, and certainly a way to break in. (More about that in Chapter Six.)

In the absence of a written bible, if you're a freelancer needing the rules of a series, my advice is watch it a lot and check the websites. If the series is so new that nothing can be found, and you've been invited in to pitch, the producer will messenger the pilot and some scripts to you. Maybe you'll get ten minutes on the phone about their current story needs. Yeah, it's tough, but if they like your writing, and you bring areas the show can use, someone will guide you a little once you have an assignment.

Writing continues steadily until all 22 shows are in final drafts. Don't make Thanksgiving plans except dinner time. As for the winter break you had in school, you're not going anywhere this year. You'll have a few days off at Christmas and New Year's. Or maybe you'll be finishing a draft at home before the wrapping paper is off the floor.

Depending on how well your series is pulled together (and that depends largely on the skill of the showrunner), you'll be slowing down at the end of February. In fact, your own episodes have probably been written, so you're sticking around for revisions, production, and polishes of scripts by other writers. Even if you're mostly done, follow everything through "post." Not only is the series very much alive with new episodes airing every week, but you want to preserve your position for the next year.

If the first season was a resounding success, the showrunner will have early notice it's been renewed, as happened to *The Good Wife* in 2010. But plenty of first-time series are uncertain down to the wire, just like pilots. It's awful, from a writer's point of view. You want to create a season-ender that entices viewers to watch in the fall, and yet if you're not being picked up for a second season, the impulse is to go out bravely and close the story arc.

Something like that happened at the end of the first season of *Mad Men*. This is how I heard the story: Now, keep in mind that this cable show is off the network grid, so they were hearing news on a different timetable or the tale might not have unfolded like this. Anyway, the showrunner (Matt Weiner) thought *Mad Men* didn't have a chance for a second season. At the point he planned the arc, it was so far ahead of announcements that he configured the episodes leading to the end of Don Draper's core question of whether he could be a family man, loving and loved, not unknown and alone. In the original script, Don goes home to Thanksgiving and finds his family waiting for him, and the through-line of the series is resolved. The producers wrote it, shot it, packed it up and that was that.

Except it wasn't. On the walk to the gallows, the award nominations started flooding in. Critical acclaim. People wanted more. But what more? As the industry tale goes, one of the interns on the staff (who later became a writer/producer herself) wrote a new scene. Don goes home and there's the family waiting, just as in the early draft. But it's in his imagination. The house is empty. Don sits alone on the stairs of his empty house. And tune in for next season because his troubles are only just beginning.

More often, the producer bets on his show and opts for the cliffhanger, while the staff hangs on their own cliff. This happens during:

APRIL

HIATUS

Vacation — yay! For a network series writer, spring is like summer and winter holidays rolled into a mass getaway. The hiatus might last three months, from late March until July, or be as limited as a month and a half — April to late May. If the staff is assured they're coming back, this is a fling of freedom. If everyone's worried, the agents sniff around for a jump to another show. In any case, the break is total. Many shows lock their offices and leave nothing but an answering machine; even the receptionist is gone — far away, after 40 weeks non-stop.

This brings us all the way back to where we started, as the cycle spins around and around and around.

WHAT'S NEW?

That traditional network paradigm is broadly accurate for, well, traditional networks. But in the alternate universe of cable television you'll encounter different patterns. For example, *Deadwood* on HBO did 12 episodes per year, not 22. The entire season was written in winter and spring, so all scripts were finished before any production began. They started shooting around the end of July, which is actually similar to networks, but *Dead-wood*'s next season didn't begin airing until the following March, when many network shows were winding down.

Sometimes shows have a partial season — maybe as few as 8 episodes — then take a hiatus and come back months later for the rest of the season. The final "season" of *Lost* was trickled out over two years with a very long break in the middle. Everyone knew the series would resolve years of suspense in the final segments. The challenge was how to spin that out — long enough so excitement would build; not so long that people gave up. In other cases, seasons are split so a new show can be piloted in the slot of a successful show, hoping to build on the audience used to watching that channel at that time.

New paradigms include Direct TV which paid for the first run of *Friday Night Lights* and then re-ran the episodes on NBC. No doubt, someone is out there thinking of ways to configure a Web-based season that makes financial sense to the producers. And then there's the seasonless world populated with years of episodes from every television era, sometimes downloaded (or bought) in the never-ending afterlife of a series.

Finally, it comes down to what you choose to create. In 2000, Showtime optioned a British series with the strange title, *Queer as Folk*. Everyone assumed the American version would be so diluted it would lose the guts that made it worth buying. After all, nothing like that had ever been done here. Then, one Sunday, writers Ron Cowen and Daniel Lipman, who had struggled to create television movies about gay life within network standards, happened to read about this option in a newspaper. They got in touch with Showtime, and said they'd do it... if they got complete creative freedom — unimaginable at a network. Not only did Showtime give them their freedom, but also a full 22-episode order. In the Writers Guild membership magazine *Written By*, Cowen and Lipman said, "The handcuffs had been removed; we'd been released from the prison of network television. And the question posed to any newly freed man was posed to us: 'Now that you have your freedom, what do you plan to do with it?'"

In the future, you'll be entering an industry whose long-established systems are no longer as certain as in the traditional model. The predictable cycles are changing, and new outlets are experimenting with different ways of making and delivering stories to an expanding audience. So ask yourselves a version of Cowen and Lipman's question: Now that you'll have choices, what do you plan to do with them?

SUMMARY POINTS

• Creating a new TV show follows specific steps from concept to network sale.

• Once on the air, a show also relies on definite steps of development from a pilot through writing and producing, to being renewed.

• In the earliest stages, a show creator might write a format or pilot script in the hope of getting a greenlight to produce the pilot, which is a prototype for the series. The pilot together with a "package" competes with other new series for a time slot, known as a "pick up."

• A full 22-week traditional season would occupy the writing staff through an intense 40-week schedule before hiatus. Most new series get only "short orders," though.

• On cable stations, the seasons and production times may differ, but the general development process has the same creative components and opportunities for writers.

GUEST SPEAKER: CHARLIE COLLIER
PRESIDENT, AMC CABLE TV

Pamela Douglas: Once upon a time, basic cable was something you went to for reruns, or you didn't go. All of a sudden AMC is up there with HBO and Showtime in terms of great drama. I'd love to hear how you got from there to here. You went counter-current because at the time *Mad Men* went on, the networks were still doing car crashes and trying to grab their audience by things that were as fast as possible; *Mad Men* is as slow as possible. How did this happen?

Charlie Collier: I was fortunate to get here in 2006 when AMC had already set out on a path of "distinction." My bosses, Ed Carroll and Josh Sapan, along with a talented team of tastemakers in original programming and development, had just come off of *Broken Trail*, AMC's epic Robert Duvall-led miniseries. That success gave us the confidence to set the mission of taking our film library and adding to it quality originals; originals that can stand beside the films in a way that also speaks to a passionate movie viewer. And, of course, we partnered with Matt Weiner on *Mad Men*, who put on paper, for our first series, what has turned out to be one of the true epic stories on television.

If you look at the way we launched *Mad Men,* it illustrates our strategy of originals complementing our movies, and is a great example of our mission in action. *Mad Men*'s lead-in was *GoodFellas*, one of my favorite films. Loosely speaking, it's about a group of men who think they're above the rules. It's a film that has themes that crossed over beautifully into its lead-out, *Mad Men*, also a story about a group of men to whom the rules do not apply; it's shot on film, it's cinematic, and it's of the highest television quality in every way.

PD: This is not just about *Mad Men*. Then you've got *Breaking Bad* and other great shows. How did you go forward?

CC: With *Mad Men*, we had success with a period piece. As they say, "imitation is the sincerest form of television." And, as such, many a period piece hit Development's desks soon after the series premiered — stories of flappers and Motown and the '70s. But we didn't want to become the "period piece" network. We were looking for a modern-day story that had some of the qualities of the films we curate and love. Not unlike *Mad Men*, *Breaking Bad* is led by an "auteur," Vince Gilligan. Vince delivered a story that was so wonderful in its description of Walt White's transformation, nuanced in every way; and we all fell in love with the script. We built the pilot with Sony, a great partner, just as Lionsgate is with *Mad Men*.

And in keeping with our strategy, to launch *Breaking Bad*, we did a month of films we called "March Badness." AMC featured some of the greatest anti-hero stories ever told, with Clint Eastwood, Charles Bronson, and others. Again, this yielded successful movie ratings all month long, all serving to promote our original anti-hero story, *Breaking Bad*.

We're a company — Rainbow Media — which has a tradition in film. We own the Independent Film Channel and the Sundance Channel, and several on our team who saw the *Breaking Bad* pilot remarked that if we were to add just 20 minutes to it, we could have called that pilot the best independent film made that year. I agree. It's a remarkable pilot and it has become an extraordinary series.

These serialized dramas have each been passion projects led by auteurs with clear and strong visions. It's a joy to nurture them. Everyone looks

Breaking Bad

forward to reading scripts, and I love the chances, when I get them, to sit down with the writers. I appreciate their talents, their vision, and their true craft in building the character and context.

PD: You said something unusual. Here you are the network president, and you said you sometimes sit down with writers. I can't imagine another president doing that.

CC: Don't get me wrong. That's not my role. The original programming team does that work and I'm, appropriately, far, far away from the professionals in "the room" day to day. However, I think anyone who gets into the business, and who doesn't have a healthy appreciation for the content and the brilliant people who create the best of it, is in the wrong business. It's certainly a point of distinction for AMC, and Rainbow, how deeply into the organization the creative is valued, with so many of us being true fans of the content, from the top of the organization on down. One early goal we set — and it remains our goal today at AMC — is to create an environment where the best in the business will bring us their passion projects because they believe AMC will nurture them differently, and better, than anywhere else. Our introduction to most of Hollywood is a very bright and talented development team. From that introduction on, I hope all of our partners would say AMC has a different feel than most networks, from top to bottom.

PD: Among the newer projects, you have *The Walking Dead* with Frank Darabont out of the movie field.

CC: Here we have the man who wrote and directed *The Shawshank Redemption*, which is on the top of just about every "best movie" list you can think of. Again, we have an auteur, Frank Darabont, who is bringing the voice, vision and story, and it's executive produced by Gale Ann Hurd, who has done a few huge films herself — *The Terminator, Aliens,* among many others we all love. In keeping with our strategy, we premiered the show on Halloween. That's at the end of our 14th annual movie event called *FearFest*, where for two straight weeks we turn AMC over to horror films and we curate them to make it feel like a film festival on our air. Of course we use that effort to support some of the great films in the genre, but also to point horror film fans to an original series of the same genre. *The Walking Dead* is shot on film and, with Frank and Gale at the helm, is very cinematic. It's another example of pairing the best talent and the best films in a genre with a like-minded AMC original series.

PD: What else is coming down the pike?

CC: In March we're launching a series with Fox Television Studios which is our first move into the crime genre. It's a show called *The Killing*, which is based on a series of the same name that was a phenomenon in Denmark. It's about a murder and the overlapping storylines and interwoven mysteries that arise on the way to solving the case. We are enraptured by the stories; from the family of the victim to the investigator and what she gives up in her life in pursuit of information about the crime. You've also got a politician up for re-election and how he and his life story intersects with the tragic event. When we saw the Danish series we thought it was the most engaging storytelling we'd seen in the crime genre. We're thrilled to bring this unique, addictive storytelling to America. It's piloted and there's tremendous talent attached. The writing is as good as it gets in the genre, led by showrunner Veena Sud (*Cold Case*)... we're just thrilled.

PD: In terms of development, the Danish series was brought to you by Fox Television Studios, who already had the project. In L.A., everybody is trying to come up with their own material, and people wonder how they would approach AMC. Do you actually look at new material, assuming it comes through representation? Do you have a pitch process like the networks where there's a season and people come in?

CC: Our process has a rhythm to it, as they all do, but in general we are developing all year along. The evolution of AMC has been quite rapid, so it's not as if we only take material during only one season as you say others do. We do have the typical development process and our very talented (and very overworked) development team has hundreds and hundreds of formal submissions as you might imagine. Regardless of genre, we're looking to tell the best stories on television; again, stories with distinction and with a cinematic feel.

PD: Do you think the high-quality, slower-paced, introspective dramas you're doing are something that's part of a response to the frenetic nature of current life?

CC: There's a character-development emphasis in the stories that we have an appreciation for, possibly because we have such an appreciation for movie-like storytelling. If you speak with Matt Weiner and others who have inspired us, they're telling stories where character and character-based drama comes first. And as with the "characters" you love in real life, it takes some time to understand who people really are. *Mad Men* and *Breaking Bad* each do wonderfully well with character, sharing the little things that make the character's stories so much more than what you could ever learn about them in, for example, a typical crime procedural that wraps up in an hour. Matt Weiner has said there's drama in a phone ringing and no one picking it up. You learn from these brilliant writers that life and storytelling and character development is in the details. And we're willing to invest in these auteurs because we love the way they tell patient stories and nurture those details. We also appreciate our share of action stories, by the way. But yes, in *Mad Men* and *Breaking Bad* the pacing can be much more deliberate than a typical TV hour. Matt says, and *Mad Men* is a great reminder, that while most of us have never worked in an ER, been in a car chase or solved a crime in an hour, we've all felt the drama in hesitating when picking up the phone, not wanting to take a call for one reason or another.

PD: That's not usual on television. You said you were just fortunate, but it seems it took a level of vision.

CC: We set out to create a level of distinction for the AMC brand. The vision is and was to create "premium television on basic cable" and to do that, my amazing team sought and delivered storytelling that at times has a cadence to it that is very different from what you might find elsewhere. We're very proud of the stories we're building and supporting.

CHAPTER 3

HOW A CLASSIC SCRIPT IS CRAFTED

Constructing your episode may seem daunting at first, but hour dramas — especially primetime network shows — follow a general template. Your insights into character, talent with dialogue, inventiveness in storytelling, and the depth of meaning are all creative qualities beyond any system. But I've found that using a basic pattern can actually release your artistry because you don't have to worry whether the underlying skeleton will hold up.

Initially, I even advise students to try to separate their right-brain and left-brain functions — the creative and the analytical. We know how we are as artists, ready to run off with the circus, or an emotional explosion. Those moments when passion takes over are gifts, and if you're touched by a cinematically hot encounter between characters, go ahead and write it down. The best writing is like trying to catch the wind anyway. But then put that piece of writing aside and return to engineering your script in the cold light of the left brain.

Even if you could somehow begin at Page 1 and steam your way through to Page 50 in a single creative breath (and I don't think anyone can), television series don't work like that. As you'll discover in Chapter Five, you'll be collaborating with a staff and will have to submit an outline or beat sheet (more about those in Chapter Four) prior to writing your teleplay.

The Dramatic Beat

Before we go further, keep in mind the nature of a screenplay scene, as I'm sure you've learned in screenwriting courses or books. A dramatic scene is the essential building block of storytelling on screen and should have a complete dramatic structure. That means each scene has a motivated protagonist who wants something and drives the action to get it through conflict with an opposition, usually an equally motivated antagonist. That's just a basic statement of story plotting. If you're stuck on this point, then take a break and refresh yourself on screenwriting before you move on to TV. Seriously. Writing television drama isn't easier than theatrical movies, even though it's shorter; actually it's more difficult, because it requires all the same elements compressed in a tighter form.

When you look at the sample script pages that follow you'll notice numbers at the sides. Those are automatically generated by screenwriting software in preparing a "shooting script" (that means the final draft which goes into production), but you should not have numbers on your presentation draft. I left these numbers in to help refer to sections as I discuss them (and because these really are from shooting scripts). The numbers indicate "Slug Lines," also called "Scene Headings," but they are not scenes in the dramatic sense I'm using. For example, an establishing shot outside a building is not a full dramatic scene, though it is a location that physical production needs to plan. For our purposes, a dramatic beat may encompass one or more slug lines; the key is identifying a step of the story, not a shot. You'll see more examples when I talk about the script segments.

A-B-C Stories

We're going to look at a show that uses parallel storytelling. In this sample, the three storylines are not subplots, but independent tales each involving distinct guest cast. Since they occur within the same arena — a New York detective precinct — and they feature the same main cast, the stories are sometimes interwoven, sometimes blended, sometimes juxtaposed. Clearly, in style and tone they are part of the same show, and you might find a theme linking all the stories within an episode.

The largest (or most resonant) story is called "A." The second most important story is "B." And the third "C" story is sometimes comic relief in an otherwise serious show, or may be a "runner," such as a recurring incident or character issue. Like any description of writing methods, those distinctions are flexible. Among variations, you may find "A" and "B" stories that are equal in weight, shows where a "C" story in one episode is a seed beginning a major arc in subsequent episodes, and shows that normally have three stories but might turn up with two or four. Again, I'm giving you a sense of the overall design, not laying down the law.

Some series usually have more than three stories — *The Wire*, for example. And some primarily "A" story only, for example *Dexter*. Before you speculate a show, carefully study how it's crafted.

Each series has its own ways, but I've come up with a generic grid that fits many shows on both broadcast networks and basic cable. I use it to analyze sample episodes in my classes, and here's a blank one you can apply to the excerpts printed in this chapter. For practice, try it while you're watching TV. But here's a hint: for five acts look for which two acts are the shortest. Usually five acts are simply Act Four divided in half. But I know of one action show that divides Act One instead. If you count pages (or time the acts) it's easy to figure out how shows are accommodating themselves to this basic structure. Once you get the hang of it, you can also use this simple chart in the early planning stages of an original script. (see Chart 3.1)

Chart 3.1 Basic Four-Act Grid

ACT I	ACT II	ACT III	ACT IV
(T)			
1			
2			
3			
4			
5			
6			
7			

Chart 3.2 Sample Six-Act Grid

Approximately 20-24 scenes total

	Act 1	Act 2	Act 3	Act 4	Act 5	Act 6
1						
2						
3						
4						
	8 to 10 minutes (replaces teaser)	8 minutes or less	8 minutes or less	Less than 8 minutes	6 to 8 minutes *might have only 3 scenes*	Around 5 minutes (replaces tag) *might have only 2 or 3 scenes or very short scenes*

NOTE: First three acts may be longer

Chart 3.3 Seven-Act Concept

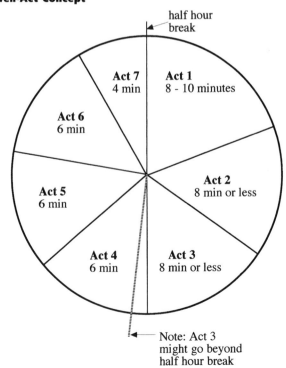

half hour break

Act 7 4 min

Act 1 8 - 10 minutes

Act 6 6 min

Act 2 8 min or less

Act 5 6 min

Act 3 8 min or less

Act 4 6 min

Note: Act 3 might go beyond half hour break

The titles on the top are the four acts of an hour episode. Remember from Chapter One that on network television (but not on premium cable like HBO) commercial breaks occur roughly every 10 to 15 minutes. Dividing 15 minutes into 60 minutes gives you the four acts. Now, an hour drama doesn't really run an hour — it's actually less than 50 minutes after commercials. And each act isn't really 15 minutes — more like 12. Dividing 12 minutes into 48 minutes gives you four acts also. But for planning a first-draft script, figure that Act One ends around page 17 or 18 if the show has a teaser (more about teasers in a minute); Act Two ends around page 30; Act Three at 45; and Act Four around 60 (or anywhere from 50 to 60).

On the left of the grid you see numbers one through seven. Those are the scenes in each act. Why seven? Well, you won't always have seven, in fact. Five solid scenes could fill out an Act in some cases, and in "vignette" shows where scenes are quick, you might find yourself counting up to nine or ten. The basis for the list of seven is the two-minute scene. Back to arithmetic, if an act is 14 minutes, and each scene is around two minutes, $14 \div 2 = 7$.

FIVE- AND SIX-ACT STRUCTURE

In 2006 some networks and basic cable shows, including the popular *Grey's Anatomy* and *Lost*, went to five acts, and ABC network mandated six acts for all its new shows. You can guess why: more commercial breaks. I don't know any writers who like this change, which seems pushed by desperation to pump revenues when network advertising rates are declining and the audience has discovered the mute button, not to mention all the people who record shows to omit commercials altogether.

Like it or not, you need to find out if the show you're speculating has four, five or six acts, and how to re-configure your structure. I suggest you begin with the four-act idea. Then take what used to be the teaser and lengthen it to around ten pages to create a new Act One. Be sure you open directly into the story with jeopardy or action or a provocative issue because this is where you need to hook the audience (and the reader).

Each of the succeeding acts will be shorter than in a four-act plan — roughly ten pages each. In a six-act structure, with acts only around eight pages long, think in terms of Act Six being a tag or the final shoe dropping, or a twist. You might see an Act Six that runs as short as five minutes. On *Nip/Tuck*, to use an example of a six-act (or teaser plus five) show, the writers experimented with completing all dramatic arcs at the end of Act Five (which is the same as a show with teaser plus four), and used the short sixth act to add a surprising twist that, in a way, was a teaser for the next episode because it incited a new issue or challenge rather than concluding the current storyline.

THE MORE THINGS CHANGE...

...The more they stay the same. After all the uproar about going to five, six, even seven acts in an hour series, by the end of 2010 the pendulum had swung back. I asked around and discovered two phenomena: First, writers are planning their stories in the traditional four acts and making the adjustment to five or six in a later draft. Second (and this amazed me), writers I've never met on shows I don't know were turning up at meetings with the grid from this book. Sometimes they knew where it came from, sometimes a colleague had just handed it to them on a piece of paper. So this little grid I invented for myself — and for you — has taken on a life of its own. Be fearless if you want to use it!

Among the producers I asked about act breaks are two of my former students, Kelly Souders, who is now Executive Producer on *Smallville*, and Wendy West, a Co-Executive Producer on *Dexter*. Both of them are interviewed more extensively in Chapter Seven, but their insights into this subject may be helpful here.

Kelly explained, "*Smallville* used to be in four acts and we had a very long Act One. So we split Act One in half — three scenes and four scenes. It used to be six to seven scenes. Now it's a teaser and two small acts. We can do that because at the end of Act One we have an action beat."

I asked Wendy how *Dexter* is planned since it has no act breaks as aired. Keep in mind that movies have often been discussed as having three acts (beginning, middle, end), in which Act Two is twice as long as Act One and Three, so in old fashioned terms, Act One of a movie is 30 minutes, Act Two is 60 minutes and Act Three is 30 minutes. But as soon as you add a midpoint in the center of Act Two (a usual dramatic turning point), you get a regular four-act structure. With that context, here is Wendy's answer to how *Dexter* is structured without formal act breaks:

"The show reverts to a three-act structure. We break the beats by character and then do a weave. We put everything up on whiteboards where each character has a beginning, middle, and end, which is why I say it has kind of a three-act structure. Although in truth we don't break anything by acts at all. We break it by character. Typically the big reversals are in the Dexter story, so we break that first, and don't worry how the other character's stories fit into it if they're not inherently a part of it. The reversals are built into what journey Dexter takes in each episode. The reversals tend to come where you'd expect — page 40 to 45 out of a 55-page script."

I also put the question to Peter Blake, a writer on the staff of *House*, when he visited my class at USC. He told us, "What I do and I recommend to all the other writers on *House* is write in a four-act structure and then add two act breaks. The doctors will go down a path — what is this disease? Then you have a diagnosis. They have a theory and at some time a treatment for that theory. And at the end of the act, it doesn't work. That's a really simple way to break the act. The audience has to be involved enough that they're not going to turn off at the act breaks. Generally, I would beat out a very simple medicine story. Then I'd beat out the personal story. I use index cards and shuffle them around. I'd see which of the later acts is the longest and I'd divide that in half."

THE TWO-PAGE SCENE

I use the two-page scene as a target for students partly because inexperienced writers have difficulty accomplishing a complete dramatic beat in fewer pages, and when they write longer than two pages, their scenes tend to lose focus or become redundant.

Historically, screen scenes used to be long, more like stage plays. If you look at great movies from the 1940s, like the ones starring Humphrey Bogart, you'll see some scenes that run five or even seven pages. They reflect a different era where the slow evolvement of a dramatic moment, gradually experienced, was part of the pace of life. Currently, AMC, which has its roots in classic movies, runs shows like *Mad Men* where scenes are paced to explore subtle nuances, and may sometimes be several minutes long.

But we're focusing here on what's usual on current TV. Whether the change was caused by the 15-second information module of *Sesame Street*, or TV ads where a one-minute commercial is long and 30 seconds is normal, or the speed of computers, where you're growling at the screen if a function takes two seconds — an electronics-savvy populace is quickly bored. If audience attention drifts, or is way ahead of where you're going with the story, you've lost your moment. On television today, a one-minute beat is more welcome than a three-minute scene, and if you're starting page four of a single encounter, that's a red flag.

Notice also that I'm using the words "minute" and "page" interchangeably. That's just shorthand. A minute per page may be an average, but it's not always accurate. Pages of dialogue move faster, while action eats up lots of time. As with all my construction advice, I'm pointing out a general design, not policing whether you color outside the lines!

USING THE GRID

If you're using the grid to help you to understand the form of an episode on TV, I suggest that you begin by recording the show. Watch it all the way through and name the "A," "B," and "C" stories (or whatever number of stories your show has). Attach each story to one of the main cast, and then summarize that particular arc in a sentence. Keep going, creating a "log line" for each story.

Once you've figured out the stories, replay the episode. This time, write a letter in each of the boxes on the grid. For example, if Act One, Scene One is about the "B" story, put a "B" in that box. As the grid fills out, it will probably look sort of like a checkerboard with "A," "B," "C" (or other) stories following each other in a somewhat random pattern.

You'll notice that the cliffhanger that occurs at the end of an act might not always be a suspenseful moment in the "A" story; it might be a turning point in the "B" story, for example. You'll also see that sometimes one of the stories continues for several beats in a row, especially if it's following a "line of interest" the writer didn't want to interrupt. On other occasions, you'll see one story interposed between beats of another; this might be used to convey a sense that time has passed between the beats in the first story (this skipping is also called an "ellipse").

No rules exist for how this "checkerboard" should look, so don't get hung up trying to match the order of scenes. You're serving the dramatic tension of the stories, not some outside system. The point is to recognize the way parallel stories complement each other.

The grid may also help you track the arcs, and especially if your show is part of a serial, you might be surprised that one of the storylines ends in Act Three, or the "C" story doesn't begin until Act Two, or Act Four is entirely about resolving the "A" story. That's all okay. Again, the structure serves the story within the general parameters of a four-act episode with cliffhangers. So learn from other shows but don't copy.

If you're using the grid to create an original script, your first foray into the grid might be to jot notes about key points in the boxes: how the show opens, the "worst case" cliffhanger at the end of Act Three, and how the show will end. You might do that for the "A" story only, or for both "A" and "B" stories, leaving room to think about the "C" story later. Particularly with the act breaks, it's helpful to reverse-engineer, stepping backward from the cliffhangers to the beats right before to fill in the actions that led to the jeopardy or collision. That reverse technique may help you to figure out your outline. (I'll explain more about outlining in Chapter Four.)

TEASERS

The excerpts you'll read in this chapter are from a show that opens with a "teaser," though not all series begin with one. A teaser, also called "a cold opening," refers to dramatic material before the titles (before the name of the series and credits). It may be a one-minute "hook," or as long as ten minutes that includes several small scenes, making it nearly as full as a traditional whole act. In any style, it exists to grab viewers faster than the enemy, which is the remote. The notion is to open the hour with an action, image, situation or character that provokes enough anticipation to keep viewers through the title sequence and into the first act.

However, increasingly, title sequences along with theme music have been dumped by networks preferring to grab viewers with uninterrupted drama. The "tease" is the story itself, and titles scroll over Act One.

Often, a teaser sets out the problem of an episode. For example, on a detective show, the crime to be solved may be enacted or discovered in the teaser. But each show is unique. Looking back at the classic *Miami Vice* series, the lush teasers featured life in Miami and a provocative crime in progress in a textured environment usually involving drugs. The main cast never appeared in the teaser. Similarly, in *House*, a cinematic vignette involving the guest cast builds to a surprising medical twist in the teaser, though House and the other doctors don't learn about it until Act One. In contrast, both *Law & Order* (in all versions) and most crime procedurals open with the cast arriving at a crime scene after the deed is done.

In many law and medical shows, a case arrives and incites the events of the episode. But in *The Good Wife* and *Grey's Anatomy*, where emphasis is on the ensemble cast, teasers have sometimes shown the continuing characters waking, getting ready for work, or traveling to work, launching their personal stories that will spin out in the episode.

HBO's *Six Feet Under* always opened with someone dying (as bizarrely as possible) who turned up in the Fisher family funeral home in Act One, underlining the show's notion that life is random. But that teaser was rarely a component of the episode's drama; its link is thematic. The prison drama *Oz*, which used to run on HBO, also opened with theme rather than continuing story — a philosophical monologue, in fact. *Dexter* uses a version of this as well, reminding viewers of the show's psychological world instead of beginning a plot.

If you're a new writer, though, I recommend sticking with story rather than message. A swiftly propelled dramatic tension will lure a reader to turn the page and a viewer to see what happens next. Real storytelling is difficult, and I've seen too many students fool themselves into thinking they can impress by opening with a weighty theme or abstruse philosophy, when they're actually avoiding the challenge of impelling an arc. The best teasers tend to be the best drama.

About These Excerpts...

With appreciation to Steven Bochco, Executive Producer of *NYPD Blue* and many other great drama series, who graciously gave permission, here is the Teaser and Act One of each of two Emmy-winning episodes that ran four years apart. I've chosen these historic examples partly because they're so clearly crafted that you can easily grasp the structure, and also because they've stood the test of time.

The first excerpt is from "Simone Says," which aired at the beginning of 1995; Story by Steven Bochco, David Milch, Walon Green; Teleplay by David Milch, Walon Green. This episode introduced the character of Bobby Simone (played by Jimmy Smits) in the middle of the second season. Other main cast — Andy Sipowicz (Dennis Franz), Lt. Fancy, Detectives Lesniak, Martinez and Medavoy, Asst. D.A. Sylvia Costas, and receptionist Donna, were established in the series at this point; the remaining names are guest cast. Read and try to identify the stories and think about the form. Following the script pages, I will analyze its dramatic elements.

After that, you'll see another episode segment, along with a discussion.

NYPD BLUE
"Simone Says"

FADE IN:

1   EXT. PRECINCT - DAY   1

To establish --

2   INT. LAVATORY - LOCKER ROOM - DAY   2

SIPOWICZ enters from the hallway wearing his jacket and
carrying a small paper bag from a drug store. He goes to his
locker, opens it takes his jacket off and hangs it on the
open locker door. Crossing to the sink with the bag, he
glances around as he steps in front of the mirror, removes a
pair of drug store reading glasses from the bag and puts them
on. A large tag hangs from the glasses, dangling against his
cheek as he unhappily studies himself in the mirror. Sipowicz
snatches away the glasses and stuffs them back in the paper
bag as someone comes in.

He turns and sees BOBBY SIMONE moving to the bank of lockers
to the left of the door, checking a small piece of paper in
his hand on which a locker number's been written.

                    SIMONE
          'Morning.

                    SIPOWICZ
          How's it going?

Sipowicz steps over to him --

                    SIPOWICZ (CONT'D)
          Andy Sipowicz.

Simone regards him, smiles and extends his hand --

                    SIMONE
          Bobby Simone, nice to meet you,
          Andy.

                    SIPOWICZ
          Yeah.

Sipowicz clears his throat, steps to the door and exits. Hold
a beat on Simone, crossing Kelly's name off the locker,
inscribing his own, then --

                                                    CUT TO:

2.

INT. SQUAD ROOM - DAY   3

Sipowicz crosses the Squad Room directly to Fancy's office.

INT. FANCY'S OFFICE - DAY   4

FANCY looks up to see Sipowicz.

                    FANCY
          'Morning Andy.

                    SIPOWICZ
          That's no good. That's not gonna
          work.

                    FANCY
          What isn't?

                    SIPOWICZ
          I just met this new guy.

                    FANCY
          Simone.

                    SIPOWICZ
          Yeah that's not gonna work out.

                    FANCY
          What happened?

                    SIPOWICZ
              (waves dismissal)
          Don't get me started.

Fancy watches Sipowicz pace. BG In the Squad Room we see
Simone meeting Medavoy, Martinez.

                    SIPOWICZ (CONT'D)
          The whole attitude's wrong. "How
          you doing," this type of thing.

Fancy's phone rings. As he picks up the receiver --

                    FANCY
          He asked how you were doing?
              (into receiver)
          Lieutenant Fancy.
              (beat)
          Okay/
              (hangs up)
          We're got a homicide.
              (MORE)

3.

                   FANCY(cont'd)
          (beat)
         You're senior in the Squad. I want
         him with you, at least till he
         learns the precinct.

Sipowicz shakes his head, disaffected with his entire lot --

                   SIPOWICZ
         I need glasses and everything else.

Off Fancy, as Sipowicz exists his office --

5   INT. DONNA'S DESK - DAY   5

Donna looks up from her desk to see JAMES ABRUZZO.

                   ABRUZZO
         Yeah, I'm here to see Adrianne
         Lesniak.

                   DONNA
         Your name is ...

Abruzzo ignores her question, crosses to LESNIAK at her desk.
Lesniak, just arrived, is putting her things away. She sees
him and a look of weary desperation crosses her face --

                   LESNIAK
         Jimmy ...

                   ABRUZZO
         What? It's not like you give me a
         choice.

Lesniak faces him from her desk --

                   LESNIAK
         Not here. Please.

He settles in a chair facing her --

                   ABRUZZO
         Then where? I can't talk to you
         outside work 'cause I don't know
         where you're staying anymore, I
         can't call you here, 'cause you've
         told that bitch at the desk not to
         put me through ...
          (louder)
         Where am I supposed to talk to you?

4.

> LESNIAK
> We've got nothing left to talk
> about.

Abruzzo sees Donna staring at him ==

> ABRUZZO
> What are you looking at?

Donna looks back to her desk. She lifts the phone.

Abruzzo leans close to Lesniak, grips her wrist --

> ABRUZZO (CONT'D)
> You don't know how much I love you.
> You don't know what I'd do for you.

> LESNIAK
> You're drunk; Let go.

She tries to snatch her wrist away as Fancy steps up behind
Abruzzo.

> FANCY
> All right, you get up and you get
> the hell away from Detective
> Lesniak.

Abruzzo slowly turns his head and looks at Fancy.

> ABRUZZO
> No, you get back. I'm holding a .38
> pointed straight at her guts.

> LESNIAK
> Jimmy.

> ABRUZZO
> Let's go. You want to keep this
> private, we'll talk in private.

He brings her to her feet.

People in the room are frozen until Fancy lunges, grabs
Abruzzo's gun hand and swings the pistol toward the ceiling.

A shot is fired, but Fancy hangs onto the gun, preventing the
cylinder from rotating to fire again. Abruzzo punches at
Fancy who hangs on with both hands.

Sipowicz lunges for him but a kick from Abruzzo catches him
in the stomach, he's hurled back and his lower spine slams
against a desk.

5.

Abruzzo is pulling at the gun, swinging it wildly from side
to aide while Fancy hangs on.

From over a desk, Simone flies through the air and hits
Abruzzo with a tackle that hurls him to the ground. Fancy
pulls away with the gun as Simone spins Abruzzo around and
twists his arms behind him.

As Sipowicz comes forward with obvious lower back pain,
Simone cuffs Abruzzo. Abruzzo is hauled to his feet in the
circle of people.

                    LESNIAK
               (miserably protective)
          He's from the two-seven,
          Lieutenant, he's on the job.   .

                    FANCY
          He's under arrest.
               (to Donna)
          Get a D.A. down here.
               (to the newcomer)
          You're Simone?

                    SIMONE
          How you doing Lieutenant?

                    FANCY
               (to Simone and the other
                Detectives)
          I got this, get to your homicide,
          Thirteenth and Third.

                    ABRUZZO
               (to Lesniak)
          Are you happy? Look what you've
          done to me now.

                    FANCY
          Shut up!

                    SIMONE
               (to Sipowicz)
          Are you hurt?

                    SIPOWICZ
          I'll live.
               (beat)
          C'mon, ride with me.

Off which --

                                        SMASH CUT TO:

6.

MAIN TITLES

EXT. STATION HOUSE - DAY   6

Sipowicz and Simone move toward Sipowicz' car as in b.g.
Medavoy and Martinez do the same.

                    SIMONE
          Lesniak and Abruzzo were going out?

                    SIPOWICZ
               (nods)
          She broke up with him, got
          transferred, he went half-wacky.

                    SIMONE
          Looks to me like he made the whole
          trip.

                    SIPOWICZ
               (beat)
          What was your last assignment?

                    SIMONE
          Intelligence. I drove for the
          Commissioner.

They've reached Sipowicz' car, are about to enter --

                    SIPOWICZ
          You were one of those guys got
          grade promotions?

                    SIMONE
          Yeah.

                    SIPOWICZ
               (flat-voiced)
          That was nice.

Off Simone, getting in, taking the hit --

                                        CUT TO:

EXT. 13TH STREET AND 3RD - DAY   7

Sipowicz' van pulls up at the crime scene and parks beside
Medavoy's car, from which we see Medavoy and Martinez
exiting. Sipowicz and Simone get out.

In front of a remodeled apartment building, a body is on the
street half under a bloody sheet.

Two units are parked with their bubble gums flashing and a
paramedic van is at the curb. Sipowicz and Simone step up to
the body.

A man in his thirties, dead in a blood-soaked linen suit.

                  SIMONE
        Anyone check for I/D.?

                  UNIFORM
        Waited for you.

                  MARTINEZ
            (to Sipowicz)
        Want me to get started on the
        canvas?

                  SIPOWICZ
        Yeah, and have a uniform run the
        plates on these parked cars.

During which Simone has pulled his gloves on, crouched to
look in the D.O.A.'s pockets for I.D. Sipowicz also crouches
effortfully beside the body.

                  SIPOWICZ (CONT'D)
            (to Simone)
        Two in the chest. You see any other
        hits?

                  SIMONE
        No.
            (reads I.D.)
        Raymond Alphonse Martarano, Jr.,
        Bensonhurst.
            (looks up)
        The wise guy's son?

                  SIPOWICZ
        Or someone too stupid to change his
        name.
            (to Medavoy)
        Greg, find out if the M.E.'s
        responding and let Fancy know we've
        got a mobbed-up stiff.

                  MEDAVOY
        Yeah, all right.

As Medavoy moves off --

                  UNIFORM
            (to Sipowicz)
        We found a shell over by that curb.

                    SIMONE
          I got that.

Simone turns to go check it out, remarks to the Uniform re
the on-lookers --

                    SIMONE (CONT'D)
          Could you move the crime scene back
          twenty feet and get me a traffic
          cone to put over this shell?

                    UNIFORM
          Sure.

Meanwhile Martinez has approached Sipowicz, points to a man
on the sidewalk.

                    MARTINEZ
          That man's the super, he said the
          victim knew one of the tenants.

Sipowicz steps over to GOLDMAN, a middle-aged man in a blue
baseball jacket.

                    MARTINEZ (CONT'D)
          Mr. Goldman, this is Detective
          Sipowicz.

                    GOLDMAN
          Yeah, hi ...

                    SIPOWICZ
               (re body)
          Did you know this man?

                    GOLDMAN
          Mr. Big Shot Ray Martarano Jr.?
          He'd tell the lamp-post who he was
          if nobody else was around.

                    SIPOWICZ
          Who did he know in the building?

                    GOLDMAN
          2C ... Miss Anderson.

                    SIPOWICZ
          You know where we can find her?

                    GOLDMAN
          She's a model. I'm supposed to call
          her agency number for emergencies.

                    SIPOWICZ
I need that.

Suddenly O.S. Shouts. Sipowicz turns. Across the street a
woman shouts from a doorway --

                    MISS SAVINO
      Help me! ... Help! My mother's been
      shot!

From the street, Simone races toward the building. He faces a
woman, thirties who is standing in the doorway of an
apartment. Her hand is covered with blood.

                    SIMONE
      Where's your mother?

                    MISS SAVINO
      In there ... in there ...

8   INT. GROUND-FLOOR APARTMENT - DAY   8

Simone rushes into the ground=floor apartment. In the room by
the window, an elderly woman is sitting in a chair, her head
to one side. Miss Savino stands in the doorway as Simone
rushes to her mother.

                    MISS SAVINO
      I was at the grocery store.

Simone looks at the woman, who is obviously dead.

                    MISS SAVINO (CONT'D)
      She's dead, isn't she?

                    SIMONE
         (puts his hand on the
         woman's shoulder)
      She is. I'm sorry.

                    MISS SAVINO
      She was in our own apartment. She
      was at her own window.

                    SIMONE
      Why don't you sit down.

                    MISS SAVINO
      That's my mother.

                    SIMONE
      I know, I'm sorry.

10.

Miss Savino raises her hands to her face and sobs as Sipowicz
comes through the doorway slightly out of breath, followed by
E.M.S. personnel, who go directly to the body.

> SIPOWICZ
> What happened?

Simone pushes back the window curtain. A hole is revealed in
the glass where a shot entered, killing the woman.

> SIMONE
> Stray from the street.

Off which --

                                                    CUT TO:

EXT. PRECINCT - DAY   9

To establish --

INT. SQUAD ROOM - DAY   10

Fancy clears the stairs, enters the Squad, approaching
Lesniak at her desk. He keeps his voice quiet.

> FANCY
> How are you feeling?

Lesniak gestures defeatedly -- doesn't say much so she won't
cry.

> LESNIAK
> I'm upset.

Fancy nods.

> FANCY
> I.A.B. Just took him to Bellevue on
> a seventy-two hour evaluation.

> LESNIAK
> And he's a collar, right?

> FANCY
> (nods)
> I alerted the D.A. and Corrections,
> if he goes into the system we're
> going to be notified.

A beat, then --

>   LESNIAK
>   What happened, that's the thing I
>   kept seeing in my mind. I kept
>   being afraid that was going to
>   happen.

>   FANCY
>   Adrianne, you want to put a twenty-
>   eight in, try it again tomorrow?

She shakes her head no.

>   LESNIAK
>   I'd like to try it today.

>   FANCY
>   Pay attention to how you're
>   feeling.

>   LESNIAK
>   Okay. Thanks.

Fancy nods, moves off, joining the just-arrived Sipowicz. Off
Lesniak --

11   ANGLE - SIPOWICZ AND FANCY   11

>   FANCY
>   I heard there was a second D.O.A.

>   SIPOWICZ
>   Eighty-two year old woman sitting
>   at her window.

>   FANCY
>   The world's coming up here 'cause
>   it's Martarano's son. Organized
>   Crime, Intelligence ...

>   SIPOWICZ
>   (sarcastic)
>   Now I know the case'll clear.

>   FANCY
>   Anything off canvass?

>   SIPOWICZ
>   No witnesses. He was banging a
>   model lived in the building.
>   Simone's finding out where we can
>   pick her up.

12.

They look toward Simone at Kelly's old desk --

                    FANCY
          How's that going?

                    SIPOWICZ
               (re Simone)
          You know he drove for the P.C.?

                    FANCY
               (nods)
          I saw that was his last detail.

                    SIPOWICZ
               (more trying this attitude
                on than genuinely
                irritated)
          I take twenty-two years making
          second grade, he gets it for
          shooing away squeegee-bums.

Fancy lets it go, heads for his office. Sipowicz moves to
Simone at his desk.

                    SIMONE
               (covers the receiver with
                his hand)
          The agency told me where she's
          working. Give me half a minute.

Sipowicz nods, looks to where COSTAS has just entered, moves
to her --

                    SIPOWICZ
          How's it going?

                    COSTAS
          I was just seeing to Abruzzo.
               (re Simone)
          Is that the new Detective?

                    SIPOWICZ
               (nods)
          Simone, what kind of name is that?

                    COSTAS
          First or last?

                    SIPOWICZ
          If it was his first he'd be a girl.

                    COSTAS
          Last name Simone sounds French.

13.

                    SIPOWICZ
           Yeah, maybe.

They're both looking toward Simone, react as he raises his
voice --

                    SIMONE
           Hey, I went through a lot of effort
           getting that red cock. I don't want
           to lose its color.
                (beat)
           I don't want to argue about this.
           You tell Billy he can't be around
           my place with his blue-barred cock.
           Okay thanks.

Simone hangs up. He sees them looking at him --

                    SIMONE (CONT'D)
           I breed birds. Racing pigeons.

Costas nods. Then quietly, to Sipowicz --

                    COSTAS
           Tell him you keep fish.

Sipowicz shakes his head no. Simone's collected his
materials, approaches--

                    SIPOWICZ
                (indicates Costas)
           Assistant D.A. Costas.

                    SIMONE
           How do you do?

                    COSTAS
           How do you do.

                    SIPOWICZ
                (to Simone)
           They gave you that address?

                    SIMONE
           Yeah, she's working on Seventh
           Avenue.

A beat, then --

                    COSTAS
           Must be interesting raising
           pigeons.

14.

> SIMONE
> It's a lot of fun, gets you
> outdoors.

> COSTAS
> You people and your hobbies.

> SIPOWICZ
> (to Simone)
> Let's go.

Off which --

CUT TO:

2   INT. A GARMENT SHOWROOM - 7TH AVENUE - DAY   12

The place is chaos, hung with cigar smoke as buyers move
among sellers and brokers beside a flood-lit ramp, where
models parade a spring line. Sipowicz and Simone push their
way through, following THELMA LEVY, a tailored fiftyish
woman, wearing a no-nonsense expression.

> LEVY
> How long will this tie her up?

> SIPOWICZ
> We won't know till we talk to her.

> LEVY
> And it couldn't wait until after
> she finishes work.

> SIPOWICZ
> NO.

She leads them into --

3   INT. A DRESSING ROOM - DAY   13

Sipowicz and Simone can't help but look around as they are
suddenly amidst a plethora of nubile bodies in various stages
of undress. Dressers move excitedly in front of them as
clothes are whipped on and off. Ms. Levy stops them.

> LEVY
> Wait here, I'll get her.

The work is so concentrated and frenetic that for the most
part they are ignored by the nude models attended by ranks of
fey male dressers and a few female fitters.

The talk level is deafening. As Sipowicz mops his brow Simone observes good-humoredly --

                  SIMONE
          What a country huh?

Ms. Levy appears with PAULA ANDERSON, good-looking, lots of make-up and a pill-assisted figure.

                  LEVY
          Make it as quick as you can.

Levy moves off --

                  SIPOWICZ
          I'm Detective Sipowicz, this is
          Detective Simone.

                  PAULA
          What's going on?

                  SIPOWICZ
          Do you know Raymond Martarano, Jr.?

                  PAULA
          Yes.

                  SIMONE
          When's the last time you saw him?

                  PAULA
          We partied last night, then I had
          to come to work.

                  SIMONE
          You left him at your apartment?

                  PAULA
          What's going on?

                  SIPOWICZ
          He was murdered this morning
          outside your building. Your
          downstairs neighbor was killed by a
          stray bullet.

Paula takes this in.

                  PAULA
          Which downstairs neighbor?

                  SIPOWICZ
          Mrs. Savino.

16.

It seems like a struggle for Paula to keep her hard edge.

>   PAULA
> I don't know anything about it.

>   SIPOWICZ
> Why don't you come to the Station
> House so we can get the background
> on this.

>   PAULA
> I'm working.

>   SIPOWICZ
> Well, now you're not working. Now
> you're coming with us to the
> Station House.

Simone holds a robe out for her to cover herself --

>   SIMONE
> Why don't you get dressed Paula?

The tone of which seems to circumvent her resistance. As
Paula puts the robe on --

>   FADE OUT.

        END ACT ONE

ANALYSIS

Before we get into content, notice that a TV drama script looks just like a theatrical screenplay. This might be news if you've written sitcoms because half-hour comedies use a unique form. Most screenwriting software will give you format options, so choose "standard," "screenplay," or whatever term your system uses for writing movies. And, of course, you know better than to use a divided page or anything called "video."

Now, I said this show starts with a teaser which precedes Act One, yet you see no heading. Some series do write TEASER in the beginning, then they FADE OUT at the end of the teaser and start a new page headed ACT ONE. Other shows start with ACT ONE at the top of Page One, whether or not there's a teaser. The only way to know what a particular show does is check out one of their sample scripts. In any case, Acts Two, Three and Four will begin on new pages and be headed ACT TWO and so forth, centered at the top.

OPENING SCENES

Look at #1, which simply establishes the Precinct building. Is that a scene? No! Remember, I told you a scene is a dramatic beat, not a production location. This kind of shot merely tells viewers where we are.

#2 opens the action with a personal detail that speaks volumes without dialogue. Think about what is revealed when a man tries on reading glasses for the first time. What do you suppose is in the character's mind? Notice how he hides them the moment Simone enters. In Chapter One, I spoke about the essential intimacy of television, and here it is: In his private moment, Sipowicz is self-conscious about aging. Insecurity that his eyesight is weakening gives viewers a window to his need to prove his status in this episode.

The Simone character is played by a younger man — tall, handsome Jimmy Smits. In comparison with Sipowicz — fat, balding and now needing glasses — the rivalry is set in motion from their first appearance. The script doesn't spell out how each man looks — that's not necessary in a TV series where everyone working on the show knows who the actors are. In fact, character tags, which are common in features, are slight if they're included here at all. Still, everything you need emotionally is on the page in this tiny moment.

Notice also that dialogue begins on Page One. That's normal for television, though you might have read features (especially older ones) where description, atmosphere, and action without speech occupy the first few pages. Look at the kind of dialogue on the first page, though. It seems like they're saying nothing except hello. That's not really what's going on, though, is it? You want to aim for dialogue that is both natural and withheld. In other words, let viewers sense the meaning under the surface without hitting it on the head, as much as you can.

You could analyze that the first scene of this teaser ends at the bottom of page one when Simone crosses off the name of Sipowicz's former partner and writes his own. It's a gesture of power in a beat that's all about relative power. But to understand the dramatic flow, I'd rather turn the page because the same tension continues into the outer rooms.

From having "lost" the unspoken battle with Simone (which is only in his own mind), Sipowicz barrels out to his boss, Lt. Fancy, in #4, and complains about the new guy. From a dramatic point of view, this page could be interpreted as a whole scene too because it has conflict between characters, however subtle: Sipowicz wants to reclaim his power by getting rid of Simone, but Fancy resists. At the end, when Fancy worsens Sipowicz' problem by ordering him to work with Simone and teach him, Sipowicz reasserts his theme that started on the first page, "I need glasses and everything else."

Though you could argue that two distinct scenes start this story, I'll group the first two and a half pages (slug lines 1 through 4) into a single beat to help you visualize the storytelling. Let's name this story "A," because it has the most resonance for the series as a whole (even though it actually doesn't occupy the largest proportion of pages in the full script). On Page 62, at the very end of the episode (not printed here), this opening moment is paid off when Sipowicz allows Simone to see him put on the new glasses, and he allows himself the vulnerability, "I got to wear glasses now." Their arc won't really end for four years, but this episode accomplishes a full step.

If you're filling in the grid, you would write "A" in the space next to the "T" for teaser. The log line for story "A" might be something like: "Sipowicz feels threatened when his new partner Simone arrives." Other wordings are also possible, of course. The point isn't what you call a story but how well you attach it to the drive of a continuing character.

The teaser's not over, though. Here comes the Lesniak story that I'll call "C." Without the full episode, you'd have no way of knowing where this one is going or how it measures against the rest of the script, so I'll just tell you. Detective Adrienne Lesniak is a continuing character whose problems with her ex-boyfriend (Abruzzo) appeared in previous shows, and this beat is part of her ongoing struggle to be free of him. But it really does more in this episode: Thematically it leverages a story with a guest cast which will begin in Act Two. That "C" story will require Lesniak to deal with women who have been abused by a man. As those female characters struggle to find courage to defend themselves against their abuser, Lesniak's personal search gives the case a deeper meaning for the audience.

The entire Lesniak/Abruzzo encounter runs almost three pages under scene heading #5, but you'll easily see it has several smaller components: the initial conflict between Lesniak and Abruzzo, then the fight which also involves Sipowicz and Simone, and finally the resolution with Lt. Fancy. By the time this scene is done, not only is Lesniak changed, but Simone has also been introduced to the squad in a dynamic way, and through the fight the balance between Simone and Sipowicz has budged a bit too.

If you're keeping notes on the grid, you'd write "C" next to where you wrote "A" for the teaser, because this opening has two beats.

The only way you know this scene ends the teaser is the transition "SMASH CUT TO" (at the bottom of Page 5 in the script) and "MAIN TITLES" (at the top of Page 6). ACT ONE begins right after the main titles, though this series doesn't state that on the page.

Scene 1

#6 is a whole scene even though it's less than a page long. Read it again and find the dramatic elements: Who is the protagonist? Who is the antagonist? What does the protagonist want which is opposed by the antagonist? Where is the climax of their conflict? How does it resolve? No, I'm not going to tell you the answers. This is good practice for tight scene writing and to grasp how character arcs are progressed. You might ask those same questions about every scene you write. Notice also that no scene exists merely to explore character. Simone and Sipowicz are on the trail of a murder while this beat happens.

Clearly, this is what we're calling the "A" story, so if you're doing the grid, put "A" in the first box in Act I.

Scene 2

In #7 the "B" story begins, and it would be routine police work at a crime scene except that we bring to it another level: the underlying jousting between Sipowicz and Simone. Clearly, the scene has three main components: first, the rising tension as they discover Martarano is "a mobbed-up stiff;" second, a guest character who leads the detectives to the next beat in their search. That construction might be flat, but the end of the scene is the third "beat," which spins the action in a new direction with the surprising shouts for help from Miss Savino. (On the grid, put "B" in the second square.)

Scene 3

#8 is an additional scene from the "B" story. You see, it's not necessary to checkerboard the order of these; more important to follow the line of audience interest. And that leads directly to the twist in this scene that raises unexpected questions about the crime. As in any mystery, the audience doesn't know which clues to value and which are red herrings, and neither do our characters — that's part of the fun of the genre. ("B" goes in the third square.)

Scene 4

Why bother with an establishing shot of the Precinct in #9? Think of a reason before I tell you. Okay, here are a few: It helps re-orient viewers to "home base" after several beats in the field; it signals the beginning of a new sequence; and it creates an ellipsis — that is, an impression time has passed — so that characters who appeared in one beat are separated from their reappearance in a next beat when they couldn't have actually traveled that quickly.

Why does the episode return to the "C" story in #10? It's not as if this beat that runs less than a minute advances the plot in an important way, so why bother? I recommend that you take a shot at questions like that because they stretch your writing muscles, even though I can't hear your responses. A few answers: It keeps that "C" story alive in viewers' minds, especially since it won't return until Act Two; it raises tension about Lesniak's state and invests us in her emotional challenge; and it delivers some information that was left unresolved in the teaser. On this last point, no scene should be written for exposition only. If you need to communicate facts, set them within an emotional context, as happens here. (Write "C" in the fourth square on the grid.)

Scene 5

Notice that the next scene is set apart merely by an Angle within the same time and place and doesn't have a new slug line such as "INT. SQUAD ROOM — DAY." You couldn't use INT. SQUAD ROOM anyway because it belonged to Scene 4, so "Angle" — which is a literary device, and doesn't intend to tell the director which angle to shoot — flags that this is a new story beat.

#11 lasts almost three pages — a little long when the material has no external action. What's actually going on? Well, first you need to know that Sylvia Costas, the Assistant D.A., is Sipowicz' girlfriend (and in later episodes becomes his wife). Costas is beautiful, sophisticated, intelligent — a step up for Andy Sipowicz. She loves him, though, and tries to help, even if he's too proud to accept advice. Now picture the smooth, attractive, newly arrived Bobby Simone in the same room. With those dynamics in mind, re-read this scene.

Look for Sipowicz' motive, his vain efforts to knock down Simone, Costas' curiosity about Simone, and how the implied threat of her interest results in lines that don't seem to be about much at all while we can almost feel Sipowicz boiling underneath. Obviously, this is the "A" story, so "A" goes in the fifth square.

Scene 6

#12 and #13 together make up Scene 6, which returns to the "B" story by introducing Paula, a guest star who may have the secret to the murder. Using resistance to the cops as they enter the showroom, and Paula's reluctance to reveal what she knows, the scene builds conflict.

This takes us to the end of Act One, which ought to be a cliffhanger. The anticipation of more unexpected turns in the Martarano case might generate the kind of dramatic tension to keep an audience through the commercial break. However, this is not such a tremendous act ender, though the "B" story has certainly been advanced. I think what holds viewers to this episode is the arrival of Bobby Simone and curiosity about how he'll affect the whole series.

After you write "B" in the box for Scene 6, you'll notice that the number of scenes in Act One doesn't go to 7. That doesn't matter. And if you add the two scenes in the teaser to these 6, that's actually 8 scenes within the first 14 minutes or so. In the original script, Act One was 16 pages, including the teaser, and set three stories in motion, so it certainly accomplished a lot of storytelling.

THE SECOND EXCERPT

Four years later, the "long narrative" of the many-faceted relationship between Sipowicz and Simone comes to a close with Simone's death. "Hearts and Souls" (Story by Steven Bochco & David Milch & Bill Clark; Teleplay by Nicholas Wootton) stretched the boundaries of episodic television as it followed Simone through a kaleidoscope of flashbacks to the afterlife, delivering an emotional and spiritual dimension rarely seen on screen.

In the Teaser and Act One we'll observe the interplay of comedy and tragedy and a gradual build of suspense before the show takes its surprising turns in Acts Two, Three, and Four. Read it before moving on to the analysis.

NYPD Blue

"Hearts and Souls"

FADE IN:

1   EXT. HOSPITAL - MORNING   1

To establish --

2   INT. HOSPITAL WAITING ROOM - MORNING   2

Present are SIPOWICZ, KIRKENDALL and MARTINEZ. Given the
configuration of the room and its proximity to the door
exiting the Cardiac Care Unit, Martinez has the prime vantage
point for viewing Simone's departure and waving greeting,
this to Sipowicz' simmering chagrin. After a beat --

                    SIPOWICZ
          You're gonna monopolize that
          position?

                    MARTINEZ
               (defensive)
          I didn't see anything yet.

                    KIRKENDALL
               (to Sipowicz)
          He wants to wave to Bobby.

                    SIPOWICZ
          That's why we're all here Martinez.

                    MARTINEZ
          Andy, I ain't moving.

                    KIRKENDALL
          I brought a harness so I could
          dangle from the ceiling.

                    SIPOWICZ
          Yeah, that's funny.

Medavoy's just arrived in a mood of happy anticipation.

                    MEDAVOY
          I take it the grand departure
          hasn't taken place yet?

                    KIRKENDALL
          Hey Greg.

2.

Sipowicz looks away, disgruntled. Medavoy surveys the room.

                    MEDAVOY
          You're in the garden spot, huh
          James? Greet Bobby without exposing
          him to any bugs.

                    SIPOWICZ
          Yeah, he came 'two in the morning
          with a pup tent.

Martinez snorts at Sipowicz. Medavoy remains sanguine --

                    MEDAVOY
          Plenty of good spots.

Sipowicz paces. Off which --

                                        CUT TO:

3   INT. SIMONE'S HOSPITAL ROOM - MORNING   3

SIMONE is sitting in a chair. His pants and shoes are on.
Emaciated from his illness, Simone swims in the shirt RUSSELL
is carefully buttoning. Russell, in whom we identify
excitement layered over physical and nervous exhaustion,
studies her husband with a hovering solicitude.

                    SIMONE
          Are you done?

                    RUSSELL
          Am I hurting you?

                    SIMONE
          No no.

                    RUSSELL
          One more.
               (completing her task)
          You've got like a little drainage,
          I wanted to go slow buttoning over
          the bandage.

                    SIMONE
          Now I'm going to lean back a
          second.

                    RUSSELL
          You set the schedule Bobby.

He tries to manage a smile of reassurance.

3.

                              SIMONE
                    Not used to all this action.

She forces a smile in return, watches as he privately tries
to measure his feeling of growing malaise. After a beat --

                              RUSSELL
                    Dr. Swan said you might get a
                    little drainage from your stitches.

                              SIMONE
                    Was my bandage wet?

                              RUSSELL
                    No, it was a little yellow
                    drainage.

Simone nods. After a beat --

                              RUSSELL (CONT'D)
                    I wonder where Dr. Swan is.

                              SIMONE
                    We got time.

                              RUSSELL
                    It's just he was supposed to
                    discharge you twenty minutes ago,

Simone closes his eyes. Though Russell has tried to sound as
if she's dealing with a minor irritation, in fact she's
growingly, irrationally afraid that if they don't leave soon
they're not going to be able to leave at all.

                                                  CUT TO:

4   INT. HOSPITAL WAITING ROOM - MORNING   4

Sipowicz has conceived an excuse to improve his position --

                              SIPOWICZ
                    I'm going to make a phone call.

                              KIRKENDALL
                    You want the cellphone?

                              SIPOWICZ
                         (shakes his head no)
                    Personal, I better use the
                    payphone.

He heads out. The others watch.

4.

                    MEDAVOY
                (admiring amusement)
            You know what Andy's doing, James?
            He's improving his position.

                    MARTINEZ
                (nods)
            He could lose five years from his
            pension, making that lame an
            excuse.

Sipowicz has reached the phones. DR. SWAN exits the
elevators, moves past. Sipowicz, feigning dismay at
discovering he lacks the proper change, keeps his head down,
re-examining this phenomenon as he moves toward the Nurses
Station.

                                            CUT TO:

5   INT. SIMONE'S HOSPITAL ROOM - MORNING   5

Simone and Russell react as Dr. Swan enters, utters his
standard discharge line.

                    DR. SWAN
            Understand you want to get out of
            here this morning.

                    SIMONE
            Absolutely.

                    RUSSELL
            Bobby has a little drainage on his
            bandage.

                    DR. SWAN
                (nods, not overly
                 concerned)
            Some of your stitches may be slow
            in absorbing.

                    SIMONE
            Diane was saying.

Russell emulates Dr. Swan's tone of unconcern.

                    RUSSELL
            He just has a little yellow
            drainage.

                    DR. SWAN
            Let's have a look.

Dr. Swan keeps his tone casual, though in his lexicon "yellow drainage" translates "big trouble." He begins unbuttoning Simone's shirt. Simone fills this silence --

>   SIMONE
>   Diane's talking about hanging her
>   shingle out 'her time off The Job.

>   DR. SWAN
>   Good, I'm looking for an associate.

Dr. Swan's undone Simone's shirt, does his best to dissemble his reaction on noting a spreading stain on Simone's bandage made by yellow pus seeping from his incision.

>   DR. SWAN (CONT'D)
>   You do have some drainage.

>   RUSSELL
>   From his stitches dissolving?

Dr. Swan keeps his voice neutral -- as if discussing an interesting chess problem --

>   DR. SWAN
>   I'm not sure. I'm going to use a
>   little Q-tip, check Bobby's
>   incision.

The camera positions itself consistent with beginning a discrete revelation of Simone's incision as Dr Swan removes the bandage. Off which --

>   CUT TO:

6   INT. HALLWAY OUTSIDE SIMONE'S ROOM - MORNING   6

Sipowicz has inched forward to the Nurses Station, glances back one last time to see if he's under scrutiny from his colleagues, then takes the last few steps necessary to gain a view of Simone's room, reacting with sickened shock on seeing Russell and Dr. Swan helping Simone back into his bed.

The eyes of the two partners meet. Sipowicz puts up his hand to Simone, waves weakly; Simone nods acknowledgement as Sipowicz moves back to the Waiting Area.

>   CUT TO:

6.

INT. HOSPITAL WAITING ROOM - MORNING

Medavoy spots Sipowicz coming out the closed door of the
C.C.U.

> MEDAVOY
> (almost chortles)
> To Andy, rule-obedience is a
> totally foreign concept. Went up
> the hall to wave.

Martinez won't concede his own position's been supplanted.

> MARTINEZ
> What I'm here for, watch Bobby
> enter that elevator.

Sipowicz re-enters.

> MEDAVOY
> You went to wave to Bobby, didn't
> you Andy?

> SIPOWICZ
> They're putting him back in bed.

Kirkendall reacts with silent dismay.

> MARTINEZ
> Is that some temporary precaution?

> SIPOWICZ
> He don't look good.

> MEDAVOY
> He went through major surgery ten
> days ago Andy.

Kirkendall's seen Russell approaching.

> KIRKENDALL
> Hi Diane.

> RUSSELL
> We have to stay awhile more.

> MEDAVOY
> (emptily)
> Yeah huh?

                    RUSSELL
Bobby has some wound infection they
have to identify. He needs a C.A.T.
scan and then they're going to
debride him.

                    MARTINEZ
Andy said he was lying back down.

Russell nods --

                    RUSSELL
You should go on to work. I'll call
if there's any news.

                    KIRKENDALL
Sure, call when you get a chance.

The Detectives put on their best face when Russell leaves.
Before she's out the door Russell gives a passing half-smile
to Sipowicz. A beat. Sipowicz seethes --

                    SIPOWICZ
                  (to Martinez)
Want to come back or you want to
keep your spot?

They're all devastated, troop out. Off which --

                              SMASH CUT TO:

MAIN TITLES

8   EXT. PRECINCT HOUSE - MORNING   8

To establish --

9   INT. SQUAD ROOM - MORNING   9

Sipowicz is the first of the Detectives to return from the
hospital. He's solemn, dour; moving as though weighted;
FANCY's going over materials with DOLORES at her desk; it's
clear they know of Simone's turn or the worse. As Sipowicz
hangs up his coat --

                    FANCY
Your ex-wife's here Andy, she's in
the lavatory.

                    SIPOWICZ
Is she all right?

8.

                    FANCY
                (noncommittal)
          Yeah, she seems all right.

Sipowicz nods; even this unexpected information can't refocus
his thoughts.

                    FANCY (CONT'D)
          Did you see him at all?

                    SIPOWICZ
                (nods)
          I saw him from out in the hallway
          for just a couple seconds.

                    FANCY
          Did he look like he was getting
          sick again?

                    SIPOWICZ
          I don't know.

Sipowicz sees KATIE SIPOWICZ, his ex-wife and mother of Andy
Jr., As she exits into the hallway. She's skittish, clutches
her handbag.

                    KATIE
          Hi Andy.

Sipowicz moves to join her in the hallway.

                    SIPOWICZ
          Are you all right Katie?

                    KATIE
          Yes, I just had to use the girls'
          room.

                    SIPOWICZ
          I mean what're you doing here?

                    KATIE
          Is this a bad time? I can talk to
          you some other time.

At this point Sipowicz is pretty sure he's smelling booze on
Katie's breath.

                    SIPOWICZ
          C'mon, let's talk in the Coffee
          Room.

Because she's been drinking, Sipowicz decides to take her the back way to the Coffee Room. As he begins to shepherd her in this direction we see Medavoy and Martinez ascending the stairs.

10   INT. HALLWAY - CONTINUOUS   10

<u>Follow</u> Sipowicz and Katie --

                    KATIE
          It's not the worst, right Andy? The
          worst already happened.

Sipowicz' embarrassment at her condition distracts him from what she's saying.

                    SIPOWICZ
          What're you talking about?

                    KATIE
          I'm in a problem, but Andy J.
          dying's the worst that can ever
          happen.

                    SIPOWICZ
          Katie when in hell did you start
          drinking?

                    KATIE
          What?

                    SIPOWICZ
          C'mon in here.

As they enter.

11   INT. COFFEE ROOM - CONTINUOUS   11

He brings her to a chair.

                    KATIE
          I had one small drink. It's coming
          to the City and seeing you. I had
          one small drink.

He's poured her some coffee, puts it in front of her, in the next instant reacts with gruff sheepishness --

                    SIPOWICZ
          You still take milk?

10.

                    KATIE
          Please.

Sipowicz provides this, watches her.

                    KATIE (CONT'D)
                (barely audible)
          I'm in some trouble, Andy. I was
          arrested in Seacaucus for a D.U.I.

                    SIPOWICZ
          On your way in to see me?

She shakes her head no.

                    SIPOWICZ (CONT'D)
          So the small drink today wasn't
          your first small drink.

She starts to cry, holds her hand to her mouth --

                    KATIE
          Please don't bully me.

                    SIPOWICZ
          All right. All right.

Katie tries to compose herself --

                    KATIE
          I'd had a glass of wine, one glass
          and the Cop says I rolled a stop
          which I did not. The person in
          front of me rolled the stop.

                    SIPOWICZ
          Did you blow impaired? Did you take
          a breath test?

                    KATIE
                (shakes her head no)
          I always heard you say never agree
          to tests.

                    SIPOWICZ
          And you told this Jersey Cop your
          ex-husband's on The Job?

                    KATIE
          It didn't do any good.

                    SIPOWICZ
          And Andy J. you told him about --
          that he'd been on The Job in
          Hackensack?

                    KATIE
          I couldn't bring myself to say
          about Andy.

                    SIPOWICZ
          Give me this Cop's name. When did
          this happen?

                    KATIE
          Nine weeks ago.

                    SIPOWICZ
               (shocked)
          Nine weeks? When the hell's your
          trial date Katie?

                    KATIE
          This afternoon.

He stares at her in angry bafflement.

                    KATIE (CONT'D)
               (apologetic)
          I was so embarrassed to come to
          you.

                    SIPOWICZ
          Were you too embarrassed to go to a
          lawyer?

                    KATIE
          I thought maybe you could help me
          keep it from that.

He slams his hand on the table --

                    SIPOWICZ
          How the hell was I going to help
          you Katie if you didn't tell me
          about it?

All his old frustration at her timidity and fear and
defeatedness wash over him. She winces as she always did when
he would shout or slam his hand down.

                    KATIE
          Oh Andy.

12.

He looks at her cower; his hand goes to his forehead. He
looks away --

                    SIPOWICZ
          You got the paperwork?

Gaze averted, she produces the summons and trial notice from
her purse. He looks at these a beat, then --

                    SIPOWICZ (CONT'D)
          Drink your coffee and let me see
          what I can do.

                    KATIE
          Am I too embarrassing to you to
          stay here?

                    SIPOWICZ
          Katie, drink your coffee.

Off Katie, as Sipowicz exits --

.2   INT. SQUAD ROOM - CONTINUOUS   12

Medavoy's with Martinez at Martinez' desk. They barely note
Sipowicz' exit from the Coffee Room, his brusque movement
toward his desk. After a beat --

                    MEDAVOY
          I'll tell you James, I never had
          the wind so completely taken from
          my sails.

                    MARTINEZ
          I got as much enthusiasm doing a
          day's work as stepping on a nail.

Sipowicz peers at Katie's paperwork, picks up the telephone.

Meanwhile MICHAEL WOLFF, 28, in sport coat and slacks, has
entered the Squad. He's carrying a manila file folder.

                    WOLFF
                (to Dolores)
          My name's Michael Wolff. I need to
          speak with a Detective.

                    DOLORES
          Just a minute.

Dolores has checked the Catching Board, heads for Medavoy at
his desk.

13.

                              DOLORES (CONT'D)
                    Detective Sipowicz is catching but
                    he's with his ex-wife --

                              MEDAVOY
                    What's the guy's problem?

                              DOLORES
                    He didn't say.

                              MEDAVOY
                    I mean did it seem like an urgent
                    problem?

Dolores, as distressed as the others by the turn in Simone's
condition, allows herself some small exasperation.

                              DOLORES
                    He didn't say. He's got like a
                    bruise above his eye, I don't know
                    if that's part of it or not.

                              MEDAVOY
                    Yeah, all right.

Martinez gives his partner a commiserating look as Medavoy
gathers his energy, starts toward the Catching Area.

13   NEW ANGLE - SIPOWICZ   13

Into receiver --

                              SIPOWICZ
                    My name's Sipowicz, I'm a Detective
                    in the Fifteenth Squad in Manhattan
                    -- you wrote my ex-wife up for a
                    rolling stop last September 8th ...

Medavoy's reached the Catching Area --

                              MEDAVOY
                         (to Wolff)
                    Can I help you?

                              WOLFF
                    I was assaulted.

                              MEDAVOY
                    Uh-huh.

Wolff points to his eye --

14.

                    WOLFF
     My name's Michael Wolff. The son of
     one of my tenants gave this to me,
     and I've had just about enough.

                    MEDAVOY
     You want to press charges.

                    WOLFF
     Yes I want to press charges.

                    MEDAVOY
     For that half-a-shiner there,

                    WOLFF
     Yes.

Medavoy abandons the forlorn hope Wolff may dematerialize --

                    MEDAVOY
          Okay, c'mon.

As Medavoy shepherds Wolff toward his desk, <u>hold on</u> Sipowicz.

                    SIPOWICZ
               (into receiver,
               incredulous)
     She don't tell you till you're in
     the Station House? You'd already
     turned the work in?
               (listens, nods)
     No, I can . . .I don't doubt what
     you're saying.
               (confiding)
     I'll tell you, we had a son on The
     Job in New Jersey got murdered --
     if she was impaired wouldn't
     surprise me if her drinking's
     ensued connected with that ...
               (rubbing his neck)
     Anyways, are you going to have a
     problem if I try reaching out to
     the Prosecutor?
               (beat)
     I appreciate it. All right, thanks
     a lot.

Sipowicz disconnects, punches in Costas' number --

                    SIPOWICZ (CONT'D)
               (abrupt)
     You know anyone in the D.A.'s
     Office in Seacaucus?
               (MORE)

                    SIPOWICZ(cont'd)
               (listens; angrily)
          I told you what I know on that --
          they kept him in and he's got a
          complication.
               (listens)
          'Cause my ex-wife took a collar
          driving drunk, Sylvia -- all right?
          -- and she don't let me know till
          three hours before her trial, and
          in between being criticized by you
          for my tone I'd like to try keeping
          her out of a jackpot. Now do you
          know any prosecutors in Seacaucus?
               (beat)
          All right. Thanks.

He hangs up. During this conversation, through the atrium
window, we've seen Katie, having exited the back door of the
Coffee Room, make her way to the landing through the rear and
side hallways, descend the stairs.

Now Sipowicz rises, starts toward the Coffee Room; as he
transits, <u>hold on</u> Medavoy and Michael Wolff --

                    MEDAVOY
          Before we make this a case, Mr.
          Wolff, have you considered how
          filing charges against her son's
          gonna affect your tenant's
          willingness to pay rent?

                    WOLFF
          I'm in my last year at Stern, which
          is the N.Y.U. Business School --

                    MEDAVOY
               (who gives a shit?)
          I see.

                    WOLFF
          I'm managing this building while my
          uncle decides if he likes living in
          Florida; I could care less how
          bringing charges against this
          steroid case affects his mother's
          paying rent.

Having found the Coffee Room empty, Sipowicz returns to the
squad --

                    SIPOWICZ
          Son of a bitch!

16.

This declaration is made in proximity to Wolff; Sipowicz
moves into Fancy's Office --

14   INT. FANCY'S OFFICE - CONTINUOUS   14

He's behind his desk. Sipowicz enters.

                    SIPOWICZ
          I need lost time.

                    FANCY
          All right.

                    SIPOWICZ
          I need to go find my rummy ex-wife.

Sipowicz starts for the door, stops --

                    SIPOWICZ (CONT'D)
          I need the cellular.

Fancy nods; Sipowicz collects the cellular, exits --

15   INT. SQUAD ROOM - CONTINUOUS   15

He heads for the door, stops at Dolores' desk.

                    SIPOWICZ
          I got the cellular.

                    DOLORES
          Okay.

                    SIPOWICZ
          If my wife calls, or there's news
          on the other front.

Dolores nods. Sipowicz exits.

16   NEW ANGLE - MEDAVOY AND WOLFF   16

Medavoy's begun filling out a 61; Wolff corrects Medavoy's
spelling of the tenant's name --

                    WOLFF
          U, not O on his name, and two l's --
          Bullinger.

Medavoy looks up, considers Wolff, shakes his head and
laughs.

                    WOLFF (CONT'D)
          What's so funny?

                    MEDAVOY
          Nothing, Mr. Wolff.

                    WOLFF
          I guess you and I don't share the
          same sense of humor.

                    MEDAVOY
          I guess I don't really care about
          that, okay. Let's just you and me
          fill out your complaint how his guy
          only hit you the one time while you
          dunned his mother for her rent.

Off which --

                                              FADE OUT.
                    <u>END ACT ONE</u>

ANALYSIS

Let's start by naming the stories. "A" is about Simone dying; "B" is Sipowicz and his ex-wife Katie; "C" is Medavoy and Wolff. I've used simple tags, and that's fine for identification, but when you plan your own script, I suggest that you create real dramatic log lines. That way, you'll be sure your stories have conflict — that they're actually stories, not just situations. Using the example episode, you might phrase log lines something like this:

A: As Simone's death becomes imminent, he fights until he ultimately makes peace with his memories. Within this arena, Russell, Sipowicz and others have story arcs from denial and anger to acceptance.

B: When Sipowicz is challenged by Katie's drinking and desperation, he must overcome his anger, guilt and his own alcoholic history to be able to help her.

C: Medavoy struggles to stay professional while an arrogant man's complaints escalate.

Notice in each case I've stated the stories as issues for main cast, not the guest cast, though the guests (Katie and Wolff) are bringing the inciting incidents.

COLD OPENING

This teaser is entirely "A" story (slug lines #1 through #7), though it's comprised of several beats. In planning an important opening like this, I would begin by making a mini-outline, planning each beat to build suspense. See if you can make your own list of the turning points in these first pages that end with "SMASH CUT TO," which signals the end of the teaser.

Did you get these beats?

• The Detectives spar with each other in anticipation;

• The first reveal: Russell discovers the drainage;

• Sipowicz schemes to find out what's happening;

• Tension mounts when Dr. Swan confirms the problem;

• Sipowicz discovers it; we see his personal stakes;

• Sipowicz and Russell reveal the crisis to the detectives, who leave, apprehensive.

Those six beats ramp quickly into the drama using a basic storytelling progression: Anticipation — Expectation — Surprise. That is, viewers are led to *anticipate* an event, which holds people through the set-up. As the action advances, we come to *expect* certain outcomes. Instead, the story turns (twists), generating a sense of *surprise* which then begins a new sequence of suspense. You can readily create tension on screen that way, as this teaser demonstrates so well.

Also, consider the use of humor in this heavy episode. Here's another age-old practice: increase the impact of tragedy by setting it against a comic foil. Shakespeare played his fools and foolishness — sometimes for belly laughs from the audience of his day — in his most tragic plays. Here, the episode begins with a moment so light it's almost silly — jockeying for position at a window. Then, as the drama moves into Act One, an outrageous fool appears in the person of Mr. Wolff. With all that in mind, let's get into the first act.

Act One

The "B" story about Sipowicz and Katie (#8 to #12) begins with several beats that are emotionally challenging to Sipowicz in the midst of the already heartbreaking news his partner isn't getting better. I just spoke about the value of comic relief, yet here's more stress. So why do you think the writers chose to come out of the title sequence and open Act One with this?

Here are some possibilities: While the Simone illness is suspenseful, it does not involve action for our continuing cast — except, of course, Simone and Russell, though even for them, the conflicts are internal, and their decisions result mainly from reflection. In dealing with Katie's very tangible distress, followed by her wandering off, Sipowicz is able to vent the claustrophobic hospital.

Katie's story also provides an opportunity for Sipowicz to externalize his feelings about Simone (including his anger), without which he'd be stuck brooding. Throughout *NYPD Blue*, a prominent quality of Sipowicz as a character is his determination not to yield to helplessness even in the face of the dregs of society, or, in this case, death. Often, Sipowicz fails, but here, Katie's needs provide a way for him to be the rescuer when he cannot rescue Simone.

See if you can discover other reasons for choosing this "B" story in this episode, and why it's an effective opening for Act One.

Throughout this act, take note of the fluid blend of scenes within the Squad Room. In the first sample script, the scenes tended to be easily separated. Here, you'll find multiple scenes in the same time and place, choreographed directorially. For example, at the end of #9, while Sipowicz takes Katie into the hallway, we see Medavoy and Martinez ascending the stairs. The point is that we don't lose the persistence of the other characters and dilemmas. The action directs the camera to "Follow" them, moving our attention with this scene, but we're also aware of material which is concurrent in the room we've left.

Similarly, the "C" story with Wolff commences as Sipowicz goes toward his desk in #12. In fact, notice that the "B" story is literally interspersed with the "C" story in #13. Toward the end of #13, you'll see multiple visual layers: While Medavoy and Wolff move to Medavoy's desk, they pass Sipowicz at his desk, and while Sipowicz speaks, we see Katie sneaking away in the background, followed by Sipowicz crossing the room, leaving us holding on Medavoy and Wolff. It's a complex, but elegant way to create depth (multiple levels) on screen.

This layering style — scene on scene in the same time and place — is found in many other sophisticated series too, so watch for it. In writing your own script, though, I suggest that you separate the stories when you plan them initially, and weave them together only when you're ready to go from outline to teleplay. (You can read more about this technique in Chapter Four.)

What You Should Do Next

Read and analyze all the good television scripts you can find from many different series. Sure, you've watched TV all your life, but observing how episodes are crafted on the page prepares you to work as a writer.

If you'd like to see how these two example shows turned out, they can be read and watched at the library of the Writers Guild and at the Museum of Television and Radio. Both institutions have award-winning shows available to the public. (You'll find those and other resources in the Appendix.)

Once you have a solid sense how the best dramas are constructed, you're ready for the steps to write your own, which I'll show you in the next chapter.

SUMMARY POINTS

• Many (though not all) drama series use parallel non-sequential stories denoted by letters A, B, C, and so forth. Three stories per episode are typical, though some shows have more. Each story is usually "driven by" one character in the main cast.

• Scenes tend to run two minutes or less. Five to seven scenes comprise an act in a classic network drama. With four acts, that adds to around 28 scenes total in an hour episode. However, certain shows that have quick dialogue-intensive scenes have more beats per act; shows with action sequences might have fewer. Shows with five or six acts may have as few as 20 scenes total.

• A "teaser" is a prologue to an episode and may incite one or more of the stories.

• By analyzing a quality show using the "grid," you can see its structure at a glance.

• The best television shows demonstrate the principles of dramatic art that apply to all quality screenwriting.

GUEST SPEAKER: STEVEN BOCHCO

Steven Bochco is the Emmy-winning co-creator and executive producer of *NYPD Blue* and many other series including *L.A. Law* and *Hill Street Blues*. I spoke with him for this book twice, in 2004 and 2010; highlights from both conversations follow.

Pamela Douglas: You're generally regarded as a pioneer, from *Hill Street Blues* all the way to now. Do you see any trajectory in what you want to do with television?

Steven Bochco: Yes and no. I don't think we started *Hill Street* with any grand notion of changing the medium. I mean, we just created the show and then, at some point in the process, the show began creating the show. And by that I mean that certain things that we committed to conceptually forced us to do other things that complemented the original things we'd done.

When you end up creating a show with seven, eight, nine characters — in response to that, ask yourself how can you appropriately dramatize that many characters within the framework of an hour television show? And the answer is that you can't. So you say, okay, what we have to do is spill over the sides of our form and start telling multi-plot, more serial kinds of stories. Even though any given character may not have but three scenes in an hour, those three scenes are part of a 15-scene storyline that runs over numerous episodes. So that was simply a matter of trying to react to the initial things we did. The show began to dictate what it needed to be. Probably the smartest thing that Michael [Kozoll] and I did was to let it take us there instead of trying to hack away to get back into the box. We just let it spill over the sides.

PD: So you didn't go into it thinking you were going to have fourteen characters?

SB: No, we just sort of started out knowing what we didn't want to do. We didn't want to do the typical cop shows that we'd been involved in writing and producing for years because we didn't feel like we had a lot more to bring to that kind of programming. So the idea of focusing, to some degree, on these cops' personal lives was appealing. But that's all we had when we started, and it just kind of organically evolved.

PD: It's generally considered the progenitor of a whole wave of television that is not necessarily about cops at all.

SB: The next show that adopted our style was *St. Elsewhere*. That came on the next year with my friend Bruce Paltrow. They were downstairs, we were upstairs. One of the reasons people, to this day, erroneously credited me with *St. Elsewhere* is that it had so much similarity in style and form.

But then it's time to move on. When we started looking at *NYPD Blue*, I didn't have a lot of interest in doing another cop show unless I could do something with the form that would really change television. That was the only time that I really, consciously thought, here's an opportunity to do something in the medium that could change it.

PD: What were some specific things you wanted to change?

SB: It was nothing exotic. I just really wanted to expand the language and visual palette. And a cop show seemed a more legitimate canvas on which to do it rather than a family or legal drama. There's just something so gritty and blue collar about a cop show that the language seems organic. So I thought if you're going to fight that battle, you have to justify doing it on the grounds that not doing it is really less than realistic.

PD: I think that's what's struck me about all of your shows. Above all, they're honest and real. These people are the way people are.

SB: Some of them are racist and some are cowards and some are frightened and some are mean-spirited, and you know, some people just don't like each other. It's politics in the workplace, so that's the stuff you always go to. And, you know, David [Milch] and I had always wanted to work together again. He wanted to do a cop show. I was less interested in a cop show but wanted to do this thing to change television. I didn't want to do it in a vacuum, but there really hadn't been a one-hour hit since *L.A. Law* in 1986 and here we were in 1991. The hour drama was in the toilet and that's my business, so my business was in the toilet.

I thought the only shot we had at reviving the form is if we were willing to compete with cable television. So that was my pitch to ABC when they wanted a cop show from me. I said: I'll give you the cop show you want, but be careful what you wish for, because the price is this, the language and the nudity. It's one thing to say yes to that theory, and it's another thing to get that script, and you've got something that's never been seen or heard before in television. Originally, the show was supposed to go on in the fall of 1992, and it didn't because we couldn't agree on language and sex. I refused to water it down. I said you take it as it is or we'll move on. So it got postponed a year.

In the months before the show went on we were getting thousands and thousands of pieces of mail — they were coming in sacks every week, from the religious right who'd spent a million dollars taking out full-page ads in major newspapers in America, beating us over the head for being pornographic. But, of course, no one had seen the show, which was very offensive. It would have been one thing if they'd seen it and taken issue with it. But these ads were so cynical, manipulative, and untrue about the content of the show — I mean, everything I wanted to do, I wanted to accomplish.

Interestingly, we succeeded, not by the show itself but by the panic-stricken religious right because they created a stir that no publicity machine in the world could duplicate. And thank God they did because given all the anxiety about the show, if we had faltered a moment in the ratings then I think we would have been gone in three weeks. But we came out of the shoot huge.

PD: Do you think that the same story could be told today if someone went in with something the religious right opposed in the same way?

SB: No I don't, I don't. Not today. Maybe next year, maybe five years from now, because all that is cyclical. A lot of it is tied to election cycles. More than anything right now, it's a function of corporate terror. As the television industry has become more and more vertically integrated, all the networks are now divisions of huge corporate entities, and in that environment they're fearful of the government and of advertisers and of their own stockholders, that it's just fear of not rocking the boat, it's just get the ratings, make the ad time, get the dollars. Ultimately, it's a self-defeating attitude. I've had a show on primetime continuously since 1981, and, you know, that's a real responsibility and a real trust.

PD: What do you think you owe the audience?

SB: A good story.

PD: And a good story to you means…?

SB: A good story to me means all kinds of things. First, a good story has a beginning, a middle, a complication, and resolution. In some fundamental way, that gives the audience a certain pleasure and satisfaction in having spent their hour in a worthwhile pursuit; and if, in addition to that, it makes them think about something or gives them a different point of view about something, then great. If it engages their sensibilities in a way they haven't anticipated — great. Those are all wonderful bonuses but that all stems from a good story.

PD: I got more than that from the best episodes of *NYPD Blue*.

SB: You know why? The good ones all have good stories, and the great ones have great stories. And when you're telling a great story, the inherent elements in great storytelling are complex thematic moral and ethical ambiguities, considerations of big human elements and conditions. Those are the kinds of big-theme issues that are embraced when you are telling great stories.

But it always starts with the story. If you say, "I got to do an episode about free speech" then you're [lost]. You're starting from the wrong place. You tell a great story and themes emerge, so that's just "Writing 101." I'm just a nut about story, story, story, story.

PD: At one point you were developing three shows at the same time. How could you stay close to all of them?

SB: First of all, I've been doing it for over 30 years, so I've learned how to be really good at it. And also it's just an issue of time management. I'm good at managing my time. Every one of those shows is at a different part of its evolution, so a show like *NYPD Blue* required a fraction of a time that a new show would require because all of us spoke a common language. The show has such a long and complex memory to think about that you don't have to invent what's there. My only chore in the last season of *NYPD Blue* was to make sure we finished the series in a way that's really satisfying to an audience and make them feel like they didn't get schmucked.

And, again, storytelling, except it's a different consideration of story. You're not considering story events, although you have to, as much as you're looking at character arcs. How do you take all of these characters on a season-long journey that organically spins them into their next life? So the audience goes, ah, that felt good, and I'm sad but I get it and I'll miss these people. But that's a different type of thinking, and that's been going on in my head for a long time. The time that I spend with the writers of a new show is almost exclusively devoted to character arcs because they'll come up with the stories, whereas we had a well of stories from cops we collected, so that part of it almost took care of itself.

A new show requires a lot of effort because it's new guys and new concepts, but it's always fun with a good new show because you get to turn over cards. It takes about two years, maybe three, to turn over all your major cards in a new show — gross character revelations in a drama — *ohhh*, he's a drunk; *ohhh*, she's gay. After three years, the job changes, the task of maintaining a show is a different task. So at the beginning, when everything's working right, it's huge fun because it's invention.

PD: You're developing several new shows for both basic and premium cable. Would you walk us through the process? When you decide, okay this one is interesting, what do you actually do? Pick up a phone and call somebody....

SB: Ideas come in so many ways. When you do what we do, you become an idea machine. I have a very close friend in the music business and we were joking about how the music business is just imploding. There is no music business any more. Discs are throwaways now — they exist only to promote the concerts. We were bemoaning all of that. Even the television business, it's all sort of upside down, trying to figure it out. So I said if you really want to make a buck, we'd start a religion. He said if you're going to start a religion, the way to do it is Michael Jackson. We were joking, you know. And I said, obviously you can't do Michael Jackson. But I said there's a television series in that idea. We laughed about it. Then I called Chris Gerolmo, who is a song composer and musician as well as a screenwriter, and I said I want to talk to you about a project. So he came over and I pitched this thing to him. I said let's spend a couple of weeks trying to figure this thing out. So he and I and another person sat here over the course of a couple of weeks and came up with a way of pitching it.

PD: Did you come up with the characters? The world? The pilot story? What exactly did you come up with?

SB: We came up with the single main character, our guy: who he is, what his background is. We came up with themes, basic thematics. I have to know what a series is fundamentally about. Then we wrote — not a scene-by-scene outline — but a shape. We came up with a beginning, middle, and end. And once we had that we whipped it into ten pages with a hook, I thought this was Showtime — that's where this should go.

PD: Did you think about casting or locations or different episodes?

SB: We thought about episodes. But since we didn't want to waste our time or Showtime's time if they were not fundamentally interested, I had my agent call to just take their pulse. And they expressed an interest.

PD: How much of that is because of your name and how much is the idea itself?

SB: It's the idea. If they weren't interested I didn't want to put them in an awkward position, or me. So we went over there. We didn't bring anything written. We pitched it. They bought it there in the room.

PD: When you say they bought it, what does that mean?

SB: They committed to the pilot script. Then we went and expanded all our pages into a real outline. We sent that over there. It's not a typical kind of show, so they wanted to get a sense of its shape. That's legitimate. By the time we gave them pages, we were all very comfortable with it. They had a couple of notes that were smart. So we made the revisions and they said let's go. Chris Gerolmo actually wrote it.

What's really interesting in the world of cable is that it's a much tougher sell. It's not like the broadcast networks that develop thirty pilots. When a cable network develops something, they won't push the button to begin with unless they're genuinely enthusiastic, and so while it's harder to get them to bite, once they bite you have a much better chance of actually getting a pilot made and possibly getting a series made.

PD: How does that compare with your other experiences in television?

SB: I worked on my first television series in 1969. So I have worked on shows in six decades. So when you really look at the life span of television... I started work at Universal in 1966 while I was in college. The irony of it is that the system I started in evolved and came apart at the seams and resurrected itself and today is a version of the system I started in. Television in the '60s was run by a bunch of studios. They were the sole suppliers for "the big three networks." For everybody it was a license to print money.

When you worked at the studio you were essentially a hack working on assignment. We were all salaried employees under contract. And that's the way it was until the very late 1970s when by virtue of the investor tax credit there sprang up a bunch of wonderful entertainment companies like Lorimar. That's when we got into an extraordinary golden age of independent company television, in which writers became empowered.

And then they rescinded all the "syn-fin" rules and these five major media giants began to vertically integrate themselves. And it became a contemporary version of what it was when I started: giant five entities control every aspect of the business from top to bottom and killed the independents. They killed innovative programming because these are all bean-counters for whom the only thing that matters is the bottom line. Everything became homogenized and the most powerful people in the equation became the executives.

PD: What do you think TV is going to look like in five years?

SB: As a business model ... Television isn't going away. It's still a good business. The interface between television and cell phone and computer in the next few years is going to be seamless. So the Internet, which everyone is spending a lot of time trying to evolve into an actual creative medium ... I don't think it is a creative medium, I think it's a platform. It's a bridge. But what's going to happen is the Internet will become another form of television. Once all these things are interconnected this will just become a resource.

I spent about a year and a half coming up with ideas for the Web, not so much original programming as interactive websites like Metacafe. I was interested in the area because it was something different. Some smart guys from Internet companies said we'll share revenue with you 50/50, but we're not producers, and we're not going to finance any production. Who wants to do that? It's a mud pit. Whether these entities are willing to use their assets to become production companies is way in the future. Nobody knows how to monetize the Internet.

Generally speaking, the most interesting evolution in the business is the dual-stream cable model. We're getting subscription programming and basic cable. That's where a lot of the interesting shows are coming from.

PD: You don't see the Internet as altering the model?

SB: I see the Internet as ultimately becoming a delivery system. ... I tend to think it's unlikely that we'll ever go back to an environment in which small independents will flourish.

PD: So why do you do television instead of movies?

SB: Easy. Easy, easy, easy. It's a better medium. Even with all the bullshit of television, it's still a more provocative medium than the movie business. The movie business is basically appealing to kids and cretinous teenagers. That's essentially what the movie business is. Very few are, in any serious way, committed to making thoughtful, provocative medium to low-budget movies that fill a real niche in the moviegoing experience. Everybody's looking for *Spider-Man* and *Batman* and all those other men, and big high concept. Those are fun and, in the summertime, kids flock to them, but that's not what I do.

Believe me, for any writer, you're going to have more fun and learn more and be more productive writing in television than in the movies. You're not going to have to share credit with 15 other idiots. You're not going to be abused and disrespected by 15 jerks in suits who have too much time on their hands and all they want to do is eat lunch. Television is a job — you got to get it on, you got to get it out, the writers are going to write their scripts, they're going to get on the tube. And that's great. If you're lucky enough to get on a successful show, you're going to do more credited writing in two years than most movie writers do in a lifetime. So it's a much more satisfying medium for writers.

PD: Would you like to share a bit of advice for students in film schools who are thinking about writing for television?

SB: Go to medical school. Not to be a doctor, go to medical school, so that when you go back into television you'll have something to write about. Have a life. It's my one beef with most young writers. If you want to be a director or producer, that's one thing. Those are skills you can learn. But, to be a writer, you got to have something to write about. Not that everybody doesn't, we've all lived lives, but when you're 21, you know, you haven't lived much of a life unless you've had an extraordinary experience to write about.

Unfortunately, most really young writers form their sense of life from watching television so what you end up getting is this sort of "Xerox" of life which is never the substitute for the real thing. So I always tell students, pursue your dream, but in the meantime, get a real job and have a real life.

SPOTLIGHT ON WRITING PROCEDURALS

WITH GUEST SPEAKERS ANN DONAHUE OF *CSI: MIAMI* AND ROBERT KING AND MICHELLE KING OF *THE GOOD WIFE*

Ann
Donahue

CSI is "the most successful franchise in television history," according to Les Moonves, president of CBS, the network that broadcasts the shows. With an original series flourishing season after season and three chart-topping progeny, *CSI: Miami, CSI: New York, CSI: Los Angeles*, not to mention off-network reruns, the franchise is inescapable, not that the tens of millions of viewers are trying to escape. When all the other "procedural" series are added, this genre, broadly defined, describes most of the hour drama series on broadcast networks (though not on cable).

Why?

Ann Donahue, co-creator and showrunner of *CSI: Miami* said it's because, in a way, procedurals are simple. People want stories resolved, to see the solutions that aren't really available in life, to be assured at the end of each episode that the bad guy gets caught.

Not that *CSI: Miami* is simple — the investigations have multiple twists, the science is intricate, and the forensic visuals are startling. But from the viewpoint of dramatic construction and the intention of the series, the format is predictable. That brings us to a general definition of "procedurals":

shows that crack their cases each episode, where the emphasis is on the puzzle more than arcs for the continuing cast. Investigation — crime-solving — is key in *CSI* and other police/detective procedurals, though *House* is an example of a medical procedural that also uses a succession of clues to reveal the culprit (in that sense, a disease), and legal procedurals (such as *The Practice, Boston Legal, The Good Wife*) use the twists of discoveries and trials to win their cases.

Procedurals have been around since the era when only three networks existed and they all required closure on every show every week. In the 1990s, *Law & Order* infused the genre with serious issues, "ripped from the headlines." But *CSI* raised the entertainment ante when it appeared in 2000. Anthony Zuiker, a writer who had no television experience at the time, had done tremendous research, even ridden with crime scene investigators in Las Vegas, to create the pilot. The network brought in experienced producer-writer Carol Mendelsohn, who in turn brought in Ann Donahue, who had won an Emmy for *Picket Fences* and had worked at Steven J. Cannell Television at the same time as Mendelsohn.

From the beginning, *CSI* was a complicated procedural with science that none of them knew and inserts showing incised flesh pierced by bullets (later dubbed "meat shots"). They had five technical advisors and had to figure out how to write the exposition and hide it.

Mendelsohn told *Written By* magazine that their fidelity to fact continued as the series grew. The three executive producers searched newspapers for

accounts of murders that inspired plots, and boned up on forensics. They went on to create the *CSI* style using super close-ups of microscopic evidence and unusual visual and sound techniques that dramatized changes of perspective, passage of time, or mood. Mendelsohn said, "The minutiae are the real essence of *CSI*. The interesting stuff is the real facts."

The challenge in writing procedurals is how to get beyond the technical to the heart. Donahue says: "The mistake we all make, including me and all of our writers on the first draft, is we do load it up with clues and we go to plot. Here's the thing: no one cares about plot. No one ever has. But story — story is not the same thing. You look around and it's the story of the guy who doesn't want to lose or who wants to go the distance. That's something people care about. Usually, that's the "A" story. The "B" story of that is his love — does he get the girl or not?

"With our shows, the "A" story is investigation, but the "B" story is the emotional line. How does one of our characters on *CSI* feel about the case and what is it doing to them personally; or one family member of the victim is involved and how can we help them through this tough time? We have to keep switching back and forth between the investigative "A" story and the emotional "B" story. If you have Act One and it's nothing but a clue takes you to this character, and that clue takes you to the next character, and our characters are only confronting them with evidence, you're failing.

"We're working on a story right now about a babysitter and there's a murder in the house where she's babysitting. We get prints of a man in the neighborhood. He says 'I went in there to steal something.' Yeah, well, why were you hanging around? Why was your nose pressed up against the window? 'Well, I was dating the babysitter, that's why.' Well, suddenly, it's not just a guy who was stealing something, but he's telling us something about our suspect who we heretofore thought was so innocent. Now we find out she's covering up the murder for her boyfriend. We find out later, they're covering up for each other. The point is you're not just interviewing the neighbor who says, yeah I robbed; I was a bad person. It's what we call upping the stakes. Someone who presented herself as innocent is having a guy over for sex. Later, that whole story becomes a 'Mrs. Robinson' story because the babysitter's mother was also sleeping with the boyfriend.

"Every person your characters investigate — and it has to be based on forensic evidence — doesn't have to be guilty, but they have to give you something else so the story builds, builds, builds. The other rule is you have to have a warm body by the end of Act One, within the first 17 pages. You have to have a real suspect that informs the audience about the story they're watching.

"A show's job is to entertain. It's plot-driven, and the writer should commit, tell the story, and let nothing get in the way — not educating the audience or political correctness or 'arias.' The hero must have desire. He must be thwarted. There must be complications.

"The difference the *CSI* franchise brought in was our production values. Each show, if it's done right, is always going to be visually intriguing and ultimately satisfying. The filmmaking is changing, but filmmaking will never replace storytelling. What I find heartening is what's always going to matter is the story and the execution of the story. When you get to the end, a good ending is surprising and yet inevitable. That's what people are waiting for.

"So every story, whether it's a medical show or a cop show or a soap opera, is a mystery. A secret is going to be revealed. When are other people going to find it out? How do we see a certain person get a comeuppance? And I don't think that's ever going to change. We want it the way we always wanted it to be. We want the ending we couldn't get in our formative years."

Of the many procedural shows on television, *CSI* is iconic — perhaps the purest example of this genre. Other shows with strong procedural drivers also feature serial stories that follow continuing characters. *House* would be a different show without Hugh Laurie's screwed-up doctor and the relationships among his team.

One of the writers on the staff of *House*, Peter Blake, visited my class at USC and gave us a peek into his own writing process. Speaking of "The Tyrant," an episode he wrote, he told us, "I asked myself 'why would a doctor kill a patient?' Well, to stop something even worse from happening. You always want to find the most difficult situations to write yourself into so you can write yourself out. You have to make the guest character as dark as possible. In this case it was a dictator who was about to commit genocide and this would stop it. Everything in the script builds to that moment.

"We had previously arced out the character relationships — where this episode stood in what was going on between Chase and Cameron. We talked about how to use that in the writers room. It got to the point that around this issue of Chase letting the dictator die leads to the breakup of their marriage.

"You lay out the bones of the procedural. Then you flesh it out. There's a question, a dilemma for the characters. An episode I wrote for *The Practice* — a legal procedural — asked 'what should you do if you represent a pregnant woman who keeps doing drugs?' If you put her in jail that's the best chance to save her life, but what if you were hired to keep her out of jail? That show often presented a moral dilemma for the lawyers.

"In *House* we look for conflict between the doctors, between the doctors and the patients, and between the patients and their families — often all of them."

For artfully balancing procedural and serial strengths, look at *The Good Wife*. Here, the lead character Alicia Florrick begins with a dilemma we've witnessed on the news side of television — the philandering husband who must make a public apology with his wife stuck miserably at his side in front of the cameras. How could a show go anyplace but her private struggle and the family drama after that? What is a legal procedural with cases that close each week doing in this most personal frame? Have two shows been conflated into one for network ease? Or is it one show with layers that continue to unfold?

In a 2010 review for *The Chicago Tribune*, critic Maureen Ryan observed, "Once upon a time, cable dramas were very different from the typical network drama. That's still often the case, but *The Good Wife* may be the most successful merger yet of the two sensibilities....

rt King
&
ll King

"Yet despite all its nods toward cable-style ambiguity and class, *The Good Wife*'s creators and executive producers, Robert and Michelle King, are mindful of the fact that their show airs on CBS, the most traditional broadcast network, and follows detective shows in which the bad guy is always caught by the end of the hour."

I asked the Kings how they make the combination work.

"I'll start with what brought us to it," Robert King began. "We are not people who run away from the more procedural aspects of the show. We enjoy procedural when it's really in top form. We enjoy it in movies. Some

The Good Wife

of the most interesting movies are ones with twists. Hitchcock is nothing more than very well executed procedural. So we like it. But we also know TV has flattened out the genre by having so much of it. Some of it's very good, much better than movies. But there's still a lot of it.

"Our interest when we were writing pilots is that the best procedural is something that has repercussions for the characters and there's only so many ways you can do that. Usually what TV does is have someone known to the hero having an impact on their lives. This hero — whether a cop, a lawyer, or a doctor — has to work to help the person who is in jeopardy. So it's a little bit of a cheat because the only way you get people caring is they care about that person who needs help.

"We wanted to find a way that the caring, the personal aspect, was really about people's lives. We wanted to personalize their home life and their work life. So that meant creating a real structure that was about character and only character. Clearly, you can't just do that and say audiences will be interested. You do need issues and even procedurals within the personal lives so the story has plot twists and revelations. We enjoyed the human part of it and wanted that to become an essential part of the show."

So, unlike *CSI*, the *Good Wife* was fashioned from character from the beginning. But amidst lots of character-based shows involving marriages and betrayals, this one brought an issue-based kind of storytelling from the pilot onward. Of course, *Law & Order* — a procedural empire — has always used news events, including scandals, to propel its episodes. But those came from the cases. In *The Good Wife*, the continuing cast itself has to deal with dramatic conflicts straight out of current day political campaigns.

I asked how they arrived at this choice.

Michelle King explained, "There were a series of scandals around the time we were thinking of what we would want our next show to be — Craig, Sanford, Haggard, Edwards, Spitzer. We became fascinated by the person whose story was not being told: the woman standing next to the man who was just getting slimed with his scandal. We started looking at that and noticed a pattern that, first, many of these women were staying with their husbands, which is kind of an interesting choice. And second, a lot of these women were attorneys."

Michelle King told BitterLawyer.com, "I think the show began when we asked, 'What are they thinking?' And Robert and I started talking about it from there ... We knew she had to go back to work and we had so many female lawyers to draw on."

The Kings themselves are not lawyers — though legal procedurals in the past have generally been produced by writers with law backgrounds, such as David E. Kelly, creator of *The Practice, Boston Legal*, and *Ally McBeal*. BitterLawyer.com put the question to them directly: "Neither of you are lawyers. Do you think that helps you focus more on the dramatic elements and not be bogged down in legal issues?"

Michelle answered, "I don't think it matters. We always start with the idea of a story, but we turn to technical advisors to make it more authentic." Robert added, "It's always a negotiation between creating good fiction and keeping it from being inaccurate. So a lot of times we have an idea, and a lawyer tells us that what we think should happen might not play out exactly as we see it." Michelle admitted jokingly, "There's a long, proud history of tweaking the law for dramatic purposes."

Actually, the show has three prongs, not two — family drama, legal procedural, and significantly, political satire, in its acute observations of judges and behind-the-scenes machinations that get people elected. Darkly comic moments drop in like sparks in otherwise procedural scenes, for example a scene when a tough woman military court judge enters, holding a glass of dark liquid, and Alicia is warned to watch out, "she's doing another cleanse."

In a deliciously complex dinner scene from a second season episode, the Florrick family attempts to impress a potential campaign contributor by celebrating Yom Kippur, the Jewish Day of Atonement. Everything goes wrong as they try to prove they are pro-gay rights, and pro-Israel, while the bright teen daughter confronts the donor about the Gaza blockade, Alicia's gay brother tries to persuade her to leave Peter, Peter's patrician mother bizarrely offers that she has a Jewish friend, and Alicia toasts the visitor with "atone," all while campaign manager Eli Gold (modeled on Rahm Emanuel) struggles to win the visitor's endorsement. It manages to be tense and funny, human and philosophical, rich in both character and plot all at the same time.

In some episodes, the show is closer to *The West Wing* than *NCIS*, which precedes it on the CBS schedule. It would seem a hard sell to a traditional broadcast network. The Kings had been writing and producing pilots for nine years before *The Good Wife*. Even with a strong track record, it's important to get the backing of a large production entity or studio, as I told you in earlier chapters. So before going to the network, they pitched the opening image to Scott Free, the production company run by Ridley Scott and Tony Scott. Ridley Scott's movie credits go back to *Alien* and *Thelma & Louise*, and together with his brother Tony, they have a long list of television productions since. Later, when they went into production, they staffed up with writers whose credits included *ER, Big Love, The Practice*, and *Boston Legal*.

Robert King described his pitch: "The scandal press conference was happening and the camera starts on the man, but our camera starts looking at the corner of the TV image and finds the wife next to him. That's who we're following. And then we go right into her head seeing this piece of lint on his sleeve. It was the opening sequence that we hoped would engage the listener."

That general approach, centering the viewer in the life of the character, often with a strong sense of place or viewpoint, has become a template for the show. "In all our episodes we have to know what our opening image is. It's a kind of DNA the story flows from," Robert King explained.

But once they're past the pilot and into planning the episodes, how do they navigate? On many traditional procedurals, the showrunners don't use a writers room at all. It isn't necessary when episodes are free-standing and depend on cases solved in an hour, without important memory for the continuing cast. To the extent those shows have arcs for the continuing cast, they are handled by the showrunner, sometimes just a couple of scenes added to the final draft after the credited writer is finished.

But *The Good Wife* is a hybrid, so Robert King explained, "In the first year, we mapped out where we were in Alicia's life ... We're not like cable that has only 12 episodes. We do 23, so we had to find a dramatic engine that would take us through the season. So much of television has melodramatic cliché. Anything we could do to avoid cliché, either using something on a current events level or a paradigm shift level, we did."

Michelle King told Maureen Ryan, "What's been fun with exploring Alicia is seeing how far she's come. She started out really unsure of her footing professionally. As she's gone on, she's become far more secure in what she does. And she hasn't been unethical, but she lives more in gray areas than I think she anticipated at the beginning....

"And even though it's a show about the fallout from a political scandal and a woman torn between two men ... *The Good Wife* never comes across as soapy or melodramatic. The show is too subtle for that, yet the charged attraction between Alicia and each of the men in her life isn't minimized either ... When we started out, we would have that half-page of dialogue explaining what was going on. Then we realized we didn't need it. [The cast] is so skilled that the audience gets everything."

"We were always fascinated by how the Clintons worked and how they both became powerful," Robert King told Ryan. "We kind of want to see, now that Alicia has found security in her work, how does that threaten her husband? Does she need her husband?"

The Kings explained that in the writers room the staff begins with where they are in the character's arc and then matches that to the case. That's different from *CSI*, which begin with the case, and different from *House*, which plans A, B, and C stories involving the medical mystery (A), Dr. House's struggle in the episode (B), and a relationship issue among the doctors which has to play out in conjunction with the case (C). In *The Good Wife*, the spine of the show — the series question — might be phrased something like "Can a woman maintain her identity and integrity while standing by the husband who betrayed her?" or even "How does a good person survive in a world of sharks?" So each episode answers the core question in some way, both in the family scenes and in the law firm where her personal issues are echoed.

Finally, I asked what they look for in writers, or what they suggest for students interested in speculating an episode. Not surprisingly, they never mentioned legal background — they have researchers and lawyers on staff for that. And they didn't mention expertise with procedural plotting either. What they said they look for is deep understanding of the show from having watched all the episodes and done your research (widely available on websites). Most important, bring some personal connection to the struggles of these characters, some life knowledge that fits these characters. And that bit of advice is good for any show, procedural or not.

As this book awaited publication, a procedural arrived with fresh possibilities for the genre. *The Killing,* on AMC, expands the franchise of cop shows and embraces the global nature of TV while holding an audience through a season of deep reveals. Some reviewers questioned whether *The Killing* is even a procedural because crime solving feels secondary to character development. Actually, this show is both plot-driven *and* character-driven.

We discussed how *The Good Wife* is also both. In that show, however, the legal (and political) procedural is distinct from the family drama. The franchises intersect in *The Good Wife,* but can be planned separately.

The Killing goes further because it's impossible to disengage the clues to Rosie's murder from her parent's grief and how their marriage is changed. It's equally impossible to separate the job from the life of Detective Linden for whom the search *is* her emotional reality. The various suspects, including politicians, are far more than red herrings — each struggles with his demons and angels, and we're invested in those internal tensions as much as we are involved in the case.

Based on a Danish TV series, *The Killing* is the opposite of the many fast-paced American crime shows that exploit disturbing images, delivered with a light touch, presenting and then solving horrific violence in an hour. Veena Sud, the writer-producer who runs *The Killing,* is herself a veteran of network procedurals as the former showrunner on *Cold Case.* Comparing those two shows suggests how far the genre has come.

CHAPTER 4

WRITING YOUR OWN EPISODE

HEARING VOICES

(The following impressionistic essay appeared in *The Journal* of the Writers Guild of America.)

> "...Trumpet at his lips, he listened to the notes bounce from brick rooftop to rooftop until, finally, he knew the rhythm of the echoes. He'd based his music on those intervals. People called him a genius, but he knew what they could not understand — that he had merely listened."

That's from a short story I wrote in college, when I believed music exists before it is played, that a statue is inside the marble block and the sculptor cuts away whatever is not the statue, and that for writers — now we come to it — characters exist beyond what is written, with larger lives than fit on film. They'll talk to you. You merely have to listen.

You catch a character the way a surfer catches a wave, waiting in still water until it wells up from a source as invisible as it is powerful.

Whaddya want? That was a kid talking.

Okay, okay, we know what it's really like. In some scripts, catching a character is more like catching a bug mid-flight on your windshield.

Working writers have to hear other voices. "You want it good or you want it Friday?" Yeah, yeah, I know, good *and* Friday... and it better be Friday.

The voice of my first movie business boss plays in a perpetual loop. Greenly arrived from the East Coast, I had landed a studio development job. I brought the boss a script by a New York friend and naively blazoned it with the kiss of death. I called it beautiful. I can hear the boss now, over his thick cigar, "Don't tell me that shit!" He's making boxing moves like Norman Mailer. "Man to man! Action! Action! Get it? *Mano a mano!*" He's snapping his fingers in my face. "Is it going to make 100 million? Is it? Is it? That's what you tell me. You come in here and prove it's going to make 100 million." A sucker dare. No one can prove any movie will make a dime. But I didn't know.

He didn't snap his fingers in your face. You're over the top, and that character is running wild. Stop him!

Okay, okay. He didn't snap. But the rest is true. I soon left the studio job for a writing career. The denigrated New York author went on to win a Pulitzer. And the executive retired richer than both of us.

What's that got to do with the voices?

They don't come easy. Sometimes you have to snare them.

My field is television drama. I've had the chance to learn from a few great writer-producers who provoked their staffs to what drives a real person, not just what gets a laugh or twists the plot. Where else do you find a 22-hour narrative of evolving characters? Immediacy. Intimacy. Power. Like a hard-charging river. But we all know what's along the banks: some cesspool shows.

When I was a beginner, I went for an assignment on one. It wasn't exactly a cesspool, just stagnant. The series characters were moved like toys to fit a franchise. While the producer described contrivances he wanted me to write, the characters in my head screamed, "Can we have the bathroom pass?" With enough craft, you can do an assignment like that. Fake it. Kind of like a worn-out love affair, and as deadening.

Then, in the midst of the script, a character surprised me with a line that could only have come from her. Gotcha! The sound of her voice was like having her address. And once I knew how to find her, she forced the characters who answered her to be as real. And they made their world whole. Once you've had it good, you don't want it any other way.

Right, like you do that every day.

No. Staring at the computer screen with a belly full of caffeine and terror, I know what it's like to have nothing on a character besides every *thing*. Facts. Stuff that has to happen at the act break. Wind whistling on deserted shores. But I've learned something: craft can be a tugboat that pulls you out to where you can hear the voices.

So, you gonna get to Joan of Arc, or what?

Not Joan. But there is a connection. The high when you're flying with a scene rolling out like it's alive — that euphoria is worth putting up with the detractors and distractions. It's like an all-nighter when you can't get enough of each other, you and the characters, and no one wants to sleep again ever, and it's already all there... just listen.

* * *

I decided to begin this chapter about preparing you to write your own script by quoting that article so we don't lose sight of the source — where writing really comes from — as we focus on the nuts and bolts of craft.

Finding Your Stories

Whether you're setting out to write a spec script or you're on a staff vying for an episode assignment, you'll need to choose subjects which (1) fit the medium, (2) complement the specific show, (3) contain events that will play on screen, and (4) express your unique experience or fresh insights. Yes, you can do all four.

Ideas that will work on television have the scale and intimacy I discussed in Chapter One. So look for character-based subjects that benefit from scenes with dialogue.

To fit an existing show, you need to have watched that series so much you can hear the characters' voices in your head. And you'll have figured out the kinds of springboards the show uses to impel stories, and its pace and style.

As you know, externalized actions are basic to any screenwriting. Just as in a feature screenplay, you plan your structure around things that happen. That sounds simplistic, and I wouldn't bring it up but I've seen otherwise-sophisticated students become so involved with the psychology of TV characters they forget that character is expressed in a series of events on screen.

Finally, what do you bring to the party? Of course, you'll consider ongoing relationships among the cast; those kinds of continuing stories are called "on series," and are fine to write, but be warned: the large turns in a season's arc are planned by the showrunners. It would be naïve to spec an episode where Don Draper of *Mad Men* goes for a sex change, or an episode of *House* where the character is nice to everyone, or a *Friday Night Lights* where the Coach realizes he hates football, or where the cast of *The Wire* breaks into a Bollywood dance routine. Don't do episodes that change the central characters or the course of the show.

Instead, think about incidents you know (or know of), and then play them out in the world of the show. If that's scary, you're not alone. Even Aaron Sorkin, creator of *The West Wing*, *Sports Night*, *Studio 60*, and movies including *A Few Good Men*, sometimes has difficulty beginning. He confided at a Writers Guild Foundation seminar in 2004: "It's bad enough trying to have ideas. When you really start you're trying to get one. Every day you're flipping through instantly dismissible ideas, so my head is like the worst movie you've ever seen. Horrible, horrible ideas that go nowhere. It's like being bludgeoned with your own inadequacies."

One way to break the logjam is through research. Some writers maintain files of clippings from quirky magazines and small town newspapers; others hit the Internet or books. For example, if you were planning a *CSI*, you'd be smart to investigate scientific clues that can be visualized under a microscope, especially if they might reveal a personal secret. If you were researching for *Big Love*, dig up little-known events in Utah or find a fresh angle on running a Home Depot-type store. For a *Law & Order*, you might come across a topical issue on an op-ed page, but come at it with an unexpected interpretation of the law. Now, none of that means you should rely on gimmicks. Clever bits of information do not make stories. But they might turn your own creative wheels.

And here's how they turn: Make your subject live and breathe through the experiences of your continuing cast. That's key. The most common error is to tell the story through guest cast. I'm going to repeat that in other words because it's so important: Don't write a story that can be told without your continuing cast. If your story could work as a movie without your show, then you haven't made it work for your show.

Here's an example of wrong and right ways to approach your story. Let's make believe you're planning an episode for a series about Jane and Sally, who are detectives, and you've come upon an item about a woman cat burglar who scales tall buildings to steal Manolo Blahnik shoes.

A *wrong* log line would go like this: Portia Pedi, a former rock climbing champion, attempts to scale the Trump Tower at night to acquire the world's most expensive stilettos, but her clever plan is foiled when she's caught by Jane and Sally.

A better approach to an episode log line would be more like this: Jane confronts her fear of heights on a ledge of the Trump Tower at night when she must rescue Sally, who has been taken hostage by a woman cat burglar, and together Jane and Sally foil the plan to steal the world's most expensive stilettos.

See the difference? In the wrong version, the guest cast drives the action of the show and leaves the main cast as mere witnesses or pawns of the guest. In the second version, the challenge, jeopardy and viewpoint belong to the main cast, whose decisions create the turning points.

Once you've identified a subject for your spec episode, write it as a log line. (Log lines are discussed in Chapter Two, in case you want to refer back.) That's easier said than done, because in order to state your story in a sentence, you need to know the whole dramatic arc. I understand that's difficult, but I advise you not to skip ahead. Once you're clear about your story's conflict you'll be secure you really do have a plot, not only a premise.

If you're working on an "A"-story series, you can move on as soon as you have a single log line, though you'll need to make sure your one story has sufficient substance for around 28 scenes. If you're doing a show with three or more stories, you'll need separate log lines for the "B," "C," or other stories, and you do have to figure out each one. With that done, you're now ready to get to work.

BREAKING YOUR STORIES

"Breaking a story" means identifying the main turning points. On network TV it involves structuring the episode so strong cliffhangers occur at the act breaks and the story engine runs all the way from the inciting incident in the Teaser (or the beginning of Act One) to the resolution in Act Four or Five.

It's not a process to take lightly, and even experienced writing staffs wrestle with stories for hours, even days. In addition to placing the act breaks, apply these two basic dramatic tests:

(1) **Credibility:** What would real, normal people do in the situation? Are you forcing the plot twists by contriving actions that stretch believability, or do the actions and responses of the characters follow naturally from the jeopardy or conflict? What's honest here?

(2) **Rooting interest:** Do you care whether the characters succeed? Are the stakes clear enough and high enough to make an audience root for your protagonist? Will people be emotionally involved?

Once you've settled on your essential stories, you can sneak up on the structure by figuring out some tent-poles. The easiest may be your opening because the event that propels the episode is often what attracted you. But even with the most obvious story, you'll have options: Do you want to open with the guest cast who will present the challenge, or with an internal problem for one of your main cast, or with a goal for one of your main cast which becomes subverted once the guest cast arrives?

Aaron Sorkin told the Writers Guild Foundation seminar how he starts: "I have an idea for the first page and a half for *The West Wing* — which, by the way, no joke, if I know what the first page and a half is of something, I don't want to say I'm half way home, but I can see the house."

Whatever it takes for you to see the house — the voice of a character, picturing a place, coming upon a crime scene, getting a case, or confronting a conflicted relationship — close your eyes and make that come to life. Then you'll be centered in your show's world, which makes it easier to be real about what happens next.

The second easiest tent-pole is probably the ending. When you chose this subject the final outcome might have been inherent. The body is found at the beginning and the real killer is the one who reported it, or the nice witness, or the secret lover, or whatever. Your challenge is how to arrive at that ending through the main character's process of discovery or growth, not mainly to solve a crime or cure a disease or manage to survive. So even when you know the ending, you have to get to it, and therein lies the craft of storytelling.

The third tent-pole occurs at the end of Act Three. It's the "worst case." Remember, in drama, the worst event is whatever opposes the protagonist's goal (or the triumph of the antagonist), not necessarily bad stuff that happens. For example, in the hypothetical show about detectives Jane, Sally, and Portia the shoe burglar, the worst case might be that Jane, who is afraid of heights, is forced to venture out on a ledge to rescue Sally. The jeopardy here is not only to Sally, who has been taken hostage, but that Jane has to confront her darkest demons in making herself climb out, and is shaking so badly because of her fears she's going to blow her one chance at the rescue. That's the cliffhanger before the Act Three break.

Here's another example: A doctor fears his wife doesn't love him anymore and is struggling hard to win her back. During the episode, he has a patient who needs surgery. At the same time it's raining outside. From a dramatic viewpoint, the worst case is that the wife rejects him, not that the patient dies or the rain turns into a flood, though those circumstances could certainly complicate the character's quest.

When you know the Act Three "worst case" you've nearly solved your basic structure because you can begin figuring backward to how your characters arrived at this crisis. Even if you can fill in no more than one or two beats prior to the act break, you'll begin to feel the progression.

Now you want to pin down the cliffhangers at the ends of Act One and Act Two. Developing the antagonist might give you some clues. Often (but, of course, not always) the second act is where the opposition that began in Act One gains strength. You know that at the end of Act Three this opposition will appear to have won, so see if you can come up with two surprises. You might discover that the protagonist underestimated the antagonist in the first act but is forced to fight back after a reveal at the end of Act One. In Act Two, maybe the antagonist is not exactly what was expected, or your characters follow a red herring, or they even believe they've won, when the antagonist (or problem) re-asserts itself at the Act Two break.

Using our make-believe Jane and Sally show, you might introduce the challenge that someone is stealing shoes in Act One and reveal at the Act One break that the culprit is a woman cat burglar who scales skyscrapers — and that brave Jane is paralyzed by this case because she's afraid of heights. So in Act Two Sally has to go it alone as Portia becomes more and more bold, endangering many shoes. In fact, Jane's inability to work on the case leads to Sally being taken hostage at the Act Two break. As the jeopardy deepens through Act Three, it becomes urgent that only Jane can save Sally, and that she has to go out on that ledge or all is lost at the

Act Three break. Act Four is pure resolution, and would emerge naturally from the "worst case."

Of course, that's a silly story, but I'm trying to give you a broad sense of how to find the big bones of your structure. Your writing is more subtle, more complex, and doesn't rely on cartoon-like action, right? Still, these "tent-poles" can help you plan:

THE GRID

Yep, here it is again, doing an encore since the last chapter. This time, though, you're not noting the various stories of someone else's script. Now, you can use the grid for your own rough ideas by filling in the major beats I've just described — opening, ending, worst case, Act One break, and Act Two break.

The grid is something I've created for myself because it helps me see the entire hour at a glance in the earliest stages of figuring it out. If this doesn't help you, don't worry about it. The grid is just a planning tool because everybody has to start somewhere, and a blank page might be daunting. Make copies and play with it if you'd like, and vary it for five or six acts if that fits your show.

Chart 4.1 Basic Four-Act Grid

ACT I	ACT II	ACT III	ACT IV
(T)			
1			
2			
3			
4			
5			
6			
7			

THE OUTLINE

The first step of writing involves listing the scenes in your script. This process has several names in addition to "!@#$%^&*()+," which is what you might want to call it when wrestling down the structure. Actual names include "outline," "step outline," "beat outline," "beat sheet," and "treatment," but they all amount to figuring out the order of events in your teleplay.

"Treatment" has a specific definition, usually observed only in the breach, and it's not a word you'll hear much in television. Technically, a treatment would be a half to two-thirds the length of a finished script written in prose (not screenplay form) that includes every scene in the order it occurs, as well as tone, style and descriptions, and is virtually the entire script lacking only dialogue. Believe me, nobody writes treatments like that. If someone asks you for a "treatment" of your story what they really mean is a few pages that summarize it. Even for full length features, I've heard the term "treatment" apply to a three-page pitch. Don't bother with it unless you're asked.

A "beat sheet," as used by some producers, is midway between a treatment and an outline. It parses your show into acts and describes the big story elements, though it doesn't spell out specific scenes. So we're talking about seeing the dramatic turns, not a diagram for writing.

"Beat outline" is sometimes used interchangeably with "outline" because it's a list of what's actually written in the teleplay, and usually those "beats" are scenes. On one show where I worked, the producers asked writers for a very full outline (like a treatment with numbers), but when the staff met, they would reduce the narrative in the outline to a more skeletal list they called a beat outline so the construction could be analyzed.

For example, an outline scene might say something like "While Jane clings to the ledge, frozen in fear, desperately trying to convince Portia to release Sally, Portia taunts Jane to climb out to get her." The simplified beat might say "Jane on ledge — Portia: "Come get her." It's an internal cue used for planning though it might not make sense to an outside reader.

This brings us to your outline. As you know from Chapter Two, an outline is a step in the professional development process. It's a contracted stage of writing that generates "story by" credit and pays almost as much as a whole script. If you have a contract with "cut-offs," you might get no further if the outline doesn't work; but a successful outline means your option for a first draft will be "picked up" (you'll go ahead to write the script).

What if no producer or payments are involved, though? Un-fun though outlines may be, you really should write one, even if you're working alone on your spec. I advise: Don't travel without a road map — hour episodes are too complex, especially if you're juggling multiple storylines. If you're on your own, though, hand-written notes might be enough, and initially you could get away with being vague, noting only what you need to accomplish for the characters within a scene. Personally, I've found that the time it takes to type a complete outline and weigh each beat saves me oodles of time writing because I'm not worrying about being lost or redundant, and it saves me from writing scenes I'll have to delete because they don't move the story ahead. To me, grief-avoidance is worth the effort.

HOW TO WRITE YOUR OUTLINE

Nobody launches into an outline at number one and trucks on to number 28 in a straight line. Instead, start with the tent-poles I mentioned and fill in the grid until it's complete enough to write the scenes as an outline. Or you could begin with index cards, as many writers do. Cards are wonderful because they're not threatening. If you don't like an idea, toss it out. If your order doesn't make sense, re-arrange the cards. And you can "download" your thoughts in any order, which lets you reach creatively to scenes you'd enjoy whether or not they fit next in the script.

One technique is to choose different color cards for each story. If you do all the beats of the yellow story, then the green one, then the blue, and assemble them, you'll see at a glance whether you've lost your green story in the second act, and whether the blue is paying off in Act Four or if it petered out in Act Three (which might be okay, but at least you'll have a chance to ask the question).

Remember, in a multiple-story show, the stories are probably uneven. So, if you'll have around 28 scenes in an hour episode, and your "A" story predominates, it might have as many as 12 to 16 beats; the "B" could have 8 to 12 beats or so, and the "C" has whatever is left, as few as 3 or 4 beats, up to maybe 8. Of course, if you're dealing with vignette writing, with seven or eight parallel stories, you might have a whole little tale in a single beat, though that's not typical of most dramas. Understand, I'm not suggesting exact numbers of scenes that should go with any story. I'm illustrating the kind of planning you might do.

Let's say you start with your "A" story. Make cards for every scene that tells your story. Count them. If you've got 40 cards you have a problem. Maybe the cards are fragments rather than whole scenes. See if you can condense many of them together until you have 10 to 20 cards. Or maybe your story doesn't fit in an episode. What portion of this story is the essential conflict that could work within an hour? Or maybe you're rambling, including backstory or side incidents that aren't part of the forward motion. Whatever doctoring you need to do, get that "A" story down to size.

What if your beats are too few? You can trouble-shoot by asking the opposite questions. Maybe you have combined a few scenes on one card. See if you can separate them into two-minute blocks, and then see if this story becomes the right size. Of maybe you don't have enough material for a major story. If it truly doesn't have enough meat, then you might look for a larger story to "marry" with it. Or maybe it does have fine potential but you haven't yet spelled out the moments that would unveil it on screen. Again, see if doctoring will get you to a useable scale.

After you do that with one story, go to the next and the next. Some scenes from different stories may play at the same time and place, so you'll actually get more mileage out of your screen time than you'd have if each story was a free-standing little movie. And once you weave them, you'll discover interesting contrasts, where telling one story enables you to ellipse time in another, or a scene from "A" resonates thematically with "B" in an interesting way. Putting the stories together can lead to discoveries, so you want to be flexible here.

After your individual stories are filled out, and you've ball-parked which beats occur at the act breaks, read the cards through with the feeling of watching on screen. Don't kid yourself. If you're bored, the audience will be too. But they're only index cards — change anything you want at this stage.

Once your basic structure is in hand, write it out. Here is a cheat-sheet for how a standard outline looks:

<u>"Title of Episode"</u>

TEASER
Summarize the teaser in a few lines, usually with more
description or tone than the beats that follow. In shows
where the teaser is a single scene it's one paragraph.

— However, complex ensemble series may begin several
stories in the teaser and break them into separate blocks.

— Teasers with two or three (or more) distinct scenes
may have two or three (or more) segments like this.

<u>ACT ONE</u>

1. EXT. LOCATION — TIME
The beats of the outline are numbered, beginning with #1 in
each act, and headed by slug lines, as in a script. Keep
them short like "log lines" for the scenes.

2. INT. LOCATION — TIME
Each step is a scene with dramatic structure. Every scene
has a protagonist (a character who drives the scene), a
goal, and an antagonist or opposition to the goal, even in
scenes one minute long, even where conflict is subtle.

3. INT. SAME LOCATION — LATER
These are dramatic scenes, not production scenes. In other
words, beats are determined by the content, not merely by
time or location. If in the same location you have a new
conflict it is a new outline beat.

— However, in a show where multiple stories converge at
a single moment, and you use a fragment of a different arc,
it may be easier to follow if you note it after the scene.

4. EXT./INT. A FEW LOCATIONS — DAY TO NIGHT
A single dramatic scene may cover several places, beginning
when characters meet, continuing with them in and out of
a car, concluding elsewhere. In this case use an inclusive
slug line, as above, though you wouldn't do it in a script.

5. INT. SQUAD ROOM — DAY
An example: Jane arrives saying a mantra about her fear of
heights just as Sally accepts a dare from Pedi to try on
the stolen shoes if they meet her on the roof right now.

6. 7. See if you can fit one Act per page. The hour outline would then run around 4 pages total. However, every series has its own pace and style.

If you use that outline form to specify locations and times for each scene, it will help you be real about what's actually on screen. Here's an example of an *incorrect* beat in place of #5 on the sample:

```
INT. SQUAD ROOM — DAY
Jane says the mantra to herself while driving to work
and stopping to feed the pigeons. While petting one, then
releasing it, she thinks about how scared she would be to
fly like the pigeons. Meanwhile Sally gets a call from Pedi,
who is trying on shoes on the roof, inviting Sally and Jane
to join her up there, where we can see her dancing in high
heels. Sally worries whether Jane would be able to go up
there too. When Jane enters, saying her mantra, Sally tells
her, etc.…
```

That's awful, right? That example is like one of those children's games where kids try to pick out all the things that don't belong in a picture. Before I tell you the answers, find the mistakes, yourself.

Okay, ready?

• Engage each scene as close as possible to its conflict or problem. Here, Jane meanders while screen time ticks away before we get to the purpose of this beat.

• Animal wrangling is expensive and consumes production time, so it's an example of the kind of material TV series spend for only when essential to the drama.

• If you're inside the squad room, you can't see Jane outdoors. All that would be exterior (EXT.) action. In an outline, you can use an inclusive slug line, but if you really mean to place the dramatic conflict in the squad room, omit the driving.

• Jane's fear of flying is not visible on screen. Don't put it in the outline if you can't put it in the script. If you do intend to put it in the script, though, indicate how you'll show it.

• A similar problem recurs with visualizing Pedi on the roof. Sure, there should be a place in the script to establish Pedi. If this is it, be clear in the outline — and give it all it's due as a meaningful location — or omit it from this scene and allow Pedi's dare to be heard on the phone or communicated in Sally's dialogue.

Once you delineate your usable beats, you can easily turn your index cards into an outline a producer (or you) could track. Or maybe not so easily. When you move from hand-written notes to a typed structure you'll probably realize some facts slipped by: You've indicated a scene is in daytime. Oh, it can't be day because the scenes before and after are at night. But it doesn't make sense for the characters to be at work at night. Okay, should you move this scene elsewhere? Or can the other scenes occur in the day? If so, how does that change the tension? What day of the story is this anyway?

That's just a hint at the reality-check awaiting you, but better to resolve it in the outline than after you've written 50 pages!

ALTERNATE OUTLINE FORMS

Not every show, or every writer, does outlines so detailed or specific. Some prefer to plan the characters' arcs but leave the actions (where, when, and how the characters play out their conflicts) to whoever writes the scripts.

I once wrote for *A Year in the Life*, which began as a beautiful "limited series" that followed a Seattle family in the aftermath of the mother's death. The short run proved so successful that the family drama was picked up for a full season. The showrunners, Josh Brand and John Falsey (who also created *Northern Exposure* and *I'll Fly Away*), had planned complete character arcs for the season, and since this was very much a serial, all episodes were like puzzle pieces that had to fit a larger picture.

The first outline Brand and Falsey handed me was unlike anything I'd encountered at the time. It followed the psychological and emotional progress in the hour, but suggested only a little that could be termed "plot" or even incidents. Yet, it was an important point in the season. In the "A" story, the family patriarch, widowed for less than a year, proposes marriage to an independent woman who has a fulfilling life as a doctor and no need to marry. The "B" story dealt with the teenage granddaughter who is arrested for driving without a license. In the "C," the newly married daughter-in-law tries to get a first job; and she and her husband have a fight. So it's not as if the hour was devoid of content, but the outline I was presented had hardly any guidance about how to relay these stories.

For instance, one beat said something like: "Coming into the kitchen after arguing with his wife, the son wants to confide in his father, but can't. The father's proposal has just been turned down, and he'd like to tell his son, but he can't confide either. During the scene neither man ever says what is on his mind, though they comfort each other." That was all.

I loved the challenge, but before I could write that scene I had to create a mini-outline for myself. In this case, the scene was set in the family kitchen late at night, each man surprised to find the other there, not wanting to show vulnerability. I kept the dialogue entirely "off the nose" (indirect), each man emphasizing his strength for the other, while they comforted themselves with food. No chase scenes or car crashes or anything larger than two people at a table, but the delicate moment did have tension because the audience knew what was being withheld. I tell you, this is the most difficult kind of scene to write because you have no external jeopardy to lean on; the conflict comes entirely from character, and much of the opposition is internal.

Because it was so difficult, I made notes for the turning points within this tiny scene — the optimal place to enter, when to take the milk from the fridge, exactly when the son would ask what happened with the proposal, the moment he'd let his dad off the hook by mentioning football tickets, the spot where the father would sigh and pointedly reveal nothing, and so forth. It helped me to have that map even though no one else saw it.

Many writers use outlines somewhere between the specific, detailed "cheat sheet" and the loose emotional agenda from *A Year in the Life*. On *ER*, for example, the outlines didn't tend to have numbers, but each step was a fully realized scene with dramatic structure. That's especially impressive when you consider how short the scenes on *ER* may be. Here is a fragment of an actual *ER* outline of the Emmy-winning episode "Love's Labor Lost" written by Lance Gentile. I'm grateful to Warner Brothers, Executive Producer John Wells, and writer-producer Lance Gentile for permission to print it here.

Episode 18

TEASER 7:00 AM

— ROSS and GREENE toss a football outside the ambulance bay. An ambulance races past, a familiar face in the window. "Was that Benton?" Ross goes long for a pass as a car careens down the street and a bloody gang member is tossed out into the street.

— Ross, Greene and HATHAWAY race the gang member down the trauma hallway, passing HALEH, who takes us into Trauma One, where she finds a distraught BENTON. The old lady with the broken hip is MAE BENTON, his mother.

— In Trauma Two, CARTER and JARVIK join the heroic resuscitation of the trauma victim. Carter witnesses Greene at the top of his game, impressed.

— Mae is shy about her son seeing her naked, exposed and in pain. Haleh reassures him that she'll give her special attention. Benton wants to write out the orders as Haleh has been insisting. She lightens up on him: "Don't worry — I'll take care of it. Go see if Greene needs any help."

— Benton enters Trauma One as Greene is prepping for a thoracotomy. As Benton pulls on a trauma gown to do the procedure, Greene says he doesn't need any help — go be with your mother.

— When orthopedic resident JANET BLAIR arrives to admit Mae, Benton insists that the chief of orthopedics be called in.

— Greene and Hathaway escort an OR team out of Trauma Two. As Hathaway heads home from the night shift, she passes DR. GREGORY NELSON, chief of orthopedics, steaming into Trauma One.

— Nelson, none too happy about being pulled from his department meeting by Benton's persistent calls, does agree to do the case. Benton tries to get him to say that he, not the resident, will actually do the case. Nelson flatly refuses, and he and Blair take her off to OR. When Benton tries to get on the elevator, Nelson flatly forbids him to go anywhere near the OR.

All of that occurs in the first several minutes, so you can see how fast television storytelling needs to move, how packed it is with dramatic stakes, and why you'd need to be at the top of your craft to write a show like *ER*. The episode you're writing might not be as intense, but you can learn a lot from *ER*'s skillful blending of the arcs and the way this outline blasts each story out of the opening like cannonballs.

For example, in the very first beat, a peaceful "status quo" is immediately broken by the inception of the "A" story when Benton arrives in an ambulance, but rapidly diverts attention to the urgent "B" story when the gang member is tossed onto the street. Talk about grabbing attention!

Re-read your own outline and read it to friends until it's as powerful and clear as you can make it.

Sonny's List

One of my former MFA students, Sonny Calderon, told me he taped reminders around his computer, mostly tips that came from my response to someone's work in class. He thought these four might be useful as you begin your first draft.

- Every beat is an action. A character "realizing" something is not a scene. Each scene involves a character who wants something but faces resistance.

- The antagonist must be as strong and motivated as the protagonist. The more equal the sides, the more suspense. See the world from your antagonist's viewpoint also.

- Aim at the turning point where the protagonist must make a difficult choice, a moral equation which is nearly balanced.

- Anchor your story with the Worst Case Scenario three-fourths through. This is where the protagonist seems to fail and must overcome his internal problem to deal with the opposition.

YOUR FIRST DRAFT

How close should you stay to your outline? That depends how close your outline is to what works on screen. If you're on an assignment from a show, you will have vetted your outline with the head writer (and maybe the whole staff), so you're sent off to your first draft with an implied contract to deliver what they expect. Sometimes an outline is considered "locked," which means you're committed to the beats on the page and you'd better stick to them. In hasty or ultra-low-budget productions, some companies have been known to start prepping (preproduction) based on the outline. (That may mean scouting locations and rough scheduling, for example.)

But what if you come upon something you want to fix? Say, in the outline, a beat exists to reveal a character's secret, but while writing, you realize the secret is already apparent from a previous scene, so you need to cut the extra beat. Or you might want to make a larger change: The guest cast pops out, speaking in a way that's more interesting than appeared in the outline, and the "voice" of the character demands that certain scenes be angled differently.

If you're doing a spec, absolutely go for the revisions if you're sure of them. You don't get points for sticking doggedly to an outline that doesn't make sense! But if this script is for a producer, it's better not to make large changes without asking. I made that mistake once. I was doing a script for a show and had thoroughly worked out my outline with the showrunner. But as I approached Act Four, I was inspired by what I thought was a more clever resolution, so I went ahead and wrote it.

Well, one day after I delivered the script, the producer was on the phone complaining I hadn't given him the ending we'd discussed. Surprised by the emotional tenor of his reaction, I listened silently as he went on about this single point before I appreciated what he was really saying. The original ending had been his idea. Whether or not my version was better, his feelings were hurt — not just because I hadn't used his suggestion, but because he felt I'd disregarded him. This was about respect. Aha, I made a mental note: In the future, pick up the phone and ask. If you get the boss on board, he'll probably say okay to write what you think is best.

Now, how do you actually do the script? You've written screenplays before or you wouldn't have reached this point, and this one is not so different. Once you get past the structural requirements of the hour format, and you've told your stories via the show's continuing cast, the next special factor is speed. Episodes are usually due two weeks after the outline is approved, and that feels fast if you're used to mulling over a feature for months. Of course, if you're speculating, no one will know how long you took to write, but a concentrated schedule is a habit you'll need if you're going to work in television.

I'll show you how easy it is to deliver in 14 days. Let's say you have an outline with 28 beats (four acts with around seven scenes in each). I like to follow my outline exactly, so I write just two scenes each day. *Voila!* 14 x 2 = 28. When I'm writing at home (not on staff), I begin each morning reading over what I wrote the day before, fine-tuning it. Then I take a breath and get ready for the first scene of the day. I approach it as if these next pages are the single most important piece of writing I'll ever do. I want to bring to this screen moment the richest experience, full of subtext and nuance, while delivering the action in the tightest way I can. I might imagine the whole scene before writing a word, or take a walk and jot down ideas, or close my eyes and wait for the characters' voices. Whatever it takes. Then I write two or three pages. And stop.

I find that pushing on diminishes quality, and I want to come to the next scene fresh. So I'll take a break. Lunch, errands, gym, calls — I try to take my mind off it, though when I'm most relaxed, not even trying, I'll have ideas for a way into the next scene or a perspective on one I wrote. Much later in the day, in the afternoon or night, I'll re-read the morning's scene and revise it. Then I repeat the process of finding, forming and writing the second scene of the day. And stop.

I've found that by the time I reach the end of the script, my first draft has already been edited because I refine my work each day. Of course, not everyone works like this, nor should they. I have a writer friend who starts work at 4 AM and smashes through as many pages as she can before she runs out of steam, hardly looking back. She tells me she'd never let anyone see that "mess" that rambles, repeats, and wanders into tangents. She regards it as raw material which she edits away after she arrives at the end. You could think of it as the difference between painting and carving a sculpture: The painter pays attention to each brush stroke, adding one after another until the picture is formed. The sculptor begins with a hunk of material, and cuts away "everything that isn't the statue," to paraphrase Michelangelo. One method isn't better than another — whatever works for you is right.

If you're frightened by a blank page, put something on it — anything. A painting teacher once taught me that as I stood staring at a blank canvas. He walked over and threw ink on my pristine surface, and that got me moving, even if only to clean up the ink. Some writers break the emptiness with automatic writing or anything a character might say, even if it's not the way to open the scene. Some people write by hand for the visceral feel of words flowing from the mind onto paper. Others talk into a tape recorder.

Aaron Sorkin commented at the Writers Guild Foundation Seminar: "When I try using a tape player, I freeze up immediately. It's walking around and talking to myself; it's driving and talking to myself. Ultimately, it's about typing. The problem I have with these new-fangled computers is that they don't make a good sound. It used to be... a typewriter makes a sound like you're working. I like the clack."

So do whatever spins your wheels. But stick with professional form when you turn in your draft. You already know you need specialized screenwriting software, and you ought to be up on how scripts look. It might help to refer to the samples from *NYPD Blue* in Chapter Three. And in case you need a quick refresher, here's a "cheat sheet" on standard form.

ACT TWO

FADE IN:

EXT. LOCATION - TIME OF DAY

The action is in a paragraph at the outside margin and goes
all across the page, single-spaced.

When you introduce a character for the first time, use
capitals. Example: CHARACTER ONE enters. But when Character
One is mentioned again, that name will not be upper case
(except when heading dialogue, of course).

                    CHARACTER ONE
          Dialogue. Try to keep this to under
          5 lines per speech, and always
          condense to minimum.

                    CHARACTER TWO
          Responses can include pauses, often
          indicated by...
               (beat)
          And then the dialogue continues
          after the parenthetical.

                    CHARACTER ONE
               (parenthetical)
          The parenthetical above should
          modify or describe how a line is
          said, but not give a large action.

If you want Character One to go across the room and do
something, that belongs here in action, not in a
parenthetical.

                    CHARACTER ONE (CONT'D)
          When the same character continues
          speaking after an action, indicate
          it with (CONT'D) after the name.

INT. LOCATION - TIME OF DAY

Give only enough description to build dramatic tension or
reveal an essential insight into character or plot. Do not
indulge in set decoration.

                    CHARACTER ONE
          Notice that after a new slug line,
          you don't need to write "CONT'D"
          though the same character is
          speaking.
                    (MORE)

2.

                    CHARACTER ONE(cont'd)
          When dialogue goes on long like
          this and breaks in the middle of
          the page, use "more" and "cont'd"
          as illustrated. Do not write long
          dialogue speeches like this though!

SECONDARY SLUG LINE

A secondary slug line might include ANGLE ON A DETAIL, or one
specific room or part of a scene, such as CLOSET.

In spec scripts and all first drafts, do not put numbers on
the scenes nor "continued" on the tops and bottoms of pages.
That happens only in the final shooting script.

And when you reach the end of each Act and the end of the
script...

                                        FADE OUT.

Remember, you're writing a "selling script," not a "shooting script." You want to entice a reader, especially if this is a spec, so write what will keep someone interested. Mr. Sorkin shared this insight at the Seminar:

> "The selling script is the most important right now. I'm not writing a script right now for a line producer to sit and budget, for a DP [Director of Photography] to work at. I'm writing a script for you to read, to sit there at night — you can't stop turning the pages, this is so much fun. Even now in the scripts that I write, I only, frankly, describe what's important for you to get that moment. It's possible that I'm going to describe, 'and the camera pushes in and pushes in and pushes in' and I'm probably going to write it like that because I'm building tension for the reader at that point .. Mostly I write for dialogue, and dialogue is what you read fastest when you're reading a screenplay. Description just slows it down."

Aim toward Page 17 to end your first act (including the teaser if you have one), Page 30 to end Act Two, around Page 45 to end Act Three, and somewhere between Pages 50 and 60 at the end of Act Four. Those are approximate guides, not rules, though. A filmed episode might run anywhere from 44 to 52 minutes (without commercials), depending on the outlet, but you won't know the actual length of your script until several drafts from now when a shooting script is read through by the cast and timed with a stopwatch. I gave you that page count only so you can check yourself. If you're way off — for example an hour script that's 30 pages or 90 — it's time to troubleshoot. Here are some quick diagnostics:

TROUBLESHOOTING

IF YOU'RE RUNNING LONG:
- Are the speeches overwritten, explanatory, or redundant? Tighten the dialogue.
- Have you indulged in set decoration, directing on the page, or over-blown description? Take a sharp knife to these.
- Are certain acts long, though the script is the right length? Move the act breaks by enhancing a different cliffhanger or re-ordering scenes.
- Have you indulged in backstory or secondary characters or tangents? Return to your original outline and stick to a clean, clear telling.
- Have you engaged the scenes as close as possible to the conflict? Have you ended scenes immediately after the climax or goal? If you have written prologues or epilogues to your scenes, get rid of them.

- Is there too much story? If your outline was accurate, this shouldn't be a problem, but you might have fooled yourself in the outline by counting sequences of scenes as one beat. If so, you need to re-think the stories themselves, or delete an entire arc. This is major work, not editing (see the discussion of "second draft").

IF YOU'RE RUNNING SHORT:
- Have you fleshed out your scenes? A script is not merely an outline with dialogue. It requires re-imagining each dramatic moment as an experience. Make sure you've fully told your story, including reactions as well as actions.
- Do you have enough story? If your outline only seemed to be complete, but actually contained mostly a premise or the circumstances in which a story would occur, you'll need to go back to the outline stage and create more events, more real turns — more of a plot. Rewrite the outline before you rewrite the script in this case.

At the End of It All...

Sorry, there isn't an end, at least not anytime soon. This process will go on for as many more drafts as you can stand, and if your episode is produced, some writers revise all through postproduction and only quit fixing things when they're forced to because the thing is on the air! In television, this obsessive tinkering is limited, fortunately, because shows get on the air very quickly.

If this is an assigned script, you probably have to deliver it to the head-writer now. But if you're ahead of schedule by a day or so, don't hand it in early. Take that day to let the script "cool," then re-read it with as much distance as you can muster and refine what you can, but deliver on time. TV schedules don't have much slack, and slackers don't get much work in TV.

If this is your own spec with no deadline, now is an opportunity for feedback. Have your draft read by everyone, not just other writers or your grandma who thinks everything you do is perfect. Sometimes an outside reader will ask what you need to hear: "Why would she do that?" "I don't get why they don't just make up." Or you might hear awful reactions: "Is this supposed to be a parody of *Buffy*?" Don't be crushed by one stupid reader. On the other hand, the reader might be on to something. It's a gift to have the chance to reconsider.

If readers are too polite, or don't know how to give feedback, ask them three simple questions:

- Do you care about the people in the stories?
- Were you rooting for something to happen?
- What do you think this script is all about?

After all the input, I suggest setting the draft aside for a couple of weeks, if you can manage that. With enough distance, you might see what you need to change by yourself. You'll also see typos that your eyes glazed over no matter how well you spell-checked and proofread. My favorite was a student script for the series *Boston Public* innocently handed in with the letter "*l*" missing in the title on the first page.

YOUR SECOND DRAFT

You need to understand the difference between revising and rewriting. The kind of editing you do every day — fixing spelling and punctuation, tightening lines, omitting a speech, clarifying an action, lopping off the heads or tails of overlong scenes — all those corrections are parts of normal writing. Rewriting is a whole other job.

A rewrite means rethinking the structure and sometimes characters as well. You're still dealing with the same general story, but you want a fresh way to tell it. You can't do that by crossing out lines or replacing words. Go back to the drawing board.

Start by putting aside the script. I mean it. As long as you cling to the precious moments you've written you'll be tied to your first draft. Take a breath and let go. Maybe you'll be able to use many of the pages you've written; and certain scenes, even sequences, might survive intact. But when you begin a rewrite, everything is on the table or you'll turn into a pretzel trying to fit a structure around scenes that don't belong.

Depending on the notes you got from the producer or readers, your episode may require a new outline. Can you work with your existing outline as a reference to re-organize the beats, or do you have to start over? Either way, boldly get rid of what hasn't worked and add completely new elements, even a new arc, if necessary.

Then begin the second draft using the new outline, though, again, you might be able to keep much of your first draft. Now, I'm not saying to throw out the story the show bought (if indeed it was bought). On that point — being told to do a second draft on an assignment is terrific news. The alternate is being cut off after the first draft and having your script given to another writer. Don't imagine for a minute that anyone's first draft is shot exactly as first written, not even when the showrunner writes it himself! And if you're on assignment, the second draft generates a payment.

I had a funny experience with a rewrite. I'd handed in a first draft (this was actually a TV movie) and the network called for an in-person meeting at their office. That didn't bode well, because if notes are minor they're often given on the phone or in a memo. So, in we went — the producer, a company executive and me — anticipating a high level effort to save the project. As it happened, this particular network exec wasn't experienced, and she sat there going page by page through the script. Two hours. And at the end of it she'd asked for changes in five lines. Five lines! The producer was so steamed that he told my agent to bill the network for a full second draft, which amounted to something like a thousand dollars per word. Don't count on that kind of waste in episodes, though. Showrunners mean it when they want a rewrite.

If you're speculating, draft numbers make no sense. Every selling script is "First Draft," even if you've written this thing eleven times. To keep track for yourself, you could put the date of the draft in the lower right corner of the title page. Or you might run a header showing the revision dates of specific pages (some screenwriting programs have this application). But submit your script with no draft numbers or dates. And no colored pages — that's for production revisions after the shooting script. Remember, the sample you send to a producer is always shiny new, hot off your printer.

YOUR POLISH

Technically, a "polish" means what you'd think — a small revision, like polishing a surface, fine-tuning. Frequently the term is used for a dialogue polish where a writer goes through a script and sharpens the speeches. Polishes do not include re-structuring or creating new characters or story arcs.

Sometimes a cultural "wash" is called a dialogue polish too. That occurs when a character's background is not familiar to the original writer and a second writer is brought in to make the character speak naturally. Usually that kind of polish is not credited.

For you, if you're working on a series, a polish may or may not appear in your contract, and if it does, the payment is slight. That shouldn't matter. If you're fortunate enough to be kept on an episode after your second draft, cling with your teeth and fingernails and polish anything including the boss's chair. Scripts keep changing, and the more you're willing to do, the more the final product will be yours. Of course, if you're on a staff, you'll be polishing other people's scripts routinely, sometimes because the original writer is busy with something larger. It's a normal stage in preparing a script for production.

As for your spec script: Polish until it gleams.

What's Next?

Do it again! If you're speculating, write another spec for a series that demonstrates you can work in a different genre. If you're writing on assignment, you'll have the thrill (really) of seeing your creation on screen. And if it's well received, you'll get another assignment in the future.

No matter how this script turns out, the best way to write better is to write more. If this is your first dramatic episode, you've taken a great leap. Just think how much you learned. And next time it will be easier. Just kidding. If it's easy, you're not stretching. So don't expect easy, but once you're comfortable with the basics, next time will be more fun.

Finally, when you have a few writing samples in your portfolio, you're ready for the next step: joining a staff.

SUMMARY POINTS

• In writing your own spec script, go through all the steps, from outline to first draft, second draft, and polish.

• An outline is a list of scenes or beats in the order they will occur in your script. It's the first professional step and generates a payment and "story by" credit if you're writing on assignment. You may create the "A," "B" and "C" stories separately and weave them together, watching that cliff-hangers fall at the act breaks.

• All teleplays are in normal screenplay format, written on standard screen-writing software, using the submissions option rather than as shooting scripts.

• Rewriting a script is not the same as editing, and involves re-thinking structure or characters.

• A polish is a smaller revision that refines dialogue and tightens scenes before presenting your script.

• Ask for feedback on your finished script and be willing to rewrite many times before giving it to a producer or agent as a writing sample.

GUEST SPEAKER: DAVID SIMON

A recipient of a MacArthur Foundation Fellowship and multiple writing awards for *Homicide: Life on the Street* and *The Wire*, David Simon also co-created *Generation Kill* and *Treme*.

Pamela Douglas: Would you share something about your creative process, the writing process that might help new writers?

David Simon: It's very hard when you haven't experienced a lot of life to comment on life. I had the benefit of spending the first part of my career as a newspaper reporter, for about fifteen years, from the time I was in college until I left the [Baltimore] *Sun*. Those fifteen years grounded me in lives other than my own. A lot of beginner's literature tends to be singular and onanistic because people don't know much of the world when they start writing. They might become a craftsman as a writer and people could do it at a young age because they're smart. They read and learn other writers and they get the dynamic. But that doesn't answer the question whether they have anything to say about the world.

To speak to something serious about life or about society it helps to have lived awhile, endured a bit of loss and tragedy and the things that happen to you when you get older. Not to mention, as you get older you see the cycle of political behavior and you're better able to parse things for what they are rather than what they claim to be.

What I look for are writers in their forties and fifties who have seen a little bit of life, and if they've been in situations or places in the world where they can bring something to bear on the subject at hand, that's even more important.

The notion that you "age out" of the grand themes is bull. Ancient Greeks were writing about this stuff. The great issues endure. The political issues endure. The arguments Socrates was making, for which they gave him hemlock, or the themes inherent in Aeschylus or Sophocles — they're still there. The political dynamics they were arguing over in Athens are still there. The power strategies in the War of the Roses can still be put to dramatic use because our world has not changed as much as we think it has. The human dynamics don't change.

But if you want to be current, maybe you have to go and research dialogue, do reportage. If I want to write something about New Orleans in 2007, it matters that I was paying attention, that I was down there in 2007.

PD: At that time *The Wire* was still on. Were you thinking ahead to doing *Treme* back then?

DS: Yes, I was there in November and then again in December after the storm for several weeks. We sold the pilot idea to HBO in 2005 right after the storm. I needed to get down there while *The Wire* and *Generation Kill* were both still in production. I needed to start doing reportage.

PD: So you did a reporter's work to develop these characters long, long before they were scripts.

DS: We took about two and a half years before we tried a first draft. We also needed time to see what was going to happen with New Orleans. How can you know how to arc the thing until you know what you're trying to say?

PD: I had the opportunity to see a draft of the original proposal for *The Wire*. I noticed that it was unlike any other show treatment or proposal I'd ever seen because of how full it was, minute by minute. Would you share why you did that?

DS: Try to imagine yourself in the room trying to explain *The Wire* to the HBO executives. You're asking them to do what seems to be a cop show. And HBO at that time had been successful by doing the opposite. They were counter-programming the networks by doing shows the networks couldn't touch, shows about sexually active women in New York, or shows with Mafia gangsters as protagonists, shows going to the heart of dealing with death. These are shows the networks can't deal with because they're busy selling to people every thirteen minutes. You can't convince people their rampant consumerism is essential and viable and worthy when you've just spent the past twelve minutes (in the case of *The Sopranos* or *Six Feet Under* or *Oz*) demonstrating that perhaps the underpinnings of society are not as intact as we thought they were. You can't tell a dark story. You can't be honest about the human condition, which is essentially tragic. We are all mortal and we are flawed. And if you want to deal with that honestly you can't oversell redemption. So to sell a story you have to sell the advertisers, and that's unacceptable.

At HBO that was the dynamic they understood. So I come in the room with a cop show. But my purpose was to do it in a way that proves the network shows are a fraud. Well, that's not the purpose of the show. The purpose is to tell a story. But that's the added bonus. I had to sell them on the notion they were still counter-programming networks. The trouble is that unless you lay it out and they see that by episode six, the whole notion of good guys and bad guys has been reduced to farce and it's really a show about economics and sociology and how power and money route themselves in a modern American city, unless you demonstrate beat by beat what you're talking about it's very hard for them to believe you.

In that very first meeting I didn't tell them we were going to carve off a different piece of the city each season. They would have laughed me out of the room. I was trying to argue for one season there. But in a way you have to go as far as I did to say I know it will seem to have all the apparent tropes of what you've already seen on TV, but it's not going to be stuff you've seen on TV and here's why.

PD: What impresses me about your shows is the character depth. But the comments I've read you've made in the past are that *The Wire* was just about Baltimore and the socio-economic issues. You don't think of it being about the characters?

DS: No. But people misunderstand that. It doesn't suggest that as a writer you're not obligated to write good characters and sustain good characters. Your characters are your tools to tell a story. They have to stay sharp. You can't build a house with a bad toolbox. Everything — the characters, the actors, the directors — you want to have the best possible toolbox. But if all you're doing is writing characters, what's the difference between what you're doing and a soap opera except that you're executing on a better level. What do you have to say about the world? What do you have to say that hasn't been said already?

Most of television writing — probably 80% of it — is to try to get a hit and then maintain the franchise at all costs. If they want to see shit blow up, blow some shit up. It's about sustaining the audience. TV, for its lifetime until the advent of premium cable, had to exist on that level. American television at this point is only barely out of its adolescence. It's been a grown-up for a very short time. And that's because the advertising model of television destroys the integrity of storytelling. You have to maintain the maximum number of eyeballs to charge the maximum amount of money to sustain those ad rates. On that economic model, you must dumb it down. You cannot make it complicated. You cannot make it dark. You have to rely on melodrama.

The thing that happened in the last decade is somebody figured out an economic model where you could be a grown-up storyteller and do something that has meaning. And if people come, they come, but at least you're still bringing people into the tent. Some people take HBO for *Treme* and *The Wire*. Not everybody. A lot of people want it for *True Blood* and whatever. But as long as I'm bringing people to the tent I can be an asset. It's a different economic model where I literally don't have to look at the Nielsens. What I do ask is, does the thing have a tail? Does it find its audience eventually? *The Wire* DVDs are selling at a faster rate now than ever before, though the show has been off the air for two and a half years. I need to know the show finds an audience or what I'm doing is irrelevant. But I don't need it to find an audience on Sunday night.

PD: Do you have another show in mind next?

DS: Yes. We — Ed Burns, Dan Fesperman, and I — are working on another show about the post-World War II history of the CIA. I'm also working with my mentor Tom Fontana [producer of *Homicide*]. We're planning a series on the assassination of Lincoln. And there are three or four other projects.

PD: Any more wisdom you'd like to pass on to readers?

DS: Experience life before they're ready to write for any mass media. Experience the world, experience people, get outside yourself. In some ways journalism and nonfiction in any form is a great training ground for dramatists. I don't work with people who woke up one day after they dreamed about becoming a TV writer. They want to become technicians. I don't hire TV writers for *Treme*. The writers I hire love New Orleans, or are people who understand American roots music, and others who are journalists and novelists from New Orleans. That's who I'm hiring.

I find television writers give me derivative television scripts. That's why it's all so generic. They get poverty and race so relentlessly wrong. They don't even see the other America, and they don't think they have to know anything other than the television industry. They read the "trades," for God's sake. I don't need somebody who's going to tell me how to make a television show. The last thing I want to do is make a television show. I want somebody who knows New Orleans, somebody who knows the drug wars, somebody who knows the CIA. Those are the valuable voices I'm always looking for. So when guys send me their resumes — I did three seasons here and I was story editor there — hey, what do you know about the world?

SPOTLIGHT ON WRITING YOUR PILOT

In the beginning is the world. When you write a pilot script, you're the creator of a universe that includes places, people, churning and contradictory desires, threatening situations, even day jobs. And always, at the core, are secrets: mysteries so deep and intricate they will take 88 or 100 hours to discover. But most writers don't start with those specific revelations, or even with the cast. And unlike movies, particular arcs in which characters grow and change are not usually the creator's agenda on day one.

CREATE THE "WORLD"

Many pilot writers begin with total mental immersion in a location where they will dwell virtually for years. David Simon, creator of HBO's searing and insightful urban drama, *The Wire*, insists his show is about Baltimore. Each season focused on one aspect, such as the schools or the media, but he says the initial inspiration wasn't the closely perceived drug dealers and police, or the teenagers portrayed with heartbreaking realism, just: Baltimore.

For Simon, the pilot emanated from both a geographic and socio-economic setting. But sometimes the "world" is tied to a quest or special character rather than a place. No one would mistake *House* for a show about Chicago. Instead, House's world is his diagnostic unit in his hospital; and within that, the internal landscape of House's need to overcome "a world of pain" (his own) propels the stories. And no one would mistake House's hospital for the one in *ER*, although it was also in Chicago. *Grey's Anatomy*'s Seattle Grace Hospital and *Nurse Jackie*'s St. Vincent (in New York) are in big American cities too, though they claim worlds of their own. Try this exercise yourself: how do the "worlds" of *Grey's Anatomy*, *Nurse Jackie*, *House*, and *ER* differ from each other?

Damon Lindelof, co-creator of *Lost*, also began his world with a place: a mysterious island where a plane has crashed. But he advises that the

starting point for most shows is usually not as challenging: "When you talk about television shows, there is a franchise element and the franchise is the world. A hospital, a law firm, or a precinct — those are the easiest worlds for a television series. You know what kinds of stories inhabit those worlds. The harder worlds are a spaceship that is being pursued across the galaxy or you're on an island in the middle of nowhere that the audience knows you cannot leave.

"The question is who's going to be interacting with that world? That's what separates a good cop show from a bad cop show and a good medical show from a bad medical show. They both deal with the same patients, but the issue is: who are the doctors who are tending to those patients? A feel-good show like *Grey's Anatomy* is a much different show from *ER*, but only because of the people. Otherwise it's exactly the same show as *ER*."

In the Second Edition of this book, Lindelof spoke generously about how the pilot of *Lost* was created. For the full interview, please visit *www .PamDouglasBooks.com*. Here's part of what he said about the genesis of his show:

"Normally the pilot season starts in the summer when studios buy ideas from writers, and then the writers go off and write outlines, and then drafts, and usually before Christmas the networks and studios get those drafts and they come back after Christmas and in January the networks start announcing the pickups of their shows.

"But at the end of January, when all the pilots were already being picked up, Lloyd Braun, President of ABC, said he wanted to do a show about people stranded on an island. J.J. Abrams and I said independently (because we hadn't met yet) well, there's no place for the series to go. It's not a dramatic show. How do you do *Survivor*, the drama? That's a game show. Still, Lloyd was passionate about it. He had a vision; he wanted something different. At the time ABC was struggling with launching new series. They had crapped out of new dramas for several years; they were the number four network. And the police dramas, or medical dramas or legal dramas — you get those every year. But this was a different setting. The showman in him said there was nothing like this on television.

"This liberated us to create what we wanted. I called J.J., though I thought it was the worst idea ever — I didn't think it was a TV show. But I said to him if you had to do it as a series it would require certain elements such as a massive cast, and it would have to be a huge ensemble piece and you'd have to know nothing about anybody. Maybe you could dramatize their past by having flashbacks of them prior to the crash. So you'd be doing two shows — one that took place after the crash and another show that took place before the crash. We didn't know how we would make that work. And I said it has to be really weird. It has to be like an episode of *The Twilight Zone* every week. There have to be twists and turns and an external source of conflict that would send the characters into conflict with each other."

FIND THE STORY SPRINGBOARDS

Okay, let's say you've fully moved into your new mental home — the world of your series. What's next? Not writing — not quite yet, though you should be jotting notes all along. Now you need to fully imagine what makes stories happen in your world. That's not limited to the pilot episode, but requires figuring out the "motor" of the show. Do people come in with cases to solve? If so, that doesn't necessarily mean a legal or crime case, or a disease. In a sense, a case could be a relationship issue, or coping with extra-terrestrials or extra-dimensionals (as in *Fringe* and *The Event*), or your internal demons (as in *Dexter* and *Mad Men*). As long as characters have long-range quests that incur conflict, and their stories present both internal and external jeopardy, you can discover the "springboards" for stories within your world. This potential for future stories is the essential that differentiates writing a pilot from writing anything else on screen.

POPULATE THE "WORLD"

Once you know how your show "works" within a rich world, your next step is probably to draw out the main cast. I use that phrase "draw out" as opposed to "introduce" or even "create," because if your world is fully enough imagined, these people already live there. In fact, if you have a problem knowing the three or four or five people who your show is about, you should go back to step one and delve deeper into your world. That's not to say you'll know everyone in a large ensemble cast, or that characters you didn't see at first won't step out and greet you as you write. Actually, as a writer it's wonderful to be surprised like that. But beginners shouldn't tackle a big ensemble anyway. It's difficult enough to write a few people well!

Some writers do thorough bios of their characters at this point. Some sketch out moments, phrases or images that "pop" a character. I once wrote a pilot where I needed a way to tag a character (express her) in order to pitch the show. I saw her speeding into the outskirts of Los Angeles at dawn in a beat-up convertible, bare feet pressing the pedals to the metal while her butt danced on the car seat to the sound of "Mustang Sally." In another glimpse, close and tight, she took her time licking the remnants of Kentucky Fried Chicken off a paper wrapper while a motel proprietor banged on her door. Only one of those moments actually appeared in the script, but both helped me visualize her at an early stage.

In the Second Edition, Ron Moore, creator of the great dramatic allegory *Battlestar Galactica* (the 21st century version on Syfy) described how he arrived at the characters. Initially, he wasn't interested in the project because the original 1970s show by the same name lacked depth. "But," he said, "when I watched it again I was struck by the dark premise at the heart: an apocalyptic attack destroyed humanity. The show was about the survivors and the Cylons chasing them forever. I thought that was a really interesting format because the core was this disturbing notion of death and being lost in the cosmos. So I thought, what if you took the premise and really did the show and asked yourself in those circumstances what would happen to real people? If you took normal, screwed-up people who just happened to be the ones that made it, what would that show be like?

"I knew I wanted to maintain the premise: the show was about the survivors who were on this last battleship. Then I decided the old show was about a family. I looked at the family tree and decided to make some changes. The daughter in the old show didn't serve any purpose so I just lost her. Then I made Starbuck a woman immediately, and decided she's the surrogate daughter to the father figure. The father figure of Adama had no counterpart, neither a mother nor any counterpart in the civilian world. I didn't want it to be just a military show. Okay, the premise was that the remnants of human civilization were in these fleets. So how do they govern themselves? Are they going to try to maintain their democracy as they move forward? Is the president to be a real player in this show, unlike the old one? And I decided that should be a woman, and that sort of completes the family, and that's who the show is really about.

"The other character that interested me was Baltar. The human race in the original was not only attacked and destroyed; they were also betrayed. Baltar betrayed them to their enemies. But then I tried to figure out, why would he do that? There's no reason I could fathom that anybody would do that, so I came to the conclusion that he does it inadvertently as part of his weaknesses. He is, in many ways, the most human character of them all in his capacity to rationalize and always look for a way that it's not his fault. He doesn't mean to do anything evil but somehow always ends up doing amoral or even evil things.

"Those are the general parameters I thought that show was about and how I was going to translate it to this show."

MAKE A PLAN

Let's say you have your world, your springboards, and your main cast. Yes, you're creeping up on writing the thing. Remember that you must grab readers even before this pilot ever gets to viewers, so your first ten pages (or less) are critical. Don't lay back and wait for episode 88, or even 22, to reel in your audience with a revelation. Get a sense of anticipation started now.

What do you need to generate anticipation? Answer the basic dramatic questions: Do we care about (or are we intrigued by) your main character? What does the character want urgently? Why does she need it so desperately? Who and what opposes her? Are the chances of succeeding and failing nearly equal? Then you rev-up the action until we expect her to reach the goal... at which point you twist it, pulling out the rug, so we discover this quest will have way more ramifications, to be continued in later episodes.

Of course, that's oversimplifying. The point is that in the early pages you need to set your series in motion by rooting us in at least one of your main cast and establishing the series franchise. As for writing the world, I recommend that you don't write text to describe it. As vital as is creating the world for your series — so important that we began with it — it has to "breathe" through your script, not ever feel "made." That is, the world of your show *is* the show; it's where your people live. If you have to explain it, something's not alive here.

After all that, you're ready to plan your pilot as you would any ongoing episode of your show. Does it have four acts? Five? A teaser? Think about the grid and the discussion of structure in Chapters Three and Four. Since you're the creator of this show you get to make those choices (at least until some network tells you otherwise — but you should be so lucky as to have a network!). Then move right along to outline, first draft, and all the revising and polishing that follows.

Once upon a time, spec pilots were indulgences in a fantasy of running a series of your own. Now, agents and producers will read them as writing samples. And, yes, sometimes they even get made. Because of this opportunity, I asked my colleague, Georgia Jeffries, to speak to you about her experiences with pilot writing.

GUEST SPEAKER: GEORGIA JEFFRIES

Georgia Jeffries wrote and produced for *Cagney & Lacey* and was Supervising Producer of *China Beach*. She is on the faculty of the USC School of Cinematic Arts.

Georgia Jeffries: I've written eight drama pilots — the most enjoyable television writing I've ever done because of the opportunity each provided to define and explore a whole new world.

When I teach my pilot class, I tell the students that creating a series is a hybrid of short story writing, and screenwriting. It is, ultimately, the creation of a novel on film. Just as Dickens wrote "episodes" of his novels in penny magazines week by week and month by month, so must the pilot writer conceive complex characters whose stories will have the potential to evolve over the long haul.

Right now (with due respect to Dickens once again) is "the best of times and the worst of times" to be a pilot writer. There are exceptionally imaginative pilot storylines that foster a higher bar for creative product. Yet it's also an extraordinarily competitive job market. There are indeed more buyers — pay and basic cable as well as the broadcast networks. But because of vertical integration, a number of those buyers are often owned by the same conglomerate. Seventy to eighty percent of all pilots ordered by the networks are being developed by their own auxiliary companies. If it's on ABC, it's fairly certain that it's going to be produced by Touchstone. So if the pilot writer doesn't have a deal at Touchstone, chances are s/he will not get a pick-up from ABC.

Stakes are higher than ever because of multimillion-dollar production costs coupled with continuing losses at the broadcast networks. They're competing with each other to reclaim the audience they're losing to the Internet and video games. I believe that means we need to target the audience in a new way with more "limited series." That is essentially what HBO and Showtime are doing with a number of their series today, ordering only 10 or 16 episodes at a time (with a long hiatus in between) instead of 22 or 24, the usual broadcast order. That translates into more time and freedom for the creative artist behind the show — and conversely more time for the audience to discover the show amidst such a plethora of choices. The more the marketplace expands and redefines what a series can be, the more opportunity for more pilots to be written by new talent.

Pamela Douglas: When your students try to do pilots, what do you warn them about? What traps do you advise them to look out for?

GJ: My largest concern is that they come into the classroom trying to emulate only what they've already seen on TV. I encourage them to take creative risks. After they watch what's on the air and read a number of pilot scripts, they have to distance themselves, take a long leap off the cliff of their own psyche and think about what they would like to see. The only way to write effectively is to stop censoring themselves as to what is or is not possible.

PD: When you create your own pilot, where do you start? Do you start with the world or the characters? What is the creative evolution for you?

GJ: I generally have started with the world.

PD: That's interesting for you because you're such a "character" person.

GJ: Yes, but for me place *is* character. The first broadcast pilot I wrote was about young female surgeons at Walter Reed Army Medical Center in Washington, D.C. So it was a very specific location — a military hospital full of returning vets. A later script, this one for pay cable, was also set in Washington, D.C. — but in a far more rarefied world of power and intrigue on the Beltway.

In this most recent pilot I've written, the characters were alive in my mind for a while before I could put them on the page. That didn't happen until I decided to take them home to Illinois. I'm from the Midwest originally, but I've never written a pilot set in the Midwest. At last I had a place I wanted to take them.

PD: When you go into a pilot you have certain themes, certain subjects you want to explore, then how do you proceed? Did you do an outline? Did you think through a whole year of arcs? Or did you really just start with the premise?

GJ: I always did story treatments, of course, but was never required by any of the networks to do a bible of future episodes. I did that on my own, assembling a tremendous amount of research for myself. With each of my pilots I put together — and I'm not exaggerating — files that were three to four inches thick, all full of character and story ideas. I was constantly pulling out articles from magazines, recording something I heard on NPR. I never felt I could relax and assume I had enough story fodder to get to the magic 100th episode.

I remember some of the earliest direction I got on my first draft pilots was, "take us further in the opening story ... bring us into the heightened drama earlier." My initial instinct was to hold back some of the mystery to surprise the audience later, but I learned that was a luxury I couldn't afford. I had to hook the executives first, while still keeping a number of tricks up my sleeve. That meant sometimes painting in more obvious colors than I would have liked (because I think the best storytelling is subtle and "between the lines"). I kept getting notes on my pilots to go bigger and broader earlier on so viewers would know exactly what was at stake. So I learned to push the characters to the emotional brink in that first episode.

When I guide my class through the pilot process, I tell them to create at least ten questions the viewer could agonize about at the end of the first episode — what's going to happen to this or that character or story point. If viewers think they know the answers, they're not going to bother to come back for the second episode. That also helps to determine the ten short synopses students have to come up with for future episodes.

PD: Do you prefer writing a pilot to either a movie or an episode of a series?

GJ: Yes, no question, because I'm thinking long-term. I'm thinking twenty-two hours, not two hours.

PD: Even though a movie is just as original, this is much bigger.

GJ: And even more demanding. We know what it's like to live fourteen hours a day with these characters, day after day, during seasons when you have a six-week hiatus if you're lucky. I could never approach a pilot half-heartedly. Creating any successful series demands a commitment of body and soul.

CHAPTER 5

IT'S WHO YOU KNOW: WORKING ON STAFF

Recently, a student on the verge of graduating asked me what was the single most important lesson I'd learned in writing for television. Her question started me thinking. Of course, I'd acquired writing skills, some insights into what works on screen, and a few experiences negotiating the system. But that's not what she meant. She was looking for career advice gleaned from what I might have done better.

I fast-forwarded through mistakes I'd made, like the time I turned down a staff position on a series because three better opportunities were around the corner. Well, one show wasn't picked up; on a second, the producer decided to write the pilot himself; and for job three, another writer was chosen. I found myself out of work as a writer for more than six months. Fortunately, I've had a "day job" teaching screenwriting at USC throughout my writing career, but it's not unusual for writers to be "between assignments" for months at a time. I'm telling you this at the start of the chapter on staff work where the pay is consistent and you may feel lulled into a sense of security. [Here's my advice: Get yourself some other survival resource, whether that's an alternate writing venue (like journalism or Web content), or a non-writing job, or a partner who helps carry expenses.] But was that the most important lesson I wanted to pass on to the student?

I also thought about scripts I might have written better. When you see your work on screen, sometimes you're grateful — really — to the actors and directors who bring a moment to life. But once in a while you cringe, "I did not write that clunky line... did I?" Or, "Does this seem as slow to you as it does to me? Why didn't I tighten that beat? No, it was the director's fault… or was it my fault?" But all that's really fleeting.

The more I considered what mattered in building a writing career I came to a single lesson: Make friends. No doubt, you've heard the line "it's who you know, not what you know;" or, put another way, "this town is all about relationships." Those glib sayings fit certain agents, managers and producers. But I suggest you think about it somewhat differently as a writer.

Especially on TV series staffs, the act of creating is not private, though you certainly bring your unique talents. Writers tend to want to work with other writers who enable them to do their own best work. That often means choosing collaborators who make them comfortable enough to take creative risks, and who can be trusted to deliver quality dialogue or story twists or humor or tales of life. Much of this rests on what's on the page. But no producer-writer has the time to comb every writing sample. Producers hire who they know.

Now, that doesn't mean you have to party with powerful people or suck up to their families. It means forming networks of professional trust. You do that through good work followed by staying in touch. Students just out of film school often form workshops that meet at each other's apartments, not only for continuing feedback on writing, and commiseration, but also for the connections. One of my writing students formed an alliance with a producing student who wanted to be an agent. On graduating, the junior agent got a job as, well, a junior agent, and brought along the writer as a first client. In time, they rose together.

If you're not in film school, you might make similar connections at seminars, workshops, extension classes, social networks and blogs. Or maybe you'll land a beginning assignment on a small show. The people in the cubicles next to you aren't always going to be in those cubicles. Someone's going to move on to a better series, someone's going to become a producer, someone's going to be asked to recommend a writer, maybe with qualifications just like yours. Join professional groups, and when you're eligible, become active in the Writers Guild. Even if you're shy or a hermit (or so focused on the characters you're creating you don't want to be bothered with actual humans), push yourself out of your shell. That's the one thing I wish I'd done more, and I offer it to you as the career lesson I learned.

If it wasn't for my history with one particular network executive I wouldn't have been able to tell a story that meant a lot to me. A teenage friend of my daughter was visiting one day and mentioned, all too casually, that her mother had been diagnosed with breast cancer. The girl blew it off as if it didn't affect her. I realized she was in deep denial, utterly unprepared to face the reality of the upcoming surgery. Thinking about her, it occurred to me that dramas had been done about breast cancer — and the last thing I wanted to do was a disease-of-the-week movie — but no one had dealt with this serious subject from the daughter's point of view. What interested me was not the illness but the relationship and how such an event would affect a teenager's sense of what it means to be a woman, and what would happen if she lost her mother.

Had I set out to write a script, or even a treatment, or even a pitch, and asked my agent to arrange meetings with potential producers, followed by waiting for their responses, followed by scheduling network meetings, and rescheduling them after they're postponed, followed by who-knows-how-many network pitches, followed by who-knows-how-long-I'd-wait for an answer that might be no... half a year might go by before I could write this, if ever.

Instead, I picked up the phone. I had some credits at CBS — four were on series and a couple of others on original dramas — and a year earlier I'd shared a table with one of the CBS vice presidents. We were at the ceremony for the prestigious Humanitas Prize that gives awards for writing in film and television, and I was a finalist for an original drama that she'd greenlighted. When I didn't win, she leaned over and whispered something like "let's try again," or "let's do something else." I don't think I actually heard her words over the applause for my competitor.

But that was enough of a "relationship" for her to take my phone call. I did a minimal pitch, like "let's do something about breast cancer but from the teenage daughter's point of view." She said "Sure. Who do you want to produce?" I chose a company I'd worked with before because I liked their attitude of respecting the script and I believed I could trust the taste of a particular producer there. Also, I knew they'd be approved because they were a frequent vendor. The network VP said fine. One quick call to the producer's office, and the deal was done. A year later, that project, "Between Mother and Daughter," did win the Humanitas Prize. My point isn't about winning awards, of course. I'm showing you how wheels turn based on relationships — not personal ones, but through mutual respect.

At other times, I've lost out on being considered for staffs of shows because I wasn't part of a social circle — the showrunners simply didn't know me. I understand how frustrated you may feel on the outside looking in. So in the spirit of learning from my mistakes, here's a tale of:

The Staff from Hell

(Cue howling wolves and lightning)

Anyone who has been on staff has a war story. That's because the proximity of staff writing resembles a trench during a battle. You make close buddies, or have to watch your back, or both. When I entered my own staff hell, I already had a number of produced credits and had spent time on staffs before, though they were either outside the mainstream or short-lived because the series were quickly cancelled. So this was my first experience on a staff of a major network show, and I made every mistake in the book — only there wasn't any book at the time. I wish I'd had this book because I might have avoided:

MISTAKE 1: DON'T SEPARATE FROM THE STAFF.

Since the series was new, it was allotted a floor of empty offices on a studio lot. The showrunner walked the whole staff over and let each of us claim the office we wanted. I thought the quality of my writing was what mattered so I grabbed the quietest spot waaaay off in a distant corner. Meanwhile, the savvy guys nabbed offices that hugged the showrunner's. Every time he walked out of his office he saw them, and they'd be at hand for quick rewrites — the staff members he'd come to rely on. And they'd be first to overhear gossip — actors in or out of favor, network pressures, production or story glitches — and nudge their drafts accordingly.

This principle of staying in the mix infuses all the situations below, though it applies mostly to beginning staffers. At higher echelons, producer-writers can't be in the office all the time because they're on the set or away on location shoots. And on many shows "creative consultants" aren't around at all unless they're called. But these lessons are meant for you.

MISTAKE 2: DON'T MIX PERSONAL AND WORK ISSUES.

Every staff becomes a family, dysfunctional or mellow. Now imagine your family members locked in one room together all day, every day, for six months. Got the picture? A degree of intimacy is unavoidable at the writing table when the staff is delving into the feelings and motives of characters, pulling from their own experiences. "When a guy stood me up, this is what I did…" That sort of insight can inform the realness of storytelling — a good thing.

But honesty can rise awfully quickly to "TMI" (too much information). You'll know you slipped over the edge between confessions in group therapy and story beats by the discomfort in the room or the head writer saying "let's move on." Remember, this is collaboration on shared character arcs that involves "catching the voice" of existing characters. One day, if you're the series creator it may also be a more personal expression; now, you're on a team.

Even if you're cool at the writer's table, watch out to maintain "friendly professionalism" at lunch, at the water cooler, everywhere at work. The other writers may be competing with you. On the staff-from-hell, I stopped by the office of my "new friend," whom I'll call Mr. Horns. Like me, he was a lower-level staffer trying to get a toe-hold on the career ladder. Two tiny pink booties from his baby daughter hung from his desk lamp.

I related immediately — I also had a young child. Ruefully, he said he left in the morning before she was awake and came home after she was asleep and was too busy writing on the weekend to spend time with her. "I'll see her in six months when we're on hiatus," he shrugged. I commiserated and confided that juggling my schedule was an issue. He shook his head — his wife didn't work, so she took care of everything at home. "You're not going to be able to do this job," he said flatly, as I noticed the protrusions on the sides of his head. And he was sure to relay my problem to the boss.

MISTAKE 3: DON'T HAVE OTHER PLANS.

Unfortunately, Mr. Horns was partly right. Working on a series staff consumes most of your time and all your energy. It's great for people who have few outside obligations, but balancing a home life is tricky. I did work on one show where the entire staff had kids, and it was so well organized that we almost always arrived at ten and left at five. The supervising producer had the clout to negotiate a deal to arrive at 8:30 AM so she could leave at 4 PM, most days, and be around when her kids came home from school. That's rare, though.

This is not about women's issues or family versus career. When you agree to join a series staff, your life has to change. You can't take much of a lunch break with friends. Chances are you're catching lunch in the studio commissary or at your desk. You may have only an hour between the morning staff meetings and an afternoon screening, or between casting and dailies, or between a quick, urgent script polish and breaking a story for the next episode. If you drive off the lot to lunch, you'll be late for your afternoon meeting. As for your other screenplays, making YouTube videos of your cat, dating, or answering long emails — hey, that's what hiatus is for.

MISTAKE 4: DON'T WORK AT HOME INSTEAD.

Each staff member writes individual episodes in addition to work-shopping everyone else's scripts and rewriting other people's drafts. In a full season, you can usually count on two episodes, but depending on the size of the staff, how much the boss likes your work, and how clever you are at pitching stories, you might write more.

Maybe you're used to working in bedroom slippers at 4 AM, or blasting a CD in your private room, or shutting your door and hovering over the computer in silence for hours, then going to the gym before returning to your computer. Sorry, folks, none of that's likely on staff. Personally, I find it difficult to concentrate in a public office off a noisy corridor with interruptions every half-hour, having to break for screenings and meetings. But some writers tune out the world so well they can write in the office all day. And headphones may help.

On the staff from the netherworld I wanted to prove myself by bringing in a wonderful draft of the first episode assigned to me, and deliver it ahead of schedule, certainly within two weeks. So I asked Mr. Horns if he thought it would be okay to write at home. "Absolutely" he grinned widely. "Do whatever it takes to write what you want to write. Just go. And if it takes three weeks, that's cool too. Don't waste your time coming in." I asked the showrunner for permission, and he shrugged "Sure," though he was busy with something else.

So I went home. For two weeks. Let me tell you, in that two weeks the script slated to run before mine killed off the character I needed to twist my story, a pivotal location was ruled out by the network, two actors in the cast were having an affair, and an intern took over my office because "no one was in it." By the time I brought in my draft, still warm from copying, it was out of touch with the series. And so was I.

Learn from my experience: Stay connected, even if you get virtually nothing written all day and have to work all night at home.

MISTAKE 5: DON'T BE PRECIOUS ABOUT YOUR SCRIPT.

You become attached, of course. Look how wonderful your script is: [The shape of a certain scene builds to a climax then twists unexpectedly and turns the story just in time; a precise detail reveals passion felt but hidden; in a nuance of character, the backstory is deftly sensed; a phrase came so perfectly as if the character was writing instead of you. It's everything a writer would want from a script, or so you believe as you type "Fade Out." So it's difficult to bring your script to the table, no matter how supportive the staff, and no matter how often you've been through the process.]

But the day arrives when your script has been distributed to the staff by email and everyone is carrying laptops into the writers room, assembling for the meeting at which it will be discussed. I said discussed, not deleted. Let's not be paranoid. Somehow, you'll need to distance yourself from it now. Try to think what's good for the show, not what bolsters your ego. It really doesn't matter how hard you worked, or how you arrived at the reasoning under a speech or action, or how much you don't want to lose a certain moment.

If the consensus of the staff — or simply the opinion of the head writer/ showrunner — is that something isn't clear or doesn't tell the story well or is not credible or steps on something in a different episode, or any other criticism, I advise you not to argue. Of course, you may clarify your intention, but then let it go. If you're a good enough writer to be on the staff you're skilled enough to rewrite and come up with a revised draft that's even better than this.

If you don't, someone else will.

MISTAKE 6: DON'T "DIS" THE CULTURE OF THE STAFF.

Skilled professional writers fill the staffs of television shows, but that's a little like saying most human families consist of people — it's a minimum requirement but doesn't tell much about what goes on. Each staff develops a kind of culture, just as families do. This comes from shared interests, experiences, memories, and (in the best cases) shared goals. If you think you and your dog begin to seem alike after awhile, consider a room full of writers melding their minds to tell stories about the same characters.

Often the showrunner sets the tone — formal, laid back, brooding, artistic, intellectual, homespun, sex-tinged, political, romantic, drugged-out, pious… and so forth. Sometimes the culture fits the nature of the series, but not always. In the case of the Staff From Hell, the prevailing ethos had nothing to do with the subject of the series. It was blatant misogyny.

Every staff meeting began the same way: A half-hour of sports talk, football, basketball or baseball, recapping the plays from a game in detail, arguing over which man is better. And there I sat, the only woman in the room, irrelevant because I didn't know about guys doing things with balls.

Even when the sports-talk gave way to writing, the sense of the room remained. And one day, when we were working on an outline for an important episode, and it was time for a break, the entire staff (except me) convened to the men's room, where they stayed for twenty minutes, finishing the outline.

I wracked my mind to figure out how to function with this staff since watching sports and shooting hoops in the parking lot seemed more important than anything I could write. The frustration mounted until one day I erupted "are you finished with the male bonding yet?" Mr. Horns couldn't contain his smile that I'd finally sunk myself, so my future episodes would be his; he'd get the promotion, the raise, the credits and acclaim — or so he calculated. If I'd been wiser and more confident, I wouldn't have tried to join on their terms, but might have discovered other interests in common with at least one of the staff and created an ally. "Dissing" the culture of the show — putting it down — alienated me further and made it more difficult to work.

Think about high school. Everyone is in cliques and you're the new kid who just transferred. How do you begin fitting in? Probably you start with one interest, and someone else interested in it; a first friend. An important lesson.

MISTAKE 7: DON'T WORK ON A SERIES THAT'S WRONG FOR YOU.

The staff from down below was probably a wrong fit, no matter what I'd done. Lots of TV series are out there and even though you (understandably) need to start somewhere, misery is not an essential rung on the ladder. You need references as well as good work to move ahead. A show that you have to omit from your resume can hurt you more than having had no job at all. When you apply for your next staff, the new producer will certainly phone the former one, and may ask the other writers how it was to work with you.

I stayed through my entire contracted season with this show, but in retrospect it would have been better to leave sooner and get on with my writing and career. I'm not advising you to quit when the going gets rough; if the quality of the show is worth it, and you can write well despite bad vibes, stay with it and amass those credits. But if the quality of your writing is suffering, go ahead and bail after speaking with the showrunner, especially if you can negotiate a non-damaging reference from him. With all you've learned, you can go on to another, better staff. You're not alone. Almost every TV writer has had a difficult experience at least once, and everyone omits the rubble of their history from their resume. You'll survive it too.

The Good Staff

Emmy magazine, the publication of the Academy of Television Arts and Sciences, asked several showrunners, "What does it take to make a creative ensemble run smoothly?" J.J. Abrams, Executive Producer of *Alias* answered, "The key is having collaborative, smart writers who keep the room running. Whether it's the official showrunner or someone else saying, 'We have to get past this and keep going.' It's crucial to get to the act breaks and the end quickly, so you can reverse and make it better. You need people who share the same vision and are collaborative and mutually respectful."

Abrams continued, "You want to make sure the show isn't repetitive, but you want to keep doing certain reveals. How do you keep doing that so that the show isn't contrived? A show like *Alias* can be preposterous — how do you keep it real? As a viewer, I'd be furious if I invested in a show that ultimately went nowhere."

For Abrams, the best thing about working on a staff is "being in the trenches with people you admire, respect and who bring to the group ideas that make you smile. That's fantastic. When things are working, you celebrate with them, and you despair with them when things don't work. Whether you're celebrating or commiserating, you're doing it together."

A SLICE OF LIFE

For a well-run staff, let's peek in on John Wells, who headed *ER, The West Wing, Southland*, and many other shows.

Picture a long dark wood conference table dominating a conference room. Ten chairs surround the table for four senior writers, four staff writers, one full-time researcher, and Mr. Wells. At the back of the room, more chairs and a few couches for full-time physicians on the staff, and production personnel as needed. All chairs face a monitor where dailies are screened.

The walls are hung with large whiteboards covered with plot points and story breakdowns for the twelve episodes to be completed for the season. On a sideboard, colored markers list ideas for possible scenes under the headings of Big, Serious, Humorous, and Other.

The staff begins laying out the season the first week in June. Working as a group for six weeks, they come up with the entire season's episodes — ideas for them and specific storylines, and the group "pounds them out." That means the team figures out all the major turning points of the stories, where the act breaks fall, and how many episodes an arc may cover, structuring the episodes.

Then an individual writer is assigned to go off and do a story treatment. (I'll discuss outlines and treatments in Chapter Four.) When that writer returns, he gets notes from the staff. The writer does a revision. Another notes session. Then he's sent off to write the script. When the script comes in, there's a notes session. He does a second draft. If that works, the episode is ready to film. In all, the process for one script takes about eight weeks.

On a visit to *ER* in an early season, *Written By* magazine described the scene on a day a first draft has come in, so this is the first notes session on the finished script. The writers file out of their offices and head for the conference room, each holding a copy of the script. Wells is in position at the head of the table, and the room is full. Coffees are brought, but this staff gets right to business going page by page through every beat of the script.

In this episode, a teenager has cystic fibrosis and his mother is afraid her son will die. The twist is that the son doesn't want to be saved, which puts Dr. Ross in an awkward position between mother, son, and his Hippocratic oath. Someone asks about the kid's girlfriend, another about Ross' choice whether or not to save the kid. A debate breaks out over whether the writer is showing traits of Ross that the audience has already seen. While the staff throws out suggestions, the writer is busy taking notes.

However, I recommend that you use a tape recorder. This experienced writer was able to get what he needed, but you might not. Three problems: First, you're not likely to be quick enough to catch every point, or distinguish what's worth noting among contradictory remarks. Second, under pressure what you type on your laptop will have all the nuance and detail of a Tweet. Third, by keeping your head in your screen, you're absent from the discussion, and constantly behind. Unless the showrunner objects, tape the session so you can pay attention in the room, and deal with exactly what

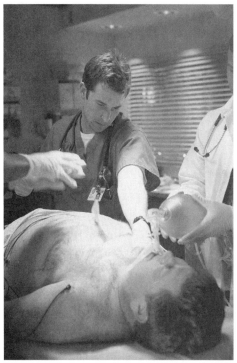

ER

was said later, when you can concentrate. Of course you might also be writing directly on the script if you have a hard copy and suggestions relate to specific lines.

Back at the meeting, Wells says the story is almost there, but it's missing a pivotal action that will define the emotional rhythm for the sequence. That propels a debate about another character's developing depression. Then Wells cues a new discussion about comic relief scenes. And on the meeting goes for four more hours as they move from scene to scene to the end of the script.

This kind of meeting happens again every Monday, Wednesday and Friday afternoon. But don't misunderstand; it's not all about logistics and group-think. Writing on a staff still emanates from each writer's art. As Wells told *Written By*:

> Writers have a responsibility, and it's sort of a particular responsibility that all artists share. You have to find a way to return yourself to that place from which you work, and not allow it to... float off of it into this pop-referential world in which we're only writing about or talking about things that we've seen or know from television and movies.
>
> I think that you, as a writer, you fight that and at whatever point you lose it, you're in big trouble. And your work suffers mightily from it, and then you'll have to find some way, if you're going to write again, to get back to it. And that's beyond all the dealings with success and all of those things which have their own problems which... you certainly don't want to complain about because you don't want it to go away, but... artistically, it has an impact on what you're doing. And that balance is very difficult to strike.
>
> I look at writing as a craft and as a gift. As a craft you have to work on it all of the time, and as a gift you have to protect it. And one of the things you do to protect it is to make certain that your world doesn't become too insular.

And, particularly, that your points of reference don't become too insular, because then you find yourself writing exactly the same things because you have nothing new to say about the subject. That's when shows become uninteresting to people, because they feel that they've already heard what you've had to say, and they're not interested in hearing it again. So there's a constant need to be looking. Not to see your name again on another show or anything like that, but just creatively, to protect that place from which you write.

THE STAFF LADDER

John Wells stands at a pinnacle of success shared by very few creators of hour series including Dick Wolf with his *Law & Order* brand; David E. Kelly, who at one time ran *The Practice, Ally McBeal,* and *Boston Public* at the same time; and Steven Bochco, who has consistently had a series on the air longer than any other producer of drama, from *Hill Street Blues* to *L.A. Law* to *NYPD Blue* to *Raising the Bar,* and many other shows.

Each showrunner was a writer first, and though the top rung involves as much skill in management as writing, the entire television ladder is built on writing titles. This differs from theatrical movies where creative power resides in the director, and financiers can buy their way to a credit or even an empire as film producers.

Beginning at the bottom, here's every step:

1. FREELANCE WRITER

A freelancer is responsible only for writing a script and is not on the staff. As an outside writer, you won't participate in story meetings or screenings or have an office at the show, or share in any of the inner workings of the series. You might not even meet the staff except for the producer who hires you and whoever supervises your episode.

But you do have an opportunity to demonstrate your skill and talent. This teleplay — especially if you receive sole screen credit — can lead to a staff offer on this series or open doors at other shows. If it wins any acclaim, and a buzz begins about you, this one break could leverage a career. (See Chapter Six for more about how to break in.)

Minimum compensation for a primetime network series under the Writers Guild Basic Agreement is more than $30,000 for "Story plus Teleplay." (All figures are approximate because the WGA schedule of minimums is revised periodically.) For comparison, that's around the same as a two-hour theatrical screenplay for a movie whose budget is under $5 million. Since networks license two runs of any episode, and successful series usually rerun, you will soon receive approximately the same initial payment a second time in residuals. Later, you'll amass more residuals if your episode reruns on cable stations or in syndication, and that can continue for many years, though the amount declines to pennies after a while. In addition, you'll receive considerable foreign royalties because virtually all successful American-made television series are sold overseas. On a series that continues to cable or syndication, you'd see well over $60,000 for a single hour you've written as a beginning freelancer.

But not all freelancing is network, and not all contracts guarantee the full ride. Network rates apply to ABC, CBS, NBC, and FBC (Fox); HBO and Showtime also pay at network levels, as do other quality cable channels. But if you write for smaller outlets, prices may dip to around $20,000 for "Story plus Teleplay." On cable, residuals are also calculated differently.

And you might not be allowed to write the episode to its finished draft. Inexperienced writers are usually offered a "step" deal with "cutoffs." That means you are given a chance to write the outline ("story"), and if it doesn't work, or it seems that you would not be capable of a quality teleplay, the deal goes no further — you are cut off. Someone else (often a staff member) takes over the project and writes the script from your outline, or even writes a new outline.

In those cases your credit will be arbitrated by the Writers Guild; you might keep credit for the story if it remains essentially what you wrote; or you might share credit on the story if more than 50% of what you wrote is in the final script; or you might lose credit altogether if the new writer had to start over and changed more than 50%. If someone else wrote the script, of course, you'll have no credit on the teleplay even if the under-lying story was yours.

The next cut-off comes after the first draft. If the head writer/showrunner believes you failed to catch the voices of the characters, or didn't convey the sense of the show, or the writing is just not excellent (for example flat or expository dialogue, unfocused scenes, lack of tension), the script will be given to a staff writer or another freelancer. Just as happened with the "story by" credit, the teleplay credit will be arbitrated and the second writer might be awarded some or all the screen credit, depending on how much he changes.

In a step deal, you are paid separately for each stage. Using network rates, the story alone is above $12,000, the first draft is around $20,000, and the second draft is the balance of whatever has been negotiated. You'll notice this adds to more than the "story plus teleplay" contract, and that's intentional. It's a kind of reward if a writer is asked to go to the next step of the project (if "the option is picked up") though the contract did not guarantee continuing.

As with the "story plus teleplay" model, you'll receive residuals for network reruns and syndication in proportion to what you've actually done (when you're cut off after the story, clearly you don't get the full residual for the episode).

If freelance assignments were abundant as they once were in television, freelancing could be a fulfilling lifestyle for a writer because you could do well on a few assignments a year, exploring various genres that interest you, and have time to write features, novels, or have a personal life. But today, most series are written by the staff.

Before I describe the staff ladder, here's one more note on freelance assignments: Many are rewrites rather than original scripts. For example, an agent sends your sample scripts to a producer who likes your writing and invites you in. You go to the meeting and pitch episode ideas (stories), but the producer might not be listening for something to buy. Instead he's hearing your insights into the show and what you bring to the creative party. If you impress him, he may give you a story he has already developed that needs to be rethought from the outline up, or a teleplay that needs to be rewritten though the story basically works, or even a pretty good teleplay that just needs a "dialogue polish" (that means revising the lines but not touching the structure). Say yes. Think of it as dues.

Back when I was freelancing, that happened at a western series called *Paradise*. I didn't know anything about the Northwest in the 1900s, though I'd watched the show and liked the characters enough to generate ideas. I had an agent and some produced credits by then, so setting up a meeting wasn't difficult, but I knew stories alone wouldn't be enough. I spent days researching the era to ferret tales from their world. Often, I've discovered vignettes and unexpected characters from research, and I've found that those gems of reality breathe life into storytelling. So armed with well-honed pitches and smart on the history, I went in.

But one after another, the pitches fell, sometimes before I completed the log line. Companies don't want to risk hearing a story that's at all similar to anything in the works. Thus I came to the end of everything I'd brought and gathered my notes to leave, when the producer reached behind him and took a script off a shelf. It was a finished draft by a good writer who hadn't been able to render one of the guest cast convincingly. Since they liked my writing and I'd brought fresh textures that fit their show (thanks to my research), the producer thought I'd understand the script's potential, and gave it to me to rewrite. Though I ultimately shared screen credit with the original writer, my next episode for them was my own.

2. STAFF WRITER

A staff writer is sometimes called a "baby writer," someone who's never been on a staff before. Think of it as a year of post-graduate education, with big differences: unlike film school, you are paid instead of paying, the work you do is measured by professional standards, it's seen in the real world, and you get no social promotions — you're up or out by the end of the season. For students from top film schools, being taught by credited industry professionals is not a novelty. But for other recent grads, this might be a first opportunity to be mentored by working writers.

Let your expectations be to learn, grow, form relationships, and write every assignment exactly as needed. If you're given one scene to tighten, don't think you'll grease any wheels by re-structuring the entire script, or rewriting scenes on both sides unless the boss says okay. Depending on the size of the staff, during a season you might be given one script to write, especially if a senior writer is available to "supervise." That means the senior writer will advise you at every stage; but that person is also standing by to write the script if you can't. No one has time to wait while you figure it out. If the staff is small, and you're on top of your craft, you might even write two episodes that are credited to you.

Staff writers receive regular salaries according to Writers Guild minimums. A beginning staff writer on a primetime network show is paid at least $3,000 per week ($12,000 per month). But your contract might be limited to 20 weeks (or less), with an "option" to renew you for the rest of the season. Off network, some beginning salaries fall as low as $1,000 per week. And if you write a script the fees will be credited against your salary, so you won't see additional payments until you go to the next step:

3. STORY EDITOR / EXECUTIVE STORY EDITOR

Once you get past freelancers and staff writers it's tricky to guess what any job title means on a particular show because those ranks may be honorary.

You see, as a writer advances in a series, his agent negotiates a new title every season. "Story Editor" is for people who are beyond staff writer, but how far beyond depends on the size of the staff and the showrunner's style. For example, a story editor may be a virtual beginner, or one of several seasoned writers on a staff where everyone except the executive producer is a story editor, or the puzzling title "executive story editor" may even indicate the head writer.

In any case, Story Editor doesn't mean someone who sits and edits stories all day. Like all the other rungs on the ladder, it indicates a writer who does all the stages of an episode from breaking stories, through outlines, through first drafts, and rewrites. Generally, a story editor would expect to write two original episodes in a season, and might be asked to polish or re-dialogue scenes in other people's scripts.

If you're first trying to break in and your pitch meeting is scheduled with a story editor, though, see if you can change to someone higher. A story editor usually doesn't have the power to hire anyone, and, worse, he wouldn't have much personal incentive to make your pitch sound usable when he relays it to the showrunner. On the other hand, if the story editor is a buddy who recommends you, that might have some weight, if the boss trusts him. In a way, we're back again to whom you know.

Story editors are salaried employees on contract for a defined number of weeks, just like staff writers. They're paid more, though — in the vicinity of $6,000 per week (depending on the length of their contract), and that's boosted by payments for writing. The minimums under "freelancing" apply to anyone above staff writer, so if you're receiving approximately $24,000 per month as a salary, and you are also assigned an outline ("story") for an episode at the same time, you'd earn around $12,000 on top of the salary, for a total of something like $36,000 that month.

Now, before you're carried away with visions of paying off your student loans, I warn you: You'll only see a fraction. Your agent takes 10%, federal, state and local taxes may add to 40% or more, guild dues are around 3%, and you'll have other mandatory reductions (disability, social security, and so forth). If you have an attorney, he'll take 5%, and if you also have a manager (though you don't need both an agent and a manager at this level), that might be another 15%. All of that comes out of the gross (off the top) before you see a dime. In fact, you won't even see the original check. That goes to your agency which takes out their share and mails you an agency check. And remember, shows get cancelled; writers are frequently out of work for months at a time. As they used to say on a cop show, "be careful out there."

4. PRODUCER

If you watch screen credits before or after a show, you'll see lots of names called Producer or Co-Producer, but they don't all do the same job. Some are like line producers on theatrical movies, dealing with equipment, schedules, budgets, crew personnel. Others are writers who have risen to the producer title but have nothing to do with physical production. Their job is to write and rewrite, much like a story editor. And some are hybrids — mainly writers, though they interact with production (especially casting, and in creative sessions with the director and editor) and have a presence on the set.

Typically, producers are invested in forming the season and are responsible for the quality of the episodes, along with the showrunner. So if an episode needs to shoot tomorrow and a script has last-minute problems (no matter who wrote it), a producer may be the one up all night rewriting, though the credit would likely remain with the original writer. Not taking screen credit is one of the courtesies that higher level staff members traditionally give lower staffers and freelancers.

Producers on a set are also expected to rewrite on the spot if a scene isn't working or the director or actors have a problem with a speech or action. Sometimes this involves staying out with the crew past midnight in the freezing rain. Offsetting the long hours is not only the satisfaction of having influence over the shape of the series, but, frankly, good money.

Producers normally are not salaried in the same way as story editors. They may have "points" (a partial ownership expressed as a percent of profits), and producing fees for episodes that air. This results in a bookkeeping oddity in which producers might work all summer without compensation to put a show on the air in the fall, but then pull in hefty sums (above $30,000 or so) each week an episode airs.

At this level, the studio may begin looking at you to create an original series while you continue up to:

5. SUPERVISING PRODUCER

The distance from Story Editor to Producer to Supervising Producer is in increments of responsibility, but all are writers. Some supervising producers actually run the writing staff, or even virtually run the show, while others spend the entire season writing and rewriting episodes like everyone else.

If you're breaking in, you're likely to pitch to someone with this title. Though your deal will need approval from the executive producer, this office usually has the power to give you an assignment and guide your script.

6. CREATIVE CONSULTANT

Now here's a mystifying title. On theatrical features "Creative Consultant" might refer to the person a movie is about, or the original writer who was totally rewritten, a famous writer who polished the final draft, an expert specialist, the financier's nephew, or the director's yoga teacher. On TV series it's a specific job, though the status depends on the situation. Normally, the title goes to a highly regarded writer who comments on drafts of scripts but is not expected to keep regular hours in the office. This person may or may not actually write any episodes or attend meetings.

At one time I was working on a show where the neighboring bungalow housed an action series that seemed to be staffed solely by four executive producers. They were all good writers in their thirties who had been writer-producers on other shows, now promoted to the top title. Writing their series was no problem, but as for managing it, each of the four was lost. Any visitor could quickly figure out what was going on — in the shadows was a semi-retired *éminence grise* with the obscure title "Creative Consultant." His credits were so eminent indeed that he didn't want to be known for this little action show, and anyway all the executive producer titles were taken. I think he educated the "executive producers" as quickly as he could and got out of there, but when I knew that staff, the "Creative Consultant" was actually the showrunner.

7. EXECUTIVE PRODUCER / SHOWRUNNER

Executive Producers come in all sizes, and it's not unusual for title promotions to create a glut at the top of a series that's been around for years. Most of those executive producers are (as you've guessed by now) simply writers. But two other categories share this title, and you want to know who's who when you go to a show, especially if you're making a first contact.

Some shows have two tracks at the very top — one is the executive producer in charge of physical production: technology, crew, schedules, location planning, construction, equipment, and so forth. The other executive producer is the head writer, in charge of content, which means all artistic aspects of creating and executing the scripts, including directing, editing and casting. These two people work as a team, a useful division of labor on some shows. Occasionally you'll also see an Executive Producer credit for a star with the clout to be called The Ultra-Grand Exalted Poobah, but don't expect that person in the writers' room.

Among all the executive producers, only one is the showrunner. Often, that's the person who created the series from its original conception, and may have written the pilot, though that's not always the case. For example, on *ER*, the pilot was written by Michael Crichton, who continued to receive screen credit as an Executive Producer, though he didn't work at the show. A bevy of other Executive Producer names also appeared in the credits. But only one — John Wells — made the key decisions and ran every aspect of the show.

If I could bless your early career I'd say: Be part of a staff where the showrunner is a great writer, because you'll want to honor that experience in your craft anywhere you work ever after.

Summary Points

- Episodes of television series are created by writing staffs that collaborate under showrunners. Staffs may range from a few writer-producers to many writers, divided into levels.

- If you join a staff, you will write your own episodes as well as participate in breaking stories and contributing to the work of other writers.

- Freelance assignments are often audition scripts for writers who are not on staff.

- Staff writer is the entry level on a show, and is an opportunity to learn from more experienced staff members.

- Story editors are a step up the ladder. They rewrite scripts and write their own episodes.

- Producers and supervising producers are senior writers who may also run the writers' room.

- The Executive Producer title may refer to the creator of the show or the showrunner, or might just be one of many senior writers on staff. The showrunner is a writer at the top of the ladder, and is in charge of all aspects of the series.

- The traditional ladder has become flexible in certain venues that seek young talent or different perspectives.

Spotlight on "Unscripted/Reality" Shows

"I can't get no respect," comedian Rodney Dangerfield used to complain. He was always answered with a sympathetic laugh because people believed he did deserve respect. Now the same line could be said about writers who work for so-called "Reality TV" shows — they can't get no respect. But here's the difference: some people don't believe the writers deserve it. In fact, the staffers who create the stories, outline each beat, mold the characters, plan the relationships and interactions, and arrange the action to make viewers laugh, cry, feel suspense or get mad, and write every word the hosts say — those staffers don't even deserve to be called writers, according to the Reality business. Instead, they are called segment producers, story editors, executives, or assistants — anything except "writers."

You see, if they were, they'd deserve the respect of being credited and paid as writers. And that would be a disaster... for companies like Freemantle Media, one of the world's largest conglomerates, which produces *American Idol*. Back in 2007 that one show made a profit of $200 million. Freemantle was sued for $250,000 in overtime wages. If the company paid the back wages to its writers, and even contributed to their healthcare, and also paid Simon Cowell his $50 million salary, their profit would be merely $199.5 million. That's one hundred ninety-nine million, five hundred thousand dollars free and clear after all production costs. Obviously that's not enough, so they can't give their writers respect as writers.

Really, the problems of working in Reality TV go beyond the semantics of what makes someone a writer. In the United States and many other countries, workers in any occupation depend on certain humane conditions including adequate time to eat and sleep, and at least a small minimum wage. A study by Goodwin Simon Victoria Research, an independent company commissioned by the Writers Guild, found that Reality writers were routinely required to work more than 60 hours a week and told by their supervisor to turn in a timecard that says only "worked." They did this work without breaks for food, sometimes without rest breaks, and with no overtime pay, netting incomes below the legal minimum hourly rate. So why would a college graduate with a film degree be willing to work under conditions worse than transient farm hands?

You know why. In fact, someone is probably reading this chapter to find out how to sign up. If you're fresh out of film school with a camera and some editing skills, supported by your parents, no credits, no hope for credits, don't think you need much sleep, survive on snack bars, and have no idea how else to break into the entertainment business, well, there's a shark — I mean Reality producer — in Hollywood willing to eat — I mean meet — you.

Let's get real about this. Most of what is on television (broadcast and basic cable) is not the kind of quality primetime drama featured in this book. Screen fiction that is written to be meaningful, insightful, revealing, intelligent, original, authentic, or that deals with life and relationships and the social fabric in any depth, together with shows that generate a good laugh or delight in creative storytelling — all of it together is maybe 25% of broadcast fare (though it's most of premium cable). The rest can be grouped under the category of "Unscripted" television, especially when you include everything from talk shows and shopping to games, how-to-do-its, contests and "docu-soaps."

This isn't new. Back in the 1940s, radio had *Candid Microphone*, which evolved in the mid-20th century to TV's *Candid Camera*. That was a template for plenty of shows with "real people" that followed. In each case, a celebrity host had scripted questions and looked for characters that were not professional actors, but were found by the casting personnel because certain kinds of responses were anticipated. Later their segments were shaped (edited) to deliver some kind of comedic or dramatic entertainment. Shows like *The Real World* and *People's Court* continued the tradition, changing only the venue and the kinds of conflicts each show would develop. Consider: The Jerry Springer smackdown has prevailed for more than twenty years, and *Dancing with the Stars* is network TV's top hit.

In his book, *Reality TV: An Insider's Guide to TV's Hottest Market* (Michael Wiese Productions, 2011), author and Reality Television producer Troy DeVolld argues, "Whether as the subject of ridicule or inspiration for more realistic dramas and comedies, Reality is now inextricably entwined with traditionally scripted made-for-TV programming and films."

DeVolld relates a story John Wells (*ER, The West Wing, Southland*) shared with him: Wells said "As a younger man, he was fascinated by the gritty realism of Bochco's police dramas until the boom in Reality TV. Suddenly, thanks to *COPS*, he would watch real police officers at work instead of fictional ones; and while his favorite police shows remained brilliantly executed classics, the shine of gritty authenticity they once wore was gone for him. With the dawn of contemporary Reality Television, John realized that scripted programming would have to work harder to emulate 'Reality' if viewers were to be expected to invest in it emotionally.

"That realization served him well just a short while later when he was asked to adapt a screenplay by Michael Crichton into a television pilot for Steven Spielberg. The long-running result, *ER*, a scripted, ultra-realistic medical drama set in a Chicago hospital's emergency room, soon became an ideal case study in how modern Reality Television's influence has permeated the sphere of traditionally scripted TV."

Now, we need a reality check. John Wells, who was President of the Writers Guild of America West two times, does not endorse the mistreatment of writers on Reality TV shows (or anywhere else). Many creators of TV drama series (who are writers, themselves) use fact-based research as a springboard or inspiration for their fictional stories. David Simon relied on his background as a newspaper journalist for the kinds of characters, situations, and social issues he dramatized so brilliantly. But in *The Wire, Treme*, and other shows, Simon *dramatized* them using professional actors and filmmaking techniques, and everyone was appropriately credited. There's a difference between having a healthy regard for underlying truths (reality) used as a basis for well-crafted stories, and, on the other hand, creating a pretend-reality while giving no credit to the people who write the pretense, and then trying to fool an audience that it is "real" and therefore unwritten.

Still, in real reality, people need to make a living, and some professional writers work both sides of television. Also, to be fair, some Reality shows do deal legitimately with writers by hiring professionals and observing union conditions. David Rupel, who wrote and produced on both fiction (*Homicide: Life on the Street*) and 'non-fiction' (*Big Brother, Temptation Island*), told *Written By* magazine, "Just like scripted television, writing and producing go hand in hand. The majority of my Reality credits are for producing, not writing, but I'm always using my skills as a storyteller. For example, when Monica and Chandler slept together on *Friends*, it was referred to as a 'plot twist.' When the tribes didn't merge as expected on *Survivor*, it's simply known as a 'twist.' The subtle language difference implies that somehow the twists in Reality magically happen on their own. Nothing could be further from the truth. There is every bit as much thought, debate and imagination behind every twist you see on Reality — both big and small."

Networks, producers, and show creators are reaching for new branding that might work for their Reality franchises. Terms like "hybrid-sitcoms" and "docu-soaps" were used to pitch shows like *The Simple Life* and *Growing Up Gotti*. "Soft-scripted" is a term the networks use for shows like *The Hills* and *The Real Housewives of (Wherever)*. These label gyrations attempt to separate Reality programming from regular scripted shows. But the further the story development gets from actual reality, and the closer to tropes used in fictional drama and comedy, the less clear is the divide. Take a show like Larry David's *Curb Your Enthusiasm*. It's highly structured, but allows for some improvisation within scenes, as do the works of indie filmmakers like David Lynch. So exactly what is the "real" part here?

That's easy. Money is what's real. In "Making Your Own Reality," an article published in *Written By* magazine, Robert J. Elisberg wrote, "Obviously, the corporations want to call game shows, comedy-variety programs and documentaries Reality TV because they can get around offering writers basic healthcare, giving lunch, paying overtime wages and paying taxes. Because this way they can get around the law... Society didn't accept such conditions 100 years ago. There's no reason to accept it today. We know better. So will the public and the city, county, state, and federal governments. That is what the issue of Reality TV is about."

Keeping all this in mind, I went to interview Scott A. Stone, a successful producer of many "Unscripted" television shows. From my first glance into his offices on a studio lot in central Hollywood, I knew I was in an alternate universe. Posters on the lobby wall were for *Curl Girls, Gimme Sugar*, and *Curl Girls Miami*. I'd read that Stone was partnering with Levi Johnston (former fiancé of Bristol Palin) to pitch a reality show to the networks titled *Loving Levi: The Road to the Mayor's Office*. According to *The Hollywood Reporter*, Johnston said "the mayoral run wasn't originally his idea but was pitched to him" by Stone. So this was a different model for a television series.

With this context, I present our next Guest Speaker, Scott A. Stone.

GUEST SPEAKER: SCOTT A. STONE

President of Stone & Co., with more than 25 years producing successful "Unscripted" TV series including *The Mole, The Man Show, Top Design*, and *The Joe Schmo Show*, Scott A. Stone revealed how so-called "Reality" shows are made, and the role of writers.

I asked, what's the pull of shows like these? Why do people watch them?

Scott A. Stone: The same reason they watch comedies and dramas. They want to see people going through the belly of the beast and coming out the other side.

Pamela Douglas: So it's the human drama.

SS: It's like all television, including game shows. You start at the beginning with nothing, you do all this hard work to get to the other side, and some people go home with nothing and others reign supreme. It's dramatic structure. It's exactly the same.

PD: Can you walk me through the process of creating a "Reality" show, keeping in mind that the people who are reading this book are looking for ways to get into the business as writers or grow their careers as writers.

SS: Reality covers many sub-genres, from classics like *New York House-wives* and shows like *Survivor* and *American Idol*, which are basically game shows, to shows like *Ice Road Truckers* that are more like documentaries, to daytime talk shows. So Reality crosses all genres.

They all come from the same place which is an idea. Somebody has an idea. It's written on a piece of paper. And I have to tell you that in my four years in film school I did very little writing and now I write almost everything. I would say 60% of my time is writing or rewriting treatments. Across the board the whole idea of television is somebody's vision — what's the big idea. So from a writing standpoint it literally can start with somebody sitting around a table at lunch saying I have an idea for a show.

I'll give you an example. My assistant said he loved *Gossip Girl*. He went to a high school in New York and *Gossip Girl* is nothing like the high school he went to. He wants to do the real *Gossip Girl*. So he sat down and wrote up an idea. Over the break he sent out a notice on the Internet through Facebook and Twitter and places like that, saying 'Hey kids, do you want to appear in a Reality *Gossip Girl*?' They all came down with their parents, and signed releases, and he videotaped them. He got some interesting characters and went on his laptop and cut some things together and put it on DVD and said I think there's a show with these kids.

There's not real writing involved in that even though he did have to write something to go on the Internet. But once he had it on a disc I said 'Now what's the show? I see these are interesting characters, but how do they relate to each other? What are their stories going to be?' The first thing the network's going to say to us is 'What drags me through all six episodes?' It's not only the story arc for the six episodes but where are these kids beginning and ending? The logical one for school kids is they start at the beginning of the school year and end at the senior prom. That's an easy story arc for us to create.

But now tell me how each character is going to be intertwined. Tell me what each episode is about because each episode has to have its own story arc. We need the episode where one of the girls breaks up with her boyfriend and she has a fight with him and wants to reconcile at the end. We have the episode when one of the girls wants to have a party and her mom doesn't want her to have a party so she sneaks around her back and has the party anyway. We have another one where one of the kids is gay but isn't out of the closet and has to tell his best friend.

Through all of those we're projecting on the characters what we think are the stories based on the interviews. But then in order to be able to sell that show — which is ultimately every writer and producer's job — we need someone else to give you the money to make your vision happen. Whether you're a writer or producer you're always convincing somebody to give you the money to make it happen. So I would have to go in to the network and lay this story out.

The only way you can do that is to write it on a piece of paper and say okay, here's the story. There are these six kids. Here are their characters. Here's how they interrelate. Here's the prototype for each one, and everyone in television has to be a big arc character, bigger than life, whether it's a comedy or a drama, because if they're not bigger than life, who cares. We write their stories, and then we tell the story in a meeting. After pitching it we show them a bit of DVD of the characters. They might ask 'If you wanted to take the six episodes and make it eight, how would you expand them?' If there was a second season, what would that look like? So you have to not only visualize all this but write it down.

The next thing the network says is 'Fine, here's a small amount of money, say $25,000. Now I want you to go out and shoot a demo reel with them interacting. Show me what the show is going to look like. It can be eight to ten minutes worth of video.' We call it a Pilot Presentation, but it's really a casting reel.

On top of that they have all these delivery requirements. Here is a list for a show about a team of people who go in and fix houses that are disasters.

• A concept synopsis.
Well, somebody's got to write that.

• A series treatment.
That's a full-on treatment of every episode.

• A detailed rundown of the first episode.
It's broken down act by act with six act breaks, so you have to understand act structure. It has to have a beginning, middle, and end with a cliffhanger. And keep in mind you're writing for a Reality show so you don't know exactly what these characters are going to do. You're projecting what they're going to do. You're writing your vision for what you think could be the show.

• Outlines for three additional episodes.

• A written description of the opening tease.

• What the show title and graphics will look like.

• Potential content ideas for the Internet.

• Full casting for the co-hosts as well as homeowners.

PD: How can they pay $25,000 for that amount of work?

SS: I have to use members of my company who are doing other shows to do this for free, basically. Or I use a kid just out of college or a producer just starting. If they shoot everything themselves, and they have the ability to write, the producer could do all this by themselves without hiring anyone. But you see this is a ton of writing.

PD: Who is doing all this writing?

SS: In this case it was an exec producer who works for me in New York. Most of the money went to her and the casting director. She writes it all and sends it to me and I rewrite it as needed.

PD: Her title is "Producer," not "Writer." In Reality is there a title called "Writer"?

SS: Not usually. We perpetuate this myth that Reality is not written.

PD: That's something I want to talk to you about.

SS: Part of it is because people who watch Reality want to believe it's real. And in a way it is because what we do is based on real emotion. We take people and put them into artificial situations and watch their real reactions, laughing or crying or angry or drunk or whatever. So they aren't technically "written," though the scenarios are written.

Everything that happens in the show is pre-produced. Take for example *The Mole*, which is a show we produce. We know the locations we're using, we know what the Mole will be doing, and we know what games he'll be playing. It's all written in a bible that's about four inches thick with all the details in it which the network approves before we go to shoot. But as soon as you put real people in there we're observing documentary-style.

Everyone involved knows there's a lot of writing to do. Most of it is written by an executive producer or supervising producer. Sometimes segment producers do some of their own writing. And there's a whole other key position that we call story editor. The story editor observes what is going on in the field and logs as much of it as they can. Sometimes you have a story editor with each camera crew. Sometimes you have one to cover the whole show. Then they go back into the editing room and screen everything they've shot. Sometimes we have a transcript of everything's that been said. So we shoot 100 hours for each one hour show. We go through the transcription and start to piece the story together from that.

The story editor puts together all that material, and for my shows they write out an entire script. The editor uses that to assemble the show.

PD: Does it look like a screenplay?

SS: That depends on the story editor. Some do and some look like time code numbers on a page. It's not exactly like screenplay with the dialogue in the center because it has a different form. But you can tell that if you're doing a one hour show the script should be around 45 pages or so.

PD: So they're writing everything except the dialogue.

SS: They are editing more than writing at this stage.

PD: Isn't that true of all films — that editing is the final phase of writing?

SS: Correct. There's also a lot of writing in the preproduction phase. For example, look at *American Idol*. Somebody has to write what Ryan Seacrest and the other hosts say. So there is a writer who is writing all those words, whether or not we call them a writer. In a show like *Survivor*, you have to multitask as a writer: you have to be able to write the details of how a game is played, then you have to write the recap at the end, "Go back to your tribes."

PD: Do you ever take a character aside and say in this scene you'll be happy or sad?

SS: Not in a show where there's a game element. That would be unscrupulous business practice because it might affect the outcome of the game. However, once contestants get used to being on camera, often they behave oddly. They realize the more odd their behavior is the more screen time they get.

PD: But in docu-soaps and docu-drama, you'd be more involved there?

SS: They know what we're out to get. We don't tell them we want you to be angry. But clearly if we're putting them in a situation where they're angry with somebody and we set up a party and that person shows up, they know what the expectation is.

We're producing it as we go along, developing the story three or four days ahead. We know we want to get these characters together because they have a discussion to have. 'He cheated on me with another girl,' so now I have to have the girl he cheated with in the scene to finish that discussion.

I need that for my editing. So I will arrange to have them meet for coffee and they go into coffee knowing we want them to have that discussion. We've told them "You arrive on 42nd Street," and "You arrive on 43rd Street," and we have cameras with each of them and say "Go" and we instruct them not to speak to each other until they reach the coffee shop.

PD: It's a kind of improv the way some indie features are made.

SS: The trick with Unscripted shows — and I prefer the term "Unscripted" to "Reality" — is casting.

PD: But they're not trained actors.

SS: But they become actors after about two or three days. There's a second season phenomenon. After they've seen themselves on TV they know what will get them more screen time.

PD: You know about the Writers Guild objections, that people who are doing writing jobs on so-called "Unscripted" shows are treated poorly. They don't get health or pension from the union because producers deny they have writers working for them, so they aren't covered by any of the normal protections of the Writers Guild.

SS: In our company we pay overtime and people have humane hours. In the beginning of the non-scripted business there was an abuse of the number of hours people worked. We were finding our way and realizing we have to shoot so many hours a day so everyone was working around the clock. It will never be nine to five, but in our company everyone gets paid proper overtime.

PD: But the production companies are mostly not Writers Guild signatories.

SS: I have done Writers Guild signatory shows before when I have Writers Guild writers working on the show. The difficulty with all shows is how to squeeze it all in the budget. And it's a question of whether the people doing the jobs want that as well, because it's not cheap to be part of the Guild. They have to join the Guild to get the benefits (such as health insurance) so it's a "Catch-22" for the younger ones.

PD: Speaking of the younger ones, of all the paths that sound like a way in for a beginner, Unscripted television sounds like an entry point. If students are interested, what should they do?

SS: Unlike with a screenplay or an original drama series, they should not feel a real proprietary interest in their ideas at the beginning. Don't feel that you have to protect your idea because somebody's going to steal it from you because whatever you're thinking is out there already.

So, yes, it is an entry into this business. And if you're really good at getting your ideas onto a piece of paper, the chances are you'd be good working on a non-scripted show because you're looking at where the story is coming together. The best thing to do, in my opinion, is write your ideas down. If anyone sat and watched MTV for a few days you could easily come up with ideas for four non-scripted shows. The trick is to get it on a piece of paper, and be a student of television enough to know what's been on and what is on. Chances are whatever you pitch, they'll say it's been done before, but understand the business and go pitch it. Literally you could get into any non-scripted company and say I have an idea. I bought a show from a student a few years ago who came in and pitched to me.

PD: What does "I bought the show" mean in this case?

SS: When I say I bought the show, I mean I actually sold the show (to a network). I made a deal with this kid for a six-month free option. And when I sold it to Spike TV, I paid him a royalty.

PD: You employ story editors and segment producers who have come from film schools where they learned the basic craft of storytelling. What do they show you? How do they get hired?

SS: The best thing is to write up an idea and shoot it. I won't read a feature script — I don't have time. But if I can click on something that's up on YouTube or somebody sends me a short DVD that takes 2 or 3 minutes, I'll look at that.

This is a producer's medium. That's why if you're a writer in non-scripted you're relegated to a lesser role because you're a cog in the wheel of putting together a story, whereas scripted series are a writer-driven medium.

Still, I spend 70% of my time every day writing. It's a cliché to say I wish I had learned to write better in school, but given what I do every day, it's a great tool to have.

CHAPTER 6

How To Break In

I want to tell you a fairy tale that really happened, or so I've been told.

Once upon a time — actually the mid 1980s — a young woman fell in love, not with a man but a television series whose main character seemed just like her. Each week at 9 PM on the day of her show, she would sit on her couch facing the screen, wouldn't answer her phone or flip a channel. Often, she found herself thinking about the motives and dilemmas of the characters and talking to her friends about stories that might happen. She noticed the speech patterns of each character, how conflicts were set up and resolved, and how the plots were interwoven. And then she made the leap: I could write this.

Gamely, she sat at her electric typewriter, knocked out a 60-page "spec" and mailed it to the show. A "spec" is a speculated script — no one asked you to write it, no one's going to pay, but it would be her ticket to ride. Except that the script was returned unread with a form letter that they don't accept unsolicited manuscripts. But she was in love, so she tried again.

Script two — somewhat better than the first simply because it wasn't her first — went off to the show. And back it came. Now, this woman had no film school degree, no relatives in the business, no screen credits, no agent. And where she lived no one else had a clue how to break in either. But she was in love.

So here came script three. By now she'd read books on screenwriting and researched the series to find hints where the stories were heading. She aimed this third script at what she thought was a gap in the series, and she included a short cover letter that showed she had something unique. So she sold this one, right?

No. But this time the envelope held something amazing: a note if she was ever in Los Angeles, come visit the office. You know how fast she bought that air ticket.

Luck, fate, or curiosity, who knows, she managed to get an appointment. And what did she have in her hands? Ah, you thought it was script four. Nope, she got smart. She brought pitches, short summaries of ten stories that were perfect for the series — twice as many as writers normally bring to pitch meetings. And she told those stories with wit and insight in five minutes each. So she sold one!

Just kidding. She sold nothing but left with an armful of sample scripts, a log of what they had in development, and suggestions for areas of interest. The producer said he'd be willing to hear her pitch again.

Next time, she finally heard the winning sentence, "have your representatives call business affairs." Does that mean she sold a script or was invited onto the staff? No way. But she'd nabbed an assignment to write an outline, which you know from the previous chapter is the first paid writing step. The producer's assistant showed her their "beat sheet" style, and she managed a workable story that — hooray! — was sent to first draft... to be written by someone else. She was too inexperienced to write, though she would receive "story by" credit. With that, she relocated to Los Angeles to watch closely as the episode developed.

And then she pitched another episode. It was good. They let her write the first draft. It wasn't so good. But she learned as the script was revised, moving through the writing staff, production, and postproduction. She pitched, outlined and wrote another episode — better. She made allies among the writing team. And finally, when the series was renewed for the next year, she was invited onto the staff.

And she rose through all the writing ranks, staff writer, story editor, producer, supervising producer. And three years later, in the last season of the series, she became the executive producer, running the show she loved. The End.

Within that fairy tale lie tips for breaking in, which I'll detail below. In fact, every writer who has broken into drama series can tell you a war story, and you can take cues from each. Here's mine:

Writing for screen never occurred to me, growing up in New York City, but I'd always written — poetry, stories, plays, journalism — and by the time I graduated from college at 20 I'd won some prizes and published in small magazines. Mostly my adolescent journalism idealized about the potentials of television if characters could reflect the diversity of our population, the true experiences of women, and the realities of urban life. (That was before HBO and the other cable channels, not to mention the better network shows, broke the old network mold and won awards for doing just that.) Based on my articles, I was hired as program director for an experimental public TV station in Los Angeles. So I arrived, with one suitcase and a winter coat that would be useless, 3,000 miles away from anyone I knew. A few months later, the station went broke.

But I'd met people and someone tipped me that MCA-Universal was searching for a young woman in feature film development because they'd never had a woman executive. In my three years at MCA, I saw predictable names always attached to movies while scripts by less-known writers (even ones with agents) never made it to the executive floors, and even when a movie was greenlighted, years passed from script to exhibition, during which time the original writer was replaced (and his replacement was replaced). But a few floors down in the television department and the units which made series, scripts were on the air in months, the writer's credit intact.

So I set out for a TV career. By this time I'd written three spec features, having learned the craft from the pros. My first job was an uncredited dialogue polish on a TV movie, a typical beginner's job. That happens when an established writer has completed all contracted drafts, and a new writer revises lines though her name would not appear on screen. In this case the young characters didn't sound real, so I spent two weeks rewriting for a flat fee.

That job got me my first agent because the producer needed to negotiate with someone, so he made a few referrals. Hey, if a producer wants to hire you that's a sure shot to an agent. I went with one who was beginning, like me, and grew with the agency for years.

Now I was ready to try the episodes. But how? I found a fresh angle: Watching episodes of *Trapper John, M.D.*, I felt one of the main cast was being ignored. I knew Madge Sinclair was a wonderful actress, having once seen her on stage, and I took a chance the series might be obligated to her after years on the air. So I asked my agent to arrange a pitch. As a kid with no experience, I didn't have a clue about "A-B-C" stories or the four-act structure, so I had to be taught by the producer. But the episode was made. Madge brought my lines to life. And later that year she won an Emmy for her performance in the first episode I ever wrote.

I didn't stay with this series. I freelanced at several others, and it was a while before I was on a staff, but that first break was a kick.

It all comes down to these rules:

THE RULES

WRITE WHAT YOU LOVE.
This is not self-indulgence; it's the way to write well. What separates you from everyone else trying to break in? For our fairy-tale heroine, passionate identification with the main character in the series, understanding the struggles and feelings that protagonist would face, gave her stories the force of reality. You might find your break-in angle from experience in a field like medicine, law, or police work, absorption in a genre like sci-fi, or even in your family background. Your passion will lead you to authentic stories.

So when you choose a show to spec, pick one you watch often. Sounds obvious, but I've encountered would-be writers who think they're playing the system by speculating shows they would never watch, thinking they're easy to break into. Doesn't happen that way. First, all shows want to hire the most gifted writers they can attract, not reluctant pragmatists. Second, never write down — it hurts you as an artist and damages your reputation. Third, it's not going to succeed. It's obvious if you don't really have a feel for the show. And finally, what you are creating in a spec is a showpiece, not an actual episode, and this brings me to the next point:

DON'T SPEC THE SERIES YOU PLAN TO PITCH.
Okay, that's opposite the lesson in the fairy tale. A few series will read specs for their own show, but most won't, and you don't want them to. Think about it — the producers know their show's minefields. Outsiders wouldn't know the producer is going to scream if he hears one more pitch about the dog, or another swimming pool corpse, or a romance between two actors who (you couldn't know) had a fight yesterday. But producers on a different show will be able to see your script for the great writing it is without the encumbrances.

So go ahead and speculate for a series you know well — then develop pitches for a different show within the same genre, or of a comparable quality. For example, at one time the producers of *ER* would read a script from *NYPD Blue* to judge a writer's ability. In 2010, producers of shows ranging from procedurals to sci-fi to family dramas were all reading specs of *Breaking Bad*, though it has nothing to do with the subjects of their shows — they were reading for ability with characters.

And ability is what you're demonstrating — talent plus skill. So choose to study and write for the highest quality series that interests you. Look for one that's been on long enough to be recognized and maybe won some writing awards. (You can find a list of award-winning series through the Writers Guild of America and the Academy of Television Arts and Sciences, both listed among resources at the end of the book.) You'll sharpen your screenwriting; and the show's multifaceted characters may pump up your dialogue.

Quality of writing is the immutable rule. And that brings me back to our fairy tale, and the next principle:

ASK THE RIGHT QUESTIONS ABOUT A SERIES.

Notice what the woman considered when she first tried the show: the motives and dilemmas of the characters, stories that might happen to them, speech patterns of each character, how conflicts were set up and resolved and how the plots were interwoven. All these can be discovered in the episodes. Once you delve into the underlying motives by asking why the characters behave as they do, you'll uncover the roots of future stories and also subtext that will color the way you write these characters. It is this more subtle layer of characterization that producers want to see in a writing sample because it suggests a source for further writing, as opposed to flat characters or "types" pushed around to serve a plot.

What stories might happen to the characters? Don't answer by using plot-lines already set in the show. Those story arcs will be complete before your script is done, and big changes that turn the series are made by executive decision, not by freelancers. Instead, ask what urges or issues come from the characters at a point of stasis — that is, when they behave normally, rather than guessing how the narrative will evolve over the year.

Or come up with an angle of your own for the main cast. For example, if you speculate a *Dexter*, in which the character often goes out on his boat, and in your real life you work as a marine biologist, what do you know about creatures in his waterways that might add intrigue to his story? When *Friday Night Lights* was still running, the most interesting spec scripts I saw were from writers who'd lived in Texas and had experienced the lore of rattlesnakes and dust storms. You could smell the authenticity in the pages.

Ideally, every character's dialogue is specific and expresses background, education, attitude, intelligence, and personality. Listen well, and ask yourself how Vampire Bill's choices of words and his phrasing differs from Vampire Eric's on *True Blood*, or how Peggy's differs from Pete's on *Mad Men*. A critical hurdle for an outside writer is to catch the "voices." You may begin with the actors, but don't let that fool you. The differences are on the page.

Conflicts and plot structures are somewhat determined by the hour format and, in network television, by act breaks, as you saw in Chapter Three, but don't let that hang you up. Do what it takes to keep readers turning pages. Production companies and agents will read only a few pages and if they're not hooked, the script gets tossed. The tension has to stay high and the reader needs to be surprised often — not by a gimmick but by a turn in the story that is true to these people. Be unpredictable within the world of the show. For example, in a story about breast cancer, give the disease to a guy because men can get it too. Be fresh, creative, unexpected.

You see, it's all about good writing, the same qualities you'd apply to writing a feature or other dramas. That's not to say you shouldn't ask about the shows you're speculating or pitching. Do your research. Unlike our woman of the 1980s, you have the Internet. Virtually all series have websites, as do all networks, and many have fan sites too. The official site will assure you basics like spelling the characters' names and a history of the series. Some include statements by the producers with hints to their taste or sources of inspiration. Watch out for the fan sites because they might not be accurate, but the best include summaries, and some list every episode that's been aired, which will save you from writing or pitching what's been done.

The right questions are always about stories and characters, not special effects, costumes, budgets, casting, gossip, or marketing gimmicks, so stay focused.

HAVE THE RIGHT TOOLS.

Our lady of the 1980s toiled on an electric typewriter; no one does that any more. For your computer you must have — *must* have — a professional screenwriting program. The Writers Computer Store (in the resource list) will advise you of your options; if in doubt, "Final Draft" is popular. "Celtx" is a free program available online. Each series adopts specific software which their writers must use, but for speculating, any program that creates a standard screenplay form is fine. As you can see in the sample in Chapter Three, the hour drama looks the same as a feature screenplay (though sitcoms are formatted differently). To be considered at all, your scripts must appear perfect and professional.

HAVE REPRESENTATION.

Easier said than done. Our heroine was out in the cold, sending scripts that were returned unread until her extreme tenacity caught a producer's attention. You could try that, but it took her years in easier times, and she got lucky. So let's talk about agents — why you need them, how to get one, and what to do if you can't.

TV series give the illusion of being so accessible, even friendly, that fans sometimes imagine they can join in. From the outside, series writing seems easier than it is, and television appears less formidable than features, so shows would be inundated with amateur scripts if they didn't have filters. Also, production companies won't risk a lawsuit from a stranger who might claim a show stole his story. That's why companies rarely read scripts that arrive "over the transom" (unsolicited and unrepresented).

You need an agent because that's who gets you read, knows where the jobs are, and puts you in the room. Without, it's difficult to know which show is looking for new writers (or at least, willing to consider one). The agency also negotiates your deal, generates your contract, and collects your pay, deducting their 10%.

While feature film companies may buy an original screenplay, television runs on assignments. The agent may know of an opportunity on a staff, or that an open episode is looking for a writer with a particular background, viewpoint or style. The agent sends over samples from several clients who meet the criteria. After reading the samples, the producer may invite you in for a meeting. Or, if you have an idea for an episode, the agent messengers over your writing samples, and if the producer likes your work enough, he might invite you in to pitch.

But a lot of good those systems do you if you don't have an agent anyway. Here's what you need in your writing portfolio before you begin your agent search:

- At least one polished full-length original screenplay that showcases your distinct voice.
- At least one hour-long TV drama script for a current series in a genre similar to your target.
- At least one more TV drama in a different "franchise" that demonstrates another tone.
- A pilot for an original series that demonstrates your unique viewpoint (or experience) and your skill to deliver a television hour with "legs."
- Original stories ready to pitch to series.

Now you're ready to begin. A long list of agents is available from the Hollywood Directory (see resources) and the Writers Guild. The guild asterisks the ones willing to consider new writers but don't take those asterisks too seriously. Some "open" agencies turn out to be filled; others who didn't offer may nevertheless be interested in a client with something they want.

How do you make your way through all those names? Try to identify those who represent the kind of writing you do. Some agencies aim mainly at Hollywood features or sitcoms, so check if their client list includes writers with credits in television drama. You'll also have to choose between the "packaging" and "boutique" agencies. Big packaging agencies supply all the talent — actors, directors, producers, as well as writers. That can be a powerful asset if you're included in a package led by experienced show-runners. On the other hand a boutique will give you the personal attention a new writer needs.

Begin on the phone. If you don't have personal referrals, cold call each likely agency. Don't ask for an agent, but focus on whoever answers or one of the assistants and say you're looking for representation for writing dramatic TV series. You may extract the names of agents who specialize in this or the new guy in the agency who's building his list. Get the names spelled. Out of a hundred calls, ten may be interested. Okay, you only need one.

Next step is a one-page letter (or email) to a specific agent emphasizing your strengths — screenwriting awards, a film school degree, well-reviewed plays, published fiction or journalism. If you don't have those, hook the reader with some specialty like having crime stories to tell from your years as a cop. Move on quickly to what's in your portfolio, for example spec scripts for *House* and *Breaking Bad*, and two features, a romantic comedy and a suspenseful drama. Your aim is to be invited to send one script.

Now comes the wait. You can probably call once every couple of weeks to remind the assistant; just don't bug people. Meanwhile, your letter is at other agencies you've contacted, and in six to eight weeks someone may ask to see your writing.

Even though you're aiming at episodic series, the first script the agent may want is an original. This is to separate your talent from the style of the series you're speculating. Later, when the agent is ready to judge your skill in series writing, the spec episodes will be useful.

Let's say you've jumped through those hoops and you're meeting with agents. Good agents are looking for clients with the talent and perseverance to grow, as interested in where you'll be in five years as whether they can place you on a staff this season. In fact, an agent who only wants a quick sale is likely to drop you if you don't make him money in the first few months. You deserve better.

You're building a relationship, you hope, so you want someone who understands your goals, can guide you to a show where you start building a career, and has the clout to push open that door. The choice is personal — the hungry young agent, the empathetic one, or the seasoned vet with a long client list? High class problems, of course.

What if you don't get a bite? Next stop is managers. The main difference is agencies are regulated by the state and have agreements with the guilds which define how much they can charge and their responsibilities. Managers are unregulated, so watch out. Professional management companies function very like agencies except they charge 15% of your earnings or more, compared with 10%. Justifying the bigger bite, managers may cover more than agents, sometimes all of an artist's business life.

For you, a manager may be available when agents are out of reach, and they can open most of the same doors. They're not listed with the guilds, but you'll find managers in the creative directory. So take the same steps: call, send a letter, send a script, and interview as with an agent.

If you zero-out with managers too, entertainment attorneys sometimes have connections to producers and may pass along your work or make an introduction. If you retain an attorney for this, the customary charge is 5% of all your screen work in lieu of an hourly rate.

Still too tough? Here are some end-runs around the representation problem.

- Get a job on the show. Any job. The top choice is Writers Assistant because you'll interface directly with the staff and might even observe in the writers room. Production assistant or even secretary are fine. The point isn't a career in photo-copying but relationships with the writers. Once they know you, they won't be able to avoid reading your work. And when you're around the series, you learn the inside tips.
- Go to film school for a screenwriting degree. The best schools promote their graduating students to the industry, and friends you meet there help each other.
- Write for an actor. Many actors have small production companies to find them material. You might get into a show by writing a compelling role for one of the less-served cast who will fight for your script. You'll need to figure how to get the script through to him or her, but it's not impossible.
- Start with new and alternative outlets. Apart from network and national cable primetime programming, dramatic writing jobs may be available off-network, in niche cable outlets, in off-hours, and increasingly on the Web. Those markets don't tend to work with agents anyway (not enough money), so you apply directly to the producers where your enthusiasm may be welcome.

BE IN LOS ANGELES.

Our heroine flew to an L.A. motel the minute she thought a producer would see her. She was lucky he kept the appointment. But a showrunner juggles delivery deadlines, last minute rewrites, and emergencies on the set, so appointments are rescheduled once, twice, three times. How long can you sit in that motel?

Some people relocate and work a day job while poring over the "trades." You know Hollywood is crowded with would-be writers, actors and directors who followed a dream and were still working as waiters — literally and metaphorically — a decade later. But as a writer you can work wherever you are, so don't leave home until your portfolio is strong, you have a bite, or you're coming to film school. The woman in our tale moved after her first assignment. Then she glued herself to the production, and that led to her next assignment.

Whether you move sooner or later, you do need to live in L.A. to write series television. A few mainstream American shows are now based in other cities — New York, Miami, Vancouver, Toronto. David Simon's shows are centered in Baltimore. But most staffs are on the studio lots. As you read in Chapter Three, TV writers work collaboratively, so there's no way to avoid the palm trees.

THE SECRET OF SUCCESS

My USC students sometimes ask how likely it is they'll make it — what are their chances of breaking in? The first year or two out of school are usually rough, but I've discovered which ones succeed five years later. They're not necessarily the most gifted, the brightest or the best connected, though talent, smarts and relationships do help. No, the ones who succeed have a single trait in common: they didn't give up.

Tales from my recent MFA graduates reflect 21st century realities both better and worse than I'd experienced a decade earlier. Worse is that free-lance assignments are tighter. Now shows depend on staff writers for most episodes, so freelance gigs are really auditions for staff.

But so much is better, more open. Okay, each show has fewer freelance episodes, but the number of series has multiplied in a world with around a thousand channels — broadcast, cable and satellite, which do orig-inal programming, plus emerging markets on the Web. When I was first breaking in, I had to pitch to guys (yes, guys only), an old guard who held a lid on traditional network formats and the kinds of plot-driven stories that had proved reliable. Too many of their shows seemed alike — mind-numbing for a creative person. Some of them are still around, but in an era when shows compete with the Internet and new venues to attract viewers, those showrunners are becoming dinosaurs.

Among new trends:

- Shows that prefer non-episodic samples (features or even stage plays) in an effort to identify original talent, along with TV specs;
- Potentials to pilot original series or use a spec pilot as a sample (see "Spotlight On Writing Your Pilot Script");
- Hybrid forms including dramedy, reality/drama and music/drama;
- More flexible act structures;
- Blends of techniques — animation with live action, for example;
- Content that includes non-traditional lifestyles, cutting edge issues, honest relationships, gutsy language, and fantasy;
- Computer generated imagery (CGI) which enables locations and effects formerly impossible.

In Chapter Seven, you'll find reprints of two articles I published in *The Los Angeles Times* and updates that bring their stories current. The first article interviewed MFA students from my USC episodic drama class six months after they graduated. I interviewed them again three years later. And the update asks where they are six years after graduation, and again fourteen years after graduation. These are today's stories from the trenches of breaking in.

Take Brian and Kelly. On graduating, they each had feature screenplays written in school, and episodes for *ER, NYPD Blue*, and *The X-Files*. But no agent signed them immediately, and both took day jobs. Brian hooked up with a young independent director and worked without pay for a year writing *But I'm a Cheerleader*, a satire about a girl sent to a camp to "cure" her of being gay, where she falls in love with another girl. The indie film was made on a shoestring but garnered Brian notice in *Variety* as a writer to watch. Meanwhile, Kelly was hired to write a script for a French actress.

A year later, they were both still at day jobs, frustrated with director-driven features, trying to break into TV, and they decided to team up. *Cheerleader* got them in a door at the WB, an off-network that hired young writers with limited credits. Here, they pitched an original series — not an episode — and actually got an assignment to write the pilot (something unimaginable in the past). It wasn't picked up. But by now the WB execs knew the team and recommended them to *Smallville*, on their network. From here, their story is traditional — they wrote an episode, joined the staff, and rose within the show. At the end of the series in 2011, they were the showrunners.

So, in a way, we've come full circle from our fairy tale. It is all possible. You *can* break in.

SUMMARY POINTS

• To break into writing for television, you first need a solid understanding of how TV drama series differs from other kinds of writing.

• Second, choose one high-quality show to learn well. Fully grasp the "voices" of all characters as well as the kinds of stories the show tells and its structure.

• Once you've learned your target show, write a spec script, but do not speculate an episode of the same show you intend to pitch. You will probably need spec scripts from several shows in different genres.

• Once your spec script is polished, try to get an agent or manager who will expose your work to producers. Ideally, you'll get meetings after your scripts are read.

• Working on a show in any capacity, including writer's assistant, researcher, or secretary, may help you make contacts who will read your script.

• It takes years for most new writers to break in, and the key is to generate many scripts that keep you growing as a writer — and don't give up.

WHAT'S NEW?

Read Chapters Seven and Eight for ideas fresh from the trenches. The new portion of interviews with my former students ("Fourteen Years Later") reveals how one of them made a connection through writing Webisodes for a car company. In Chapter Eight, Internet and international potentials are also explored.

LIFE AFTER FILM SCHOOL: CAUTIONARY TALES AND SUCCESS STORIES

CHAPTER 7

For the past fourteen years I've followed one group of MFA students who happened to take my class in writing episodic TV drama. Initially, I intended only to bear witness to how careers begin. But after all this time, the reunions have led to a rare and unexpected longitudinal exploration of how the lives of seven writers evolved. First interviewed for *The Los Angeles Times* just months after they received their graduate degrees from the USC School of Cinematic Arts in 1997, I interviewed them again for *The Times* three years later, then four years after that for the first edition of this book published in 2005, and finally fourteen years after they graduated for this Third Edition.

In hindsight, their accomplishments and struggles now seem inevitable — which is not the same as saying that standing at the door to the classroom on their last day I knew for sure what would happen. It's like looking at a seedling in my garden, knowing it could one day grow tomatoes, but I don't know how many or how big, and that's only if it survives; and that's not a sure thing. These former students came from all parts of the country, from colleges ranging from Harvard to someplace you never heard of; not one of them had a relative in the business; not one of them was personally rich; no one just lucked into their jobs. They each worked for what they achieved, they each had some hard times, and they all survived.

Together, the four sessions form case histories that hint at what to expect as you begin writing for television. Most of all, I hope their stories give you hope: When the industry appears impenetrable, they remind you that you're not alone. When the doors nudge open, they tell you what they did to walk through. And if they succeeded, maybe you can too.

THE CLASS OF '97

(The following article appeared in *The Los Angeles Times*, Feb. 8, 1998)

Reunion. Six months after graduating from USC's School of Cinematic Arts, seven students from my advanced television writing seminar meet again in our former classroom. Reunions are bittersweet. Now we gather at night, the comforting predictability of school assignments and the company of hundreds of others taking the plunge into the industry with them, all gone. A few are thrilled to have professional assignments. Others, still mailing samples they wrote in school, trying to get agents, claim they're not jealous. Right.

I've taught students like them for a decade, holding out the prospect that hour-long episodic drama in shows like *ER, NYPD Blue, Homicide, Law & Order, The X-Files* and others offer opportunities for the most incisive, challenging writing they'll find anywhere. Now the industry is dotted with stars of previous classes — not just mine but from other USC professors. It's a hot time for new TV writers.

The graduates gathered tonight understand the power they'd wield in television and feel responsible for what they give the public, quick to put down gender and ethnic stereotypes and relationships that don't seem real. It's an attitude not typical of earlier generations. Credit for it goes to the trailblazing series they've studied, and to living in a multi-cultural America very different from what was reflected in earlier decades of TV.

Drew Landis and Julia Rosen became writing partners at USC. Brought to the U.S. from South Korea by his minister father during the Amerasian adoptions in the 1970s, Drew worked in politics in Washington before entering the Graduate Screenwriting Program. Julia grew up in Los Angeles and made films that won festival competitions. Together, they speculated scripts for *ER, NYPD Blue, Early Edition, Party of Five, Frasier*, a drama pilot, and two features before graduating. That portfolio got them signed by The Artists Agency, a TV-movie deal, and a possible position on a new series. Credit all those sample scripts, and their certainty about television.

Drew: "An agent asked at one of our first meetings why we want to write for television. It's because when I watch I love the connection to the continuing characters, and having experienced that, I want to translate it every week."

Julia: "For me, it's that feature films nowadays are comedies or spectacles. But you go anywhere in the United States and everybody is watching *ER* and they know all about those characters. The way to reach people and talk about real subjects and get to people's hearts is television.

Wendy West wanted to write TV since she was a child. "I found an old diary, pink, with bunnies. I was excited to see what I did as a child. But when I opened it, I found pages and pages of 'Today on *Alice*, Flo said kiss my grits' — whatever was on TV each day."

Her *X-Files* spec won her a staff writer position on an upcoming WB series, but it hasn't been as she'd imagined. "I feel a little left out. My first script was not exactly what the show is. Working in the real world, you need to be a chameleon. That doesn't mean losing your voice but you have to adapt to the style of the show you're writing. So much of film school is spent trying to find your voice so it seems counterintuitive to think you should lose it somewhat. But only somewhat. I guess we're waiting to see the stamp of a Wendy West script, but you can bet on someone falling in love or at least tripping over her own heart."

Still hopeful, Wendy tells the group, "A good day is like our class for eight hours. One of the reasons I went into television is I like collaboration, knowing people are there to help you get through the outline. You're not alone the way you are with a feature."

That yearning for community echoes among them, all single, in their 20s. Gib Wallis wrote and performed plays off-Broadway and on London's fringe before film school. Now he works as an actor while looking for a writing agent. He chose television because: "With features if they want somebody to rewrite you, how much of the original vision is left? With a TV show, even if you're the youngest and you're rewritten, they have to see you at lunch. You have writers working with writers so they understand."

That's his dream. But it's a hard fit to the past months. "Right before graduation I sent out fifty query letters and to my surprise I got six meetings and I thought I'd hit the jackpot with people wanting to read my *ER* sample. They said give us several weeks. But every time I called I got this response of now is not a good time. Finally they wanted to hear back from me in July; only the TV staffing season ended in June. I told them I'd hoped they would have read it in time, and they said, oh, we're glad we got your script but there's no way we're going to read it because we're staffing right now. We're trying to get jobs for the people we already signed. I felt there was this little window and I wasn't able to get into it quite soon enough."

Eric Trueheart graduated in English Literature from Harvard, but is equally frustrated since finishing his MFA. He wrote five spec scripts but "It's extraordinarily difficult to get people to read ... I've had a lot of time to think about what it means to be a writer." While at USC, Eric was mentored by Glen Morgan and James Wong, then on *The X-Files*, now executive producers on *Millennium*. "They were great letting me look in on the process. But they're so busy they haven't read anything even though I wrote a *Millennium*."

With television hard to crack, some graduates accepted jobs rewriting features, like Kelly Souders. Having grown up on a ranch in Missouri, she wrote fiction before entering the Graduate Screenwriting Program, where her feature thesis won highest honors. Kelly discovered "Without the episodic TV class the feature would have been a real struggle. I had to take someone else's character in someone else's story and put the structure together, and I learned that in episodic."

She's emphatic: "The quality is in television. I can't tell you how many times I came out of a theatre and said I'm never going to a movie again. These big action things have no characters. It's like marketing people put the film together. And then you watch *NYPD Blue* and *ER* and it's the best writing I've seen."

They long for believable characters and more of the spectrum of people in the real world. Wendy describes *Homicide* as "amazing" in its depth of internal issues among African-American characters. "The scenes between Andre Braugher and James Earl Jones were riveting — how Pembleton was conflicted over covering up to protect a black hero."

Other students point to episodes on *ER* when Benton coped with the illness of his mother — how refreshing to see African-American women written with dignity. They're aware the main cast includes Latinos in *Law & Order* and *Chicago Hope*, and Asian and Native Americans on *Star Trek: Voyager*.

Wendy agrees, "We have role models in TV we don't have in features. It's great to see women doctors sticking their hands into someone's body to save his life. It's not just this season. Believable women go back to Cagney and Lacey, who had real relationships — they weren't just cops, or sex objects. Back then it was a big deal that women wrote that series. Probably they had to fight for it to be truthful."

Not everybody is into the fight, at least, not right away. I see Brian Peterson around campus, no longer in jeans, wearing a tie. He took a job at the School until he has more scripts. "After graduating, you really have to figure out who you are again." Heads around the table nod, understanding as Brian continues, "We were all zombies in the last month of school. We all felt so much was riding on our feature thesis, and we were supposed to start off the block with a big bang. I sent out my query letters and went home to Montana and regrouped. It turned out my feature wasn't useful for television. A couple of agents called me back and said I loved your *ER*, it was great. And I said so? And they said so? So, where are your other TV scripts?"

It's easier to return to the ideals of writing than cope with waiting. They retell moments from shows we studied like Dr. Greene losing a patient in childbirth on *ER*, a controversial issue in *The Practice*, gutsy innovations on *EZ Streets*, true relationships on *My So-Called Life*. Gib likes "shows to experiment with the narrative. Some of that is in *Ally McBeal*, interweaving her fantasies in a way that's provocative." Brian wants "a world I can see come to life like *Twin Peaks* that created its own world."

Revisiting friends. Shared goals. Tonight it's easier to get fired up about politicians who want to censor their art than deal with getting assignments that compromise it.

Eric argues, "In one of Bob Dole's anti-TV campaigns, he complained about *NYPD Blue*, saying the last good cop show was *Dragnet*. *Dragnet* was a cartoon. If people want cartoonish versions of morality spelled out, they're welcome to it. But the realistic dramas are supremely moral because they're grappling with issues everyone is trying to grapple with, struggling to come up with moral answers to them."

Kelly: "Television gives people a clear moral choice: the on and off button. I don't watch certain shows, but it doesn't mean they shouldn't be on. There are shows I could never be interested in because they don't have enough honest reality. To me, that dishonesty is as damaging as violence."

Left to right:
Kelly Souders,
Brian Peterson

Left to right:
Julia Swift,
Andrew Landis,
Kelly Souders

Left to right:
Wendy West,
Gib Wallis,
Julia Swift

Left to right:
Eric Trueheart,
Wendy West,
Gib Wallis,
Julia Swift

Julia: "*NYPD Blue* and *ER* challenge people in ways people who watch shows like *Touched by an Angel* wouldn't want to be challenged. Those people know they're not going to leave with a sick feeling. They want the issues simpler, but for emotions to still be there. There's room for that."

Eric challenges Kelly: "If you were offered a job, could you write for one of those "angel" shows?"

Kelly: "I don't think so. I'd be pushing away my experience. Though they say never say no to your first job."

Ah, jobs. That punctures the debate. I lead the conversation back to school. Looking back, what counts?

Drew: "Me and Julia finding each other."

Julia: "We're able to have an extended version of our class all the time. You learn the questions. Do you have the act breaks? Where do your moments come in? Whose scene is this? What's the arc of your character? You go through them, one by one, and make changes until wow, this works. Before, I wrote from my heart but had no idea how to make it powerful. When we graduated, we turned to each other and said Thank God."

Kelly: "For the rest of your life when you're sitting at a computer you'll be hearing your teachers in your head. You hope what they're saying to you will help you work."

The seven former students turn to me as if I have one more lesson, some secret I know. I do know that five years from now those who refuse to give up will have "made it," as generations before them did. They'll do it by writing unpaid script after script until the craft comes naturally, by learning nuts and bolts on shows they'll one day leave off their resumes, and finally by not losing sight of the great writing they studied on television today. Beyond craft, they've come of age in a "golden era" of television dramas. They'll stand on the shoulders of those giants.

THREE YEARS LATER

(The following article appeared in *The Los Angeles Times*, July 5, 2000)

Three years after graduating, they meet again. They had been MFA students in my class, a few months out of school and mostly out of work, when *The Los Angeles Times* first ran a feature on them. Since then, six other classes have come and gone through my course in writing episodic television drama at the USC School of Cinematic Arts, each with its own angst and triumphs.

Now the former students meet in my backyard on a sunny afternoon to talk about what happens when *Variety* (the entertainment trade daily) names you one of "The Ten Writers to Watch," and exactly how much unemployment pays; how exhilarated you feel rising to co-producer of a TV series, and how you find out your show is cancelled; how to avoid letting producers know you're pregnant, and being single with no time to date; how a chance meeting can luck into a break, and yet old friends are what keeps you going.

While they were in school, I predicted that any of them who wanted a TV writing career enough, who didn't give up, would have it within a few years. Now, let's see.

Brian Peterson went home to Montana after graduating then returned to a job in the Dean's Office by day, while sending out his scripts by night. The next fall, director Jaime Babbit, who had an idea for a movie, *But I'm a Cheerleader*, made an offer. Some offer: write a screenplay for no pay.

But Brian sparked to the subject: "a cheerleader whose parents send her off to rehab because they suspect she's a lesbian, but she discovers she really is gay, and at rehab she falls in love."

Brian says, "I spent a whole year rewriting it for nothing, and then it finally got shot. It was the kind of thing you dream about: you see these hot pink signs that say 'Cheerleader,' and you say, 'Oh my God, that's mine.'"

While the film was screening at festivals, *Variety* named Brian one of the "Ten Writers to Watch." Despite that, "every time *Variety* mentioned *Cheerleader* they said Jaime wrote and directed it. People who don't know better have this love affair with writer-directors."

Brian concluded, "After that experience, Kelly and I started pitching pilots for TV."

That's Kelly Souders, whose thesis script, "My Slut Mom," was optioned by a producer soon after we last met. But Kelly asserts, "Every meeting I had on it was about toning it down. I'm not going to tone it down."

For about a year she co-wrote another feature with an actress, but that hasn't been produced either. So she was also looking toward TV, and they remembered an idea they'd had at USC, and their agent got them meetings.

"Everybody we've met in television has been fantastic, 180 degrees from features," Kelly says. The team sold their pilot, and "we'd love to be in the situation to hire everybody at the table," Kelly offers, to a round of cheers.

In the time from their 20s to pushing 30, from being outsiders to working in the industry, Kelly says, "You start getting protective of what kind of work you want to do. It's easier on your self image," to which Brian quips, "But not always on your checkbook."

Everyone groans with understanding, even Wendy West, who was the first on a series staff. Wendy laughs that she was also first to discover that unemployment pays $230 per week, when that series was cancelled. But a producer she'd met there invited her onto yet another show... which didn't make it on the air either.

"The way we found out was we opened up the paper and it said we were being suspended. Meanwhile, our sets were being built. In fact, there was a delivery of lumber that day."

But she had made more relationships. So, when one of the producers moved on to the *Law & Order* spinoff, *Special Victims Unit*, he brought Wendy along. Now in her second year on the show, she was promoted to story editor, and this coming year she will be a co-producer.

Wendy: "It's wonderful, exciting, fantastic. [Executive Producer] Dick Wolf is so smart and talented; it's not an accident he is where he is. His notes catch exactly the little things you know don't really work, but you tell yourself, well, nobody will pick up on this. Then he sticks his finger in it, and you say, all right, all right."

Wendy looks warmly over at Andrew Landis and Julia Rosen. "Last year Drew and Julia were on the lot so it was more fun because we could get lunch."

Drew and Julia teamed up before they left school, and armed with sample scripts for five different series, they garnered an agent before anyone else, and they won contests. Julia observes, "Producers need something that says other people think you're good."

They nabbed their first real job on *Hercules*, "by going in and pitching something outrageous," Julia says. Drew adds, "They have people on staff who are going to write the show, so you can only bring something that's yours."

Between *Hercules* and the staff of the short-lived series *D.C.*, Julia married Andrew Swift, a producer on *True Hollywood Stories*, and became pregnant.

The only one of the group who is not single, Julia confides, "I hid my pregnancy while we were working on *D.C.* People think if you have a newborn you're not going to work, and that's not true for me. In order to be a good mother I have to be a happy mother." As it happened, *D.C.* was cancelled before the baby was born, and the team found themselves out of work, anyway.

Everyone at the table has done temp work while waiting for the next writing job, but Brian warns, "People don't see you as a sexy writer if you have a day job."

On the other side, Eric Trueheart, far from his Harvard literature degree, is writing an animated feature, *Guy Futomaki: Ninja Temp*, which he sold to Fox. "It's the story of a trained Ninja. His clan has been destroyed and he's forced to come to America where he can only survive by doing temp work."

Eric's route to the sale was "Hollywood," in the worst sense. "I had a so-called agent who wouldn't sign me, but he mentioned *Guy* to a studio executive. So we go over, and there's this 24-year-old development guy in an expensive shirt. I told him, you know, it's animated. He said, 'We're thinking live action.' I said, 'We're thinking like *The Simpsons, Beavis & Butthead*.' He didn't get it, but he started pitching it around town without us, when he didn't have any rights to it."

Eric shakes his head, "It was classic Hollywood. It's not that these guys are evil. They're just driven and oblivious."

Ultimately, Eric made his deal with Fox, but his success on the fringe began doing Web work at the company run by Steve Oedekerk (writer of mainstream comedies like *Nutty Professor 2*). There, Eric made a friend who occasionally asked him to write for their Internet shows. He worked on *Thumb Wars* and *Thumbtanic*, for which he also appeared as a thumb.

With an edgy reputation growing, he landed a staff writing job on Nickelodeon's new animated series, *Invader Zim*, which Eric describes as "torqued," while *Guy* is developed.

"It's the first time getting a steady paycheck for writing. It's a weird experience."

Now immersed in Hollywood, they speak of staying in touch with what's real. Drew and Brian are training to run in the Chicago Marathon to benefit AIDS Project Los Angeles. And Drew, who was brought to the U.S. from South Korea during the Amerasian adoptions of the 1970s, wishes he saw more faces on television who look like the friends everyone here has, people of diverse backgrounds.

So, it turns out, three years after graduating, my prediction came true: those who went for it succeeded in beginning their careers. Now they ask: what will they do with their new-found status; what really matters?

SEVEN YEARS AFTER GRADUATING

The class reconvened in my backyard in August, 2004. Kelly Souders had gotten married. Julia Swift showed us photos of her "baby," now grown into a beautiful little boy about to enter kindergarten. Now everyone present was drawing at least a partial income from writing and several had been able to quit their day jobs. We began by passing the tape recorder around the table, each writer bringing us up to date since we last met. As enthusiastic as I'd known them as students, though wiser, they offer their experiences to you:

Eric Trueheart: "Three years ago I was going into animation, which was a great education working on a staff. There were only three writers on the whole show including me and a comic book writer who didn't know much about structure but was really funny. Actually, I learned a lot about comedy sitting on that show. You spend time crafting a joke but sometimes a scream can just be really funny. Then it was cancelled so I was fired.

"I've also been working on my own comedy show out of a warehouse that's been the pick of the week in *L.A. Weekly* — *The Ministry of Unknown Science* — and we do these elaborate shows that are part-live, part-video. We were repped by CAA [Creative Artists Agency] for about a year but we discovered they had certain ideas how to promote our show that were different from the way we had envisioned it. So in the process we learned that what an agent can really do is step in at the last minute and help.

"Then there's just the constant therapy and self-evaluation that all creative people must do. I thought I was going to graduate and be all set, trained to do this stuff. I've been trained — it's like dental school. I still think hour-long drama is great but I haven't had the chance to do anything in it yet. And I've had a lot of trouble finding how I sell myself in the industry, but it's been like Zen. Now I'm in on another animated show. I've sort of fallen into animation but it doesn't pay nearly so well and it's not Guild.

[In other words, the production company is not a signatory to the WGA Minimum Basic Agreement, which means that writers have no protections on payments or working conditions and do not receive guild benefits such as health and pension.]

Wendy West: "I've been working in hour-long drama — I worked on some interesting shows that got cancelled, a medical show and a crime show. One was called *Gideon's Crossing* and the other, *Line of Fire*. I never wrote crime in your class but that seems to be what I do. If there's not a dead body I feel like something's missing now. I think it's interesting because you encouraged us to write from our heart and the business is just about writing what sells. I knew this guy from last year's show and I got a meeting on a current show and it was between me and another person and he helped me get it. So I owe him — a lot."

Gib Wallis: "Around three years ago the Mark Taper Forum was doing this thing, and I got tapped to do artistic response to the events of 9/11. I wrote a one-act play and that was cool because I always loved theatre. It was a 65-seat theatre and there were people sitting in the aisle. Then enough people began requesting plays for different things.

"Since I still have a day job, it's been an interesting challenge to keep being inspired. When you're in film school, you have great people around you to talk about story and character but when you go out, there are a lot of people who want to talk about selling things or setting things up. I'm a member of a playwrights group called Playwrights Six and, for me, to meet with people regularly to talk about the art — that was my favorite part of film school."

Julia Swift: "Drew [Landis] and I have been together for eight years. We did a pilot with Regency and the WB based on a weird part of my life and that was very interesting and fun. When you write a pilot you have the flexibility and the salary, which is great. But writing my own life was very difficult because I had this strange life growing up that I've always tried to hide. We were at a meet-and-greet at CBS and the executive pushed me to [talk about more ideas]. So I told him about growing up in a mob family, half in Vegas and half in L.A.

"The story was about the year I went to college. My father turned my grandfather into the FBI and took off. I watch *The Sopranos* and it pisses me off because Tony is tough at work and nice at home, which is just wrong. It was interesting because we would be on the phone with network executives and the character's name is Maia, but they would call her Julia. They brought on Carlton Cuse as a producer and we loved him, and he said to Drew, 'Your assignment is to go home and get Julia drunk and ask her questions about her family.' And we did! We got pages of stories that would blow you away. We gave it to Regency, and they loved the stories. But it ended up being too 'complicated.' The emotions weren't all on the surface and Carlton and the studio wanted it to be more complicated, and the network wanted it more on the surface. So that was interesting, learning whose advice to take.

"Now we're pitching a new pilot, more drama, and we have a studio that wants to go out with us, but the executive called us and he might be moving, so who knows? As long as you keep those relationships you can move with them, but it's difficult."

Andrew Landis: "What makes our partnership work is being able to communicate honestly five or ten times a day. It's better than working alone, to get someone else's eyes to see what I don't. Having a strong partnership puts everything in perspective."

Kelly Souders: "Three years ago was right before *Smallville* so I was writing grants for the Science Center and I didn't have a car."

Brian Peterson: "We'd partnered up and were working on these pilots. I'd taken a job transcribing EcoChallenge tapes. Then in one year we got a pilot with Fox and were on staff on *Smallville*. It was interesting because which do you take — the pilot or the staff — and we really debated that.

"After my writing credit on *But I'm a Cheerleader*, I needed to go into meetings with ideas. I got a couple of rewrites but then we had to start over in TV. It's great, though, because we learned as much in working in TV as we learned in film school."

Kelly: "In your class we really learned to write a scene, the shape of it, when to come in, and that we use everyday."

Brian: "The work-shopping we did in class, learning what notes to take and what not to take, was great."

Kelly: "On *Smallville* right now, we're rewriting other writers, dealing with production, writing our own scripts, dealing with the scheduling. People in the room tend to either be really good at story or really good at character. For us, we make a great team, but it's funny because our strengths and weaknesses are similar. For us, the story is always a weak point and, over the last three years on the show, we've really learned a lot."

Brian: "Being on a staff we have such a great group of mentors, you have a built in support group, we know about each other's lives."

Kelly: "It makes a big difference because we landed on a show where the people above us are really smart. We'd been working together for years but on our own time so it was more relaxed and we weren't depending on each other to pay our bills. Suddenly to have that switch in 24 hours was a struggle, our first couple of days on that show. The end of the first day, Brian was ready to lop off my head and, at the end of the second, I was ready to lop off his. Now, after work we'll go to dinner or to a play so we're able to separate the friendship from the work relationship."

I asked a question for entire table: If you could talk to your own young self at USC, what advice would you give?

Eric: "Get a day job because it takes forever to earn a living, but there will be breaks. A job will be a financial and psychological safety net. It gives you that freedom to figure out what you're doing without having your life depend on it."

Kelly: "Wendy gave me a magnet, 'If you're going through hell, keep going.' For me, I think this is a longevity race. If you can keep at it and hang in there, then do it."

Brian: "Have samples in a lot of different genres because people like to read different shows. Keep updating, keep going. Just as soon as someone says there's an opportunity, you can't wait a week or two weeks, you have to give them a script."

Drew: "You have to network a lot more than you're comfortable with. You really have to force yourself when you're done with your writing to meet people. Your agent can only do so much, and a lot of the jobs come from what you hear."

Eric: "Get a job on a show as an assistant. Just get in that environment, there are so many stories you hear of a writer's assistant pitching an idea and the show using it."

Kelly: "There are two freelance episodes we have a year and we give them to the assistants."

Wendy: "My advice: Keep writing. The business has changed; they want to know what's out of the box. It wasn't that way when we were getting out of school. I got a job off a short story — it's crazy. Also, it's important to be in a writing group. I think those people who didn't stay in a group just fell out of writing. It's really hard to get yourself pumped up, but having a place where you have to produce every week or two weeks is valuable."

Julia: "We were taught in school to write what we love and we came out thinking we're going to write what we love but have some action in there. You can write a genre that's not your dream genre but infuse that with you and the marketplace will respond because it has that bit of whatever makes you different."

Wendy: "One of the things that I'm constantly reminded of is that this town is run on passion, which is great. But when we send out scripts, people are so afraid that they're going to choose something that they'll get fired over, or that the advertisers are going to pull the show. You have to wind through so many obstacles until you get to the final piece and then that's pushed to the middle ground."

Julia: "I think that as this generation raised on HBO grows, then something has to change because they won't want to go back to that middle ground."

Brian: "As you mature into the industry, you realize the venues that are appropriate for your work. Every major studio wants their Emmys and Oscars so they will support certain producers. So there is a chance to be an artist, but you really have to focus on it."

Fourteen Years after Graduating

Hard to believe — in 2011, fourteen years will have elapsed since these writers went out into the industry, hopeful and scared. Now everyone was so busy we couldn't find a time when we all could get together, so we gathered at my house without Brian Peterson, though he was represented by his producing partner, Kelly Souders.

Some of the most revealing insights came privately after the tape was off. Wendy West had been nominated for an Emmy in 2010, and she told me her "arm candy" (her dates) for the Emmy Awards were her parents. Gib Wallis asked me to urge the readers not to become isolated. Eric Trueheart said he's making the transition to hour-long this year. "I'm getting good responses to my spec pilot and my manager is sending my specs out to agents hoping to get someone in time for staffing season. So it seems after all these years of weirdness, I'm finally ending up where everyone else started ages ago."

Kelly worried that her show's budget would be mentioned in the book. Of them all, she seemed to have changed the most. As showrunner/executive producer of *Smallville* (along with Brian), capping nine years on that show, she juggles huge responsibilities at work, two children at home, and a house remodel. Though she said she was stressed, she exuded executive capability, the kind of seasoned professionalism achieved at high levels in a career. But when I looked back to her comments years ago, Kelly was the one who asserted about a feature script she'd written, "Every meeting I had on it was about toning it down. I'm not going to tone it down ... You start getting protective of what kind of work you want to do." And yet she has risen to a level where she scarcely has time to write at all.

Funny thing, she and Brian had just sold a pilot back in 2000, before they started on *Smallville*, and she told the group at that time, "We'd love to be in the situation to hire everybody at the table." Well, she did hire Julia Swift and Drew Landis, sitting at the table smiling today.

Drew had also changed, it seemed to me. In his school days I thought of him as reserved and reticent to speak much about his personal life. Now he'd grown in confidence and this day he told us he was celebrating his second anniversary with his partner, since they'd been able to marry when same-sex weddings became legal in California. That's an announcement we wouldn't have heard fourteen years ago.

Former students 2010

Former students 2010

Gib, who always had a ready laugh, seemed to be carrying the weight of the world as a caregiver for his father. Back when they were recent graduates, their burdens were about getting jobs to pay student loans; life hadn't quite happened yet.

Wendy seemed to have changed the least, though she's now co-executive producer at *Dexter*, a highly regarded position earned through years of experience. I guess she's one of those people with a portrait in the attic that's getting old. She seems to be having fun as a writer (as does Julia) and I think that may be one reason they've been so welcomed onto writing staffs. Readers, that's a tip for you.

I asked Kelly what has changed from when she was a writer on *Smallville* to now when she's running the show, and also how she works with other writers.

Kelly: "The main difference is now writing is only about 15% of what I do. I miss it. That's what I got into this for. I enjoy the other challenges but I do miss writing. That's kind of common for the job — it's much more about budgets and management, a lot of phone calls.

"The way our show works — a group of writers work together to break a story and do the rough outline and somebody goes off and writes it. In some shows writers go off to break stories by themselves, but we keep it together in the group. Multiple minds are better than one mind. It's a very traditional writers room."

I asked how Julia and Drew came on the show — was it their relationship from school? Kelly said no, "They had to submit a script. On our show, when all the submissions come in we take the front page off and put numbers on them and give them to a couple of people. At least two people read every script. The ones who get a plus end up on our desk and we actually read without knowing who it is. To me, there's so much pressure from agents calling to say please put this person's script at the top. That system didn't work well for us. So we came up with this idea of anonymous reads.

Julia said she and Drew submitted a *Mad Men* spec and a pilot. That surprised me so I asked Kelly, "You read a *Mad Men* for *Smallville*, though they couldn't be more different?"

Kelly: "For us, writing action isn't very important on our show. We have an amazing crew that will make anything look incredible. What we care about is writing characters so we'd much rather read a character-based story than something that has a lot of action in it for the show because the show is much more relationship-based than you'd think."

Julia: "When Drew and I went to work for Brian and Kelly, I hadn't seen them for years, and I was sitting there in the writers room and everyone started pitching five million ideas. They went out and came back in and what they were able to keep in their minds and what they were able to keep track of and how professional they were — they never skipped a beat no matter what anyone threw at them. They were different people from whom I'd known before and I was flabbergasted. I walked out of the room that first day saying, 'Oh my God!' When you haven't seen someone for so long and they'd spent all those years learning and growing and acquiring skills I'd never seen in school, that was amazing to me. I walked around not being able to talk to them for the first couple of days."

Drew: "One thing we learned being on the show now for two years is you pitch ideas. They encourage the writers to pitch really big ideas and they'll figure out how to pay for them later. After a while we see how things go — how can we produce this, how could we actually be able to make this happen? For me it has changed how I write in terms of thinking about what could go into the scene and how to pay for it. You find a way you can afford to do it while still telling the same type of story you really want to tell. It impacts how you write scenes. You might pitch it one way but you have in your back pocket another solve that might be more practical."

Next was Gib's turn at the tape recorder. "I'm the exception to this wonderful group of TV writers because I've been writing theater," he said. "In 2006 I wrote a play that went to New York City. After I came back from New York I became the Associate Producer of the theater company and did the Christmas show that included a ten-minute monologue. The interesting thing from that is though it was just a one-off for four performances, GLAAD came (Gay and Lesbian Alliance Against Defamation) and I was nominated for a GLAAD Award for Outstanding Writing for Theatre. Most recently the same theater company asked me to become the artistic director for 2011, and I'm thinking about that. It's Playwrights Six, the oldest writer-run theater company in Los Angeles."

Eric: "The past six years I've been making my living in animation, doing some comedy as well. Mostly I've been working in family entertainment animation, which has been good because I've worked on a lot of different shows, I've pitched things, I've had pilots in various stages of production, and though none of them were picked up, I've had lots of experiences with showrunners and executives and the life of a freelancer, finding the voice of a show that isn't on the air yet, learning to operate with people. The downside is I work for a lot less money which kind of sucks. On the one hand it's been great because I've written hours and hours of television. A lot of it is stuff I wouldn't watch but it's made the kids happy, I assume. In some ways it's a really good gig for a writer because people go home early — most of them at Disney and Nickelodeon have families.

"I end up writing a lot of scripts and freelancing on other shows just to make ends meet. They are not anything I would choose to be on but it's good practice. Every writer in this city ends up taking jobs they never thought they would take."

The last time we met, Eric had been writing and producing shorts for the Internet, so I asked if he's still doing that. He said, with resignation, "Everybody is realizing you can't make money from that. On the Web with Hulu and iTunes and so forth there's finally a revenue stream going through the Internet, but it's hard to get paid. It's incredibly labor-intensive to produce your own material to post and at some point the grown-up gene kicks in: I better focus on something that, when I look back, I could say it came to something."

I knew Wendy was co-executive producer on *Dexter*, one of my favorite shows, so I was curious how she and the staff write it. She explained, "Everything is filtered through Dexter's point of view, because of the voice over too. That helps locate where you are in the story. The first thing we break is where is his emotional journey? Not so much what are the plot twists but what does this episode have to accomplish in the emotional journey of twelve episodes. The reason the show is so successful is the emotional notes it hits.

"The biggest task is to decide the arc of the season and who that character actually is. We go to 'camp' to plan it in February — we're February to October so we're off-season. We spend February talking, just talking — the eight of us writers. And then we constantly evolve all the twists and turns, but usually we know the beginning and the ending. We know what's in episode twelve and then everything has to work to that.

"The division of labor is that everyone is very much in every script. There's so much talking about every script before it gets made. Even if your name is on it and you wrote the scene, somebody else's fantastic idea may have just happened to land in your lap and there doesn't seem to be a sense of this is mine, that's yours. I think we all feel like we're in service of *Dexter*. We love this character and we want it to be all it can be. It's a show that you can give everything to and it can hold it.

"For me this is a heaven-sent gift in the sense that *Dexter* is so close to what I would write anyway. I think it's about how do we deal with what really motivates us? To what extent is Dexter aware of the different parts of himself? When does his Dark Passenger take over? Does he want to fight it? It's funny and really dark. He has such a wry view of life. For me it comes very naturally. I find myself thinking things that Dexter thinks too, which is strange and weird. I'm so thankful every day, every day."

Since Kelly had spoken about how they take in writers on *Smallville*, I asked Wendy how they take in writers on *Dexter*, or do they not?

Wendy: "I had met on the show earlier and it didn't happen. When there was an opening it was just very lucky that I was able to come in. I also had a lot of material that was very *Dexter*. I had a crazy serial killer love story and that was a good sample to have. It was a car commercial. I got hired by Lincoln to write twenty Webisodes that were two minutes each. So basically you were writing a pilot. It's the old thing: never turn down a job. I had two months off, so I said yeah. And lo and behold it turned out to be a great pilot experience. And the person who directed it directed several of my *Dexter*s and just won the Emmy for best directing. He had been on *Dexter* but he decided to do this crazy guerilla thing — we shot for five days, eight to twelve pages a day. It's back before the Internet bubble burst when we all thought maybe that's how things would get made."

Beyond their professional lives, I wondered how their personal lives had changed, how they coped, especially Kelly and Julia, who are parents. Kelly answered, "For years Brian and I talked about how do we balance having a life and the job. Now what we've come to is you can't. I don't see my kids nearly as much as I want. I try to keep my weekends open. During the week the chances of me getting home before they go to sleep is slim. So you depend on the people around you. I don't pick up dry cleaning. I don't go to the grocery store. I work and then whatever free time I have is devoted to being with them. That's very difficult, and it doesn't matter what job you have on a show. The assistants' hours are even worse than mine. I walk through the office yelling 'Go home, people. Do you have to be here? If you don't have to be here, go home.' So that's kind of hard.

You get to do your dream, which is awesome, and you're not the only one making sacrifices. The people around you are too.

"As for being pregnant and working in television — it was winter time and I literally did not tell the people I worked with until I was five and a half months pregnant. People were shocked. I wore jackets and big sweaters and scarves. I was in the middle of a contract negotiation and I didn't want it to be an issue. Finally I told my bosses. I was the only woman on staff for two years, and the only woman above the line for the first years I was on the show. No one who had ever worked on the show had ever been pregnant. I walked in and I was so nervous. I said I'm sorry I didn't tell you sooner. They said 'It's nobody's damn business if you're pregnant.' They could not have been more supportive and wonderful."

Julia: "I did hide it also when I was pregnant with my son because I didn't want it to be an issue. It doesn't mean I won't do the late nights or stay as long as I need to get the work done. The way I make that work is I make my son a part of it. He gets excited about whatever I'm working on. Mommy loves her job so much that I talk about it all the time. And when he was four years old he wrote a two-page synopsis for a *SpongeBob* script.

"We had an experience on different shows — this happened more than once — that the men would talk about their children in the room and the women don't because you don't want them to think you have something that's going to take you away from the show. One of the men was talking about his new baby, and this amazing producer we worked with, John Tinker, stopped everyone and said 'Guys, can you just realize there are women on this show with children. Have you ever heard them talk about them? Have you ever heard them say their kid kept them up at night? No. They're not allowed to.' It was amazing that he'd think to bring that to light."

Gib added, "I don't have a kid but I do have a kid — my dad. I have a 71-year-old. It's like I'm always the pregnant woman in a way because I'm the primary caregiver. He's been living with me for four years and when the phone rings at a certain time, all other calls are off. I have to step out or leave because there's an emergency. It's interesting being a man and a primary caregiver — you just don't bring it up professionally. On the other hand I got to bring my dad to opening night in New York."

Eric: "I've always been working on the side on something I hoped would get me somewhere else. So I've always had two jobs and I haven't had much time for a life. I haven't reached the point of stability where I feel I could build on something."

Drew: "One thing about my relationship with my partner that has taken getting used to is that the hours are so intense. It was kind of a learning experience the first year we were on *Smallville* — okay, what hours will I be home? This year he knows that when I'm on script he'll rent lots of movies and see other friends because I'll go into a hole and just write. One thing about being married to a therapist — he spends most of his days listening to other people's problems. So when I come home from being in the room and my brain is exhausted — we have twelve other people — he wants to talk because he listened all day. For me, it's just I want to be quiet, so that's also taken some adjusting on both our parts.

Wendy: "My life is just the same. It's just the same! I think about it when we have functions. I don't like to walk into a party alone, but I find somebody I know and we talk. It's the moment getting out of a car that I think I hate being single, but otherwise you're talking so much all day you're happy to go home and read a book. I feel like I have plenty of 'family' time. I don't feel there's something missing."

I asked them all for advice they'd like to give beginners. Eric answered, "Embrace the rewrite. New writers want to get it perfect the first time you write the scene or the outline and you never, ever do. The rewrite is your biggest friend."

Wendy: "Also your attitude toward that. We've all worked with writers who are offended when they get notes and offended when they have to rewrite something. To the extent that we're all in it to make the best script possible, embrace it with open arms."

Kelly: "If you think you don't need to rewrite your script one more time, you're naïve. Working with Drew and Julia on staff, people are impressed with how enthusiastic both of them are. When you get a note it might be from someone who has knowledge of something that happens four episodes down the road and may not have anything to do with whether they liked what you wrote. When you're running a show and you're under so much stress if there's somebody you can go to every time and say will you please help out with this, and they come up with ideas and they're positive, I can't tell you what a difference it makes."

Wendy: "The defensiveness comes out of wanting to protect your voice and when you're on a show you're not there to protect your voice. This is the big conundrum: you tell a young writer to go to school and develop your voice. And then you get a job on a show and you have to switch personas. You have to become in service to the show. As a writer you live a double life. At night or on Sundays you come back to what your voice is or what your dream show is. I wish somebody had said that to me in school: When you're in this room it's not about your voice. Make your showrunner look like a star. Give everything to that."

CHAPTER 8

THE FUTURE OF TV DRAMA SERIES

Any prediction about the future of television will be wrong. This is not because shows come and go each season, or genres fall in and out of favor, or new gadgets arrive on the market, new technologies are invented, new business models and entire industries take over TV distribution, or even that viewers are transformed by their personal lives and world events — though all those do happen and they may influence what you write for TV.

Any prediction will be wrong because predictions are based on the notion that the future is linear. Now, bear with me a moment — I'm not veering off into some sci-fi/fantasy realm. I'm leading up to advice that might be helpful long after the shows I mention in this book have all become history.

Some theoretical physicists have deduced that the Space/Time Continuum does not favor going in any particular direction, such as forward rather than backward; and for centuries mystics have invited us to experience Time as a single infinite moment. Of course, the mathematicians and philosophers could have saved their trouble by watching episodes of *Lost*, *Flash Forward*, *Fringe*, *The Event*, and anything on the Syfy channel. You are already familiar with flashbacks, flashes forward, simultaneous events told from various perspectives, and time travel in modes from silly to provocative. Personally, I think of Time as a spiral in which experiences and choices repeat, though never in exactly the same way, sort of like the DNA helix. To us in Flatland, that three-dimensional spiral would look like a pendulum swinging.

Here's my point: Television has swung widely in the past few years. Sitcoms were "dead" at the start of the 21st century, but by 2010 half-hour television comedy was on the forefront of storytelling. Quality drama series were supposedly "killed" by cheap "Unscripted" shows, but as the mistake of moving the Jay Leno show to 10 PM revealed, the audience hungered for scripted series, and hour dramas actually grew instead. Broadcast networks themselves were "dead," with the rise of cable and Internet viewing; but, guess what, broadcast audiences increased while cable also grew after 2009.

Now that camera and editing equipment is inexpensive and easy to use, and anyone can post an opus on the Internet, some observers have claimed that professionally produced full-length shows of any kind will become rare (if not "dead"), replaced by thousands of homemade productions. Right. Everyone really wants to see Junior's horror series in which he bursts out of a closet in a sheet rather than tuning into Frank Darabont's series *The Walking Dead*. Uh huh. I even hear that television itself is the walking dead, a zombie killed by Internet fever. Gimme a break.

Of course, some industries really do die out with the advent of technology. After paper became available, very few scribes preferred to carve into rocks. If you are a computer or technology specialist, venture capitalist, or an entrepreneurial independent producer with your own filmmaking equipment and aggressive energy, then yes, you probably should pay attention to the momentary swings of fortune and invention. But if you are primarily a writer, and you are interested in writing real television drama, I advise you to take a breath and stop spinning.

No matter what happens with Google TV or Apple apps or Hulu or DVRs or the number of act breaks or different financing models — *you* are what everyone needs. You bring the content. If you can continue to create credible characters with enough depth to develop long narratives, if you can be insightful in telling the stories of our times and our relationships, if you can acquire the craft to make the world of your script compelling on screen, then it doesn't much matter what platform people use to view it.

So my advice to you is to find the center of the pendulum, the spot that doesn't move (or the vortex of the DNA spiral if you prefer). Just let everything swing around you. And write your story.

With that caveat, I'm going to introduce our final Guest Speaker, David Goetsch. His enthusiasm for what he calls "New TV" led him to speak without interruption in the following interview. After David, I will return with other viewpoints.

GUEST SPEAKER: DAVID GOETSCH

Executive Producer of *The Big Bang Theory*, David Goetsch has also been a writer-producer on *3rd Rock from the Sun* and *Grounded for Life*. His interest in "New Television" brings him to our discussion of the future.

David Goetsch: The first question to ask is what is television today? It had been really clear up until ten years ago what television was, from *I Love Lucy* to *Emergency*. You knew what an hour was and you knew what a half-hour was. Half-hours were always comedy and hours were dramas that had a procedural component or an action component or a relationship component, or all of those, but they were very distinct genres.

Now TV has changed in two ways. One is distribution. How do you pay for and also show these dramas and comedies? We saw some changes with the cable revolution. But now there's a third thing farther along the spectrum — a lot of different things that generally could be called The Internet.

The second part is that it used to take a lot of money to make all of the programming, but now it's not necessarily the case. Now there can be lots of innovations and even tweaks and plays on the old forms. A drama on broadcast television is 44 minutes after commercials. But on the Internet there's no limit to the length. And there's no limit to how narrow a story or characters can be.

A television show about the world of antique wooden boats is a really small world, but you could probably get advertisers for it. If you spent little enough money to make the show it could be a profitable venture. What may become a great opportunity for invention is not limited by time constraints or budget.

On regular television you have to do a pitch, present that pitch, write a pilot, get approved, get it shot, and finally get it on the air. If you go through that process and it fails, you don't have the opportunity to make the show. You lose everything you put into it.

There's a producer who couldn't have been more on top of the world. He created *Veronica Mars*, top ten list. But after three years the network canceled it. So what does he do? He goes with his friend and creates *Party Down* in his backyard. He just shoots the pilot himself then shops it around, and Starz buys it. That's an example of a pilot they made for themselves because they thought it might be fun, but then it has a whole new life.

So the effect of that is the way a person can develop TV is different. There are new opportunities because of the low cost of production. There's a new opportunity to write something, to shoot it, to look at it, and say you know what, I was wrong. I'm going to change this and rewrite it again. You have the potential to incorporate production into part of the rewrite process if you choose because the economies of scale have come down over time. And things now can look great. You can have zero trade-off in production values between something you made yourself and something you paid millions of dollars for.

The number one most-watched drama in the world, according to the creators of *House*, is *House*. And the last episode of the show was shot using a camera I could go out and buy for about a hundred dollars. We were always approaching this time, but now we're here.

The result is that the barriers to producing ongoing television series have disappeared. All you need is the talent to do it. You're rewarded for your innovation because you get to create characters you love, which increases the chance of an audience falling in love with your show, creating characters and situations that are not mitigated by a network or studio.

So you've got innovation on the creative side, innovation on the production side, and then you have the opportunity to distribute it yourself. If nobody wants to pay you to distribute it, you can post it for free and build an audience. After a few years of building a fan base it could come to television. And then if that show comes to television and lasts a few years, you could make a deal to get it back so you could continue it. What could potentially happen is a show could be born in a creator's home, produced by the creator, run on the Internet, go to television, but the show would not have to end when it comes off of broadcast television.

What is television? What do great television shows do? They create character narratives so people want to check in every week to see what's happening. The greatest things that have ever been on television are the wonderful series, both hours and half-hours. What we now have the opportunity to do is make those shows without television, without approvals, without the financial requirements.

I love having my job in broadcast television, and I don't want to quit it, but one day it will be over and then I don't want to be limited to go out and have my specs sent around as the only test so somebody can judge me as a writer. I can do all those things, but in addition I can make my shows, put them on the Web and build an audience of not just fans, but also an audience of executives in Hollywood who know what I'm doing, and who are interested in the kinds of shows I'm making.

This is such an exciting time. When was the last time writers were presented with this kind of chance to start a new tradition? When shows migrated from radio to television, many of them kept the same traditions, with similar sponsors, similar act breaks. The televised play, the proscenium comes out of that tradition also. Now we're one step further from our grandparents' media as we go out into the real world with our cameras and interact with our audience.

Another dimension is the opportunity to have a dialogue with the audience. *Star Trek* always had its conventions people could go to. But now fans, like the fans of *Glee*, are following what the actors are doing on Twitter, are getting perspective on what writers are doing in the writers room, having an almost real-time conversation with the creators. For some creators it's a gut check for what you want to do on the show.

An extension of that is a computer innovator who has invited people to collaborate online in creating a TV show. What if a writers room is not ten people, but thousands of people who could weigh in. Managed properly, you could create a show that has thousands of loyal fans who are not only participating but also marketing that show. We'll see what can happen.

What will survive are the shows that speak to an audience, the ones that make people feel they have to check in each week and see what's happening to the characters.

A Tour Of The Future

Not really. Any attempt to tour the future will be wrong, as I explained. But, keeping in mind David Goetsch's projections, I'm going to lead you through a brief survey of the innovations circa 2011 that may affect you as television writers.

INTERNET DRAMA SERIES

Joss Whedon, creator of the iconic *Buffy the Vampire Slayer* (and its spinoffs) is a believer. His self-produced, self-funded musical *Dr. Horrible's Sing-Along Blog* was a Web pioneer, streaming online for free before becoming available for sale on iTunes, where it shot to the top of the charts. He says he was inspired by shows he'd seen online like *Star Trek: New Voyages*, a show created by fans of the original series.

It was the middle of the 2008 Writers Strike and everyone was out of work. So he pulled together members of his family and some actor friends, and everyone worked for free. When *Written By* magazine asked Joss to explain his business model, he remarked "Somebody coming to me for business advice is like somebody asking a guy who makes balloon animals how to pick up women."

When the strike ended, Joss went back to work on *Dollhouse* on traditional television, though his experiment from 2008 (available on Hulu with commercials) has had millions of downloads by now. But the question remains, as *Written By* asked, "Can his success be replicated by others? Or is it only possible for a Joss Whedon with his fervent fan base, critical support, and name recognition that's rare for a writer?"

Larry Brody, in "Field of Dreams or Mine Field" (*Written By*, January 2009) opened his article: "2009. The Year of Video on the Web. The Year that TV Viewing Habits Change Forever. The Year That All of Us Learn to Stop Worrying and Love Hulu.Com. The Eve of Destruction of Traditional Television. And the Dawn of Total Interconnectivity. Convergence Time is here.

"Pull up your comfy living room chair and surf the Internet on your TV. Pull up your even more comfortable ergonomically correct office chair and watch TV on your desktop PC. Be even hipper and more relaxed by using your laptop to do both in the intimacy of your bed. It's a Slingbox world, kids. And it's *free! free! free!*"

But when Brody spoke to actual writers of Internet shows he discovered, as one told him: "If your skill set is restricted to slapping words together to create dialog and imagery that is hilarious, thrilling, or involving, the Web can still be an exciting new medium... as long as you have the resources of a Joss Whedon. You can hire the crew and performers you need. And if it takes off, you have a calling card that could land you a 'real job.' But if you're merely a writer who spends every waking hour trying to land the next real job, becoming Web proficient... is more likely to lead you to a career working on other people's projects than to one in which you get rich writing your own."

One solution — if you're truly dedicated to making your own Internet show — is to start small. Tiny. Ross Brown, author of the book *Byte-Sized TV* (Michael Wiese Productions, 2011), works with students to create that kind of series. I asked him to describe his process:

"My premise is, this is about series. If you just make a funny video of your cat drinking Jack Daniels or you lip-synching in your bedroom, that's not a series. To be a series it has to have multiple episodes, to have a cast of characters just like a network or cable series, a consistent premise. We do write scripts. I would say half of my book is about the conceptualization and the writing. The aspects of production and postproduction are more part of the show-running, the supervision of the project.

"I insist that my students pitch a story before they write a five-page script. It's just like with a longer show, that's when you discover if you have a faulty premise or a problem with story structure. The same points in your book about knowing what the premise of the series is and understanding the characters and the long narrative — what I call the series question — you have to have that for an Internet series too. You have to know what the overall dramatic tension of the series is.

"Most of what's on now is comedic. People are struggling with how to do drama in very short form because it's difficult to build the tension in three minutes or five minutes. I think *Quarterlife*, which had eight-minute segments, did a pretty good job of it. Part of the principles of *Quarterlife* was that the producers (Marshall Herskovitz and Edward Zwick), had extensive hour television background, so they said, hey, each act is an episode. We do five- and six-act television in hour shows and that's what these episodes are. Clicking on the next episode is like coming back after the commercial.

"The essential questions are consistent: what's a series about, how do you develop a series and characters. But the market and how you market is what will change. The best of what will be on Internet television will still have story structure. It will have some version of Aristotle's beginning, middle, and end. We can't help it. That's the nature of who we are."

WEBISODES

Well, let's say you're neither Joss Whedon nor Herskovitz & Zwick. If creating an entire new Internet drama series is beyond you because you're not rich and powerful (or backed by some entity that is) and you'd actually like to pay your rent, what else is online for a writer? Consider Webisodes. Those are usually original episodes of existing broadcast series, sort of an "added value."

For example, ABC's *Lost*, which aimed for a wide audience, simultaneously played to its Internet viewers. When I spoke with showrunner Damon Lindelof for the Second Edition of this book, he noted: "We have to keep our eye on the mothership at all times and the best ideas will always end up on the show. But we have constructed very elaborate backstories to explain things, and those ideas would never end up on the show because they don't really mean anything to our characters.

"If Jack and Kate were to learn the origin of the numbers, most people wouldn't really care. So we decided let's give the fans who really care about the origin of the numbers the answer. It's a sci-fi-ish technobabbly thing and you can tell that on the Internet. So we constructed this Internet experience of a girl who investigated the Dharma Initiative and had the payoff be another Dharma film in which it was explained. But we could never tell that on the show or your head would spin.

"It's not an alternate universe. It's more like having a compendium besides a text that gives you a deeper understanding. Other mythology-based shows like *X-Files* and *Star Trek* also have a 'canon.' For us, we say we generated this and it is part of the *Lost* universe."

Terry Borst, who writes the monthly "Alt.screen" column for *Written By*, sees the evolvement of eTV (enhanced TV) and ITV (interactive TV) as both a future opportunity for writers and a source of success for shows. "The resurgent interest behind dramatic scripted programming is due not only to great writing but also to the ease in which viewers can interact with each other on the Internet, quickly creating show loyalty, and spread the word to others. As that interactivity carries over to a one-screen television format, the chance to extend and expand the world of a show further increases."

Now most shows have online components. *Dexter* boasts five million fans on Facebook (plus online games), and *Big Love* invited viewers to hear Margene confide her "secrets" about Bill. These made-for-Web episodes offer a sense of personal connection that comes partly from being viewed on your own computer screen, and partly from the feeling of access the viewers have — deciding when to how to receive their visitors.

In writing Webisodes, you'll find some stylistic differences. The *Lost* team said that their writers give a lot of thought to the final viewing platform as it directly informs the action of each Webisode, "This intimate viewing model in which the stories are usually viewed alone on a small screen seemed to us to call out for more intimate, diary-like storytelling. We purposely avoided the more epic action type scenes that fill the network show and used the Webisodes to focus more tightly on the characters."

You might think Webisodes offer break-in opportunities for new writers, and in a few cases staff is added for these non-televised episodes. But it's turning out that the same writers on the regular show are writing the Webisodes too, mostly to keep the quality consistent and because it's difficult for anyone not on staff to know where storylines are heading.

Of course, that doesn't stop anyone from creating fan-based stories (which pre-date the Internet with *Star Trek* novels about escapades of Kirk and Spock that never happened on screen). But if you're producing your own Web show, you're right back to the Joss Whedon paradigm — okay if it's a hobby and you can afford it, but unless you have the super-powers of Buffy the Vampire Slayer, it's probably not a career.

THE WEB IS DEAD

"Chaos isn't a business model."

In August, 2010, *Wired* magazine exploded into the debate about the future with a feature "The Web is Dead. Long Live the Internet." The article offers sophisticated analyses of economic and technical factors by *Wired* Editor-in-Chief Chris Anderson and Contributing Editor and *Vanity Fair* columnist Michael Wolff. If you're interested in that level of information, I commend this article which can easily be found on the "dead" Web.

Here's what's happening: Back in 2001, the top ten websites accounted for 31% of views, but by 2006 the top ten commanded 40%, and by 2010 control by the top ten websites reached 75% and was rising. Investor Uri Milner, who owns ten percent of Facebook, remarked, "Big sucks the traffic out of small." Wolff wrote that this development was "a familiar historical march, both feudal and corporate, in which the less powerful are sapped of their reason for being by the better resourced, organized and efficient — is perhaps the rudest shock possible to the leveled, porous, low-barrier-to-entry ethos of the Internet Age."

So much for the promise to put all content in the cloud and replace the desktop with the webtop. Open, free, and out of control isn't winning over the viewers, after all. Anderson wrote, "The story of industrial revolutions is a story of battles over control. A technology is invented, it spreads, a thousand flowers bloom, and then someone finds a way to own it, locking out others. It happens every time.

"Now it's the Web's turn to face the pressure for profits and the walled gardens that bring them. Openness is a wonderful thing in the non-monetary economy of peer production. But eventually our tolerance for the delirious chaos of infinite competition finds its limits. Much as we love freedom and choice, we also love things that just work, reliably and seamlessly. And if we have to pay for what we love, well, that increasingly seems OK."

What does this mean for you, the writers (known as "content creators" in new media vocabulary)? You can still post anything you want on the Web, where so much is noncommercial. As Anderson noted, "The wide-open Web of peer production, the so-called generative Web where everyone is free to create what they want, continues to thrive, driven by the non-monetary incentives of expression, attention, reputation, and the like. But the notion of the Web as the ultimate marketplace for digital delivery is now in doubt.

"The Internet is the real revolution, as important as electricity; what we do with it is still evolving."

Wolff concluded, "We are returning to a world that already exists — one in which we chase the transformative effects of music and film instead of our brief flirtation with the transformative effects of the Web.

"After a long trip, we may be coming home."

HOME IS THE WHOLE WORLD

EXHIBIT A: *The Walking Dead.*

In November 2010, AMC announced the show's renewal for a second season after ratings that reached more Adults 18-49 than any other show in the history of cable television. Simultaneously, its international distributor FIC (Fox International Channels) announced that the show had record-breaking premiere ratings in 120 countries in Europe, Latin America, Asia, and The Middle East. FIC's international distribution is carried in 35 languages, reaching around 875 million people worldwide. Meanwhile, Americans viewed the show across all platforms including on-air, online, on demand, and mobile. All that is part of "New TV."

But from a writer's viewpoint, the show is entirely traditional. It's an expensive scripted hour drama telling a "long narrative" serial through professional actors, skillfully creating suspense and character conflict, written in the same four-act structure as 20th century network dramas. The showrunner is a multi-credited American movie writer-director and the writing staff has worked on other shows. If you time-traveled from the 1980s to watch *The Walking Dead*, you'd understand how it works.

I mention that not to diminish this successful production but to keep the future in perspective. International distribution is essential to affording shows like this one, and if you're creating a new series, you might keep in mind its potential worldwide appeal. But day-to-day as writers, good work is what it has always been.

EXHIBIT B: *LITTLE YURT ON THE PRAIRIE.*

Yes, that's the real title, and it's not a joke. It's a Chinese adaptation of *Little House on the Prairie* due to premiere in China in 2011. Then there's *CSI: Mumbai*, and *Ordre Public: Intention Criminelle*, the French version of *Law & Order: Criminal Intent*. And so forth, around the world. Of course cross-fertilizing goes in all directions: *In Treatment* came to the U.S. from Israel, *The Office* was British before American, *Ugly Betty* migrated from Mexico, many series, including *Battlestar Galactica*, have been shot in Canada, and global co-productions (too many to list) include major historic series such as *The Tudors* and *The Borgias*.

Rene Balcer, a producer-writer on *Law & Order*, observed in *Written By* magazine, "Welcome to the new electronic Silk Road. Through the ages, commodities like silk, tobacco, salt, and rice, that originated in one specific area, eventually became huge engines of global commerce. The global commodities were adopted to serve their own cultures. With time, these adaptations were themselves traded on the world market. Television series… have now become such a global commodity."

It sounds like ever-more opportunity for creators of shows, especially writers who have multi-national insights or connections. But watch out: the future is not a worldwide Age of "PAX Television" (at least not yet). The kickback is a potential confrontation with distinct cultures who may regard Hollywood as a purveyor of colonialism through entertainment. When Hollywood products integrate themselves into international markets, cultural anxieties and political clashes become part of the debate about cultural trade generally. If you're interested in this subject, you can read more about it in books such as *Globalized Arts: The Entertainment Economy and Cultural Identity* by J.P. Singh (Columbia University Press, 2010).

With that caution in mind, the future looks bright for you. Writers who are skilled in American-style TV storytelling are in demand all over the world, partly to transmit skills in places where TV industries are beginning, and partly to work on American series that are being adapted. In fact, the Second Edition of this book has been translated and published in Germany, China, Korea, Spain and elsewhere to date, and I'm often asked to consult with writers from other countries.

Meanwhile, if you are still trying to create your original series for the Internet, think big — electrons don't know about countries or borders; there's money and audiences beyond the 405 and 10 Freeways in Los Angeles; that's a part of the future I can predict.

RIGHT NOW

In his 1967 book, *The Medium is the Message*, Marshall McLuhan envisioned a world where people were connected not just by what they watched but because they were watching it together — a modern "electronic hearth" that replaced the neighborhood front porch. His idea of television — especially prime-time storytelling — as the heart of a "global village" still resonates.

But most American households now have some form of personal choice when they watch through recording, or watching on demand or online.

McLuhan's vocabulary has morphed into phrases like "time shifting" and "appointment viewing." Beyond choosing when they watch, people are choosing how they watch, and directly influencing what they watch. Ron Moore, who ran *Battlestar Galactica*, said, "It's going to just become 'media,' and it will stop having distinctions that no longer mean anything. TV and computers are going to become the same thing. You're just going to have a box or boxes at your disposal, and you'll put everything on this box ranging from blogs to what we know today as TV shows and movies.

"I think fracturing the audience into various niches is a good thing. When broadcasting meant broad broadcasting, when only the 'Big Three' existed, they had to appeal to a gigantic swath of audience. To hold those huge numbers they had to make the stuff that had the most common denominators. Now, when you break it up into smaller chunks, *Galactica* and shows like *The Shield* can appeal to specific audiences. Critics say it's the Golden Age of TV because of the quality of the shows, but I don't think any of them could have survived in the three-network era. Now the high-quality shows can sustain themselves with dedicated fans who are interested in their particular kind of material."

So where does that leave writers like you? If you've read this book because you hope to create a series of your own, special opportunities lie in narrowly-defined new markets. But for all good writers, opportunities abound. A spec script that has guts and passion and the skill to deliver them professionally will always be useful. And storytellers will be as valued in the coming age as we've been throughout history. Actually, we may be needed even more to define and link cultures that have fractured.

No matter what the delivery system — broadcast, premium cable, basic cable, mobile devices, Google TV, YouTube, Web, or Internet — the creative process starts with you. So now that you've learned what's special about hour drama series, and how TV development works, and what it takes to work on staff, how a script is crafted, and how to approach writing your own episode, and you've even heard how to break in, and what the future may hold — all that adds up to just one moment: when you sit down and start to write. And now that time has come. It's your turn.

Conclusion

Thank you for completing this journey with me.

If you bought the first two editions and are holding the Third Edition in your hand you know that content — writing — is at the core of every form of television, traditional and emerging. Your growth as a writer never ends, and those who are most competitive in this industry are always replenishing their tools and ideas.

If you are new to *Writing the TV Drama Series*, welcome and congratulations! Whether you're a beginner, a pre-professional, or a working writer, producer or director, this book can help guide you in the years ahead. Thousands of readers before you have worked with the earlier editions in film schools (where it is required in many screenwriting classes), in network mentoring programs (where it is also required reading), and one by one as word has spread. I'm always pleased to hear from people who tell me they read the book a few years ago and just landed their first writing assignment or staff position, and went looking for the latest edition to refresh themselves or bolster their confidence before they take their leap. And I've heard that pointers from the craft chapters have been mentioned in writers rooms on major TV shows. So you're in good company.

Resources For You

The Writers Guild of America (WGA), West
www.wga.org
7000 West Third Street
Los Angeles, CA 90048
(323) 951-4000

WGA Intellectual Property Registry
(323) 782-4500
Office is open 9:30 AM to 5:30 PM Monday through Friday.
Drop-off is available 24 hours outside the Guild.

WGA James R. Webb Memorial Library
(323) 782-4544
Located on the first floor of the WGA.
Open to the public to read scripts and view shows.
10 AM to 5 PM, Monday through Friday, and Thursday to 8 PM.
(closed the last Friday of each month)

The Writers Guild of America, East
555 W. 57th Street
New York, NY 10019
(212) 767-7800
(WGA East does not have a script library)

Writers Guilds affiliated with the WGA are located in many countries, for example The Writers Guild of Great Britain and the Writers Guild of New Zealand.

Museum of Television and Radio, West
465 N. Beverly Drive
Beverly Hills, CA 90210
(310) 786-1000
Reading and viewing is free and open to the public,
Noon to 5 PM, Wednesday through Sunday.

Museum of Television and Radio, East

25 W. 52nd Street
New York, NY 10019
(212) 621-6600
$10 admission. Screenings and seminars.
Noon to 6 PM, Tuesday through Sunday.

Academy of Television Arts and Sciences

5220 Lankershim Blvd.
North Hollywood, CA 91601
(818) 754-2800
(The television academy does not have a script library)

GLOSSARY

A–B–C STORIES. Parallel plots within an episode. Stories are denoted by letters (A, B, C, D…). Often each story follows the dramatic arc of one of the continuing cast.

ABOVE-THE-LINE. Production elements at the top of a budget breakdown, usually: producers, directors, writers, and sometimes composer or star. Crew positions are "below-the-line."

ACT. A dramatic unit made of a number of scenes. Network TV hours usually have four acts that build to cliffhangers before commercial breaks, though some have five or six acts. Cable shows which do not have breaks may structure episodes into three or four theoretical acts.

ACTION. In a script, the description below a slug line that tells what is occurring on screen. Also see **DESCRIPTION**.

AGENT. Someone who represents talent. A literary agent advances career opportunities for writers who are signed to him and usually negotiates his clients' deals. Agents are licensed by the state, and receive 10% commissions.

ANTAGONIST. A character whose goal opposes the protagonist's goal. Though sometimes considered the "villain," in quality drama the best opponent is a "worthy antagonist."

ANTHOLOGY. A show whose installments are free-standing and do not have continuing casts, such as *The Twilight Zone*.

ARC. The progression of a character from one condition to a different dramatic state. Example: A character who is cold in the beginning loves someone in the end.

A.T.A.S. Academy of Television Arts and Sciences. Membership organization for all fields of television. Produces the Emmy Awards, among other activities.

ATTACHED. Talent (for example, an actor) is "attached" when that person commits to participating in a proposed show.

BACKDOOR PILOT. A two-hour movie that suggests potential for a series.

BACK NINE. The remaining nine episodes in a traditional 22-week season after the first thirteen are finished. Even if a series is given a full-season order, the **GREENLIGHT** to produce the back nine may depend on how well the first thirteen perform.

BACKSTORY. History before the action on screen, usually incidents or relationships that shaped a character.

BACK-UP SCRIPTS. Extra episodes beyond the pilot that a network orders to assess a show's potential when it is not given a slot on the air, sometimes called back-up pilots.

BASIC CABLE. Television channels available for free to cable subscribers.

BEAT. 1. A scene or step of the story; 2. A pause in dialogue or action.

BEAT SHEET. Also see **OUTLINE**. A list of events (turning points) in the story, often detailed in numbered scenes, though sometimes more generally in sequences or even summaries of entire acts.

BIBLE. A guide to the series, especially for writers and directors joining a show. Includes character biographies, rules for the world of the show, summaries of past episodes, and sometimes what the producers are seeking in tone, style or stories.

BREAKING A STORY. Finding the major turning points (and often act breaks) in a story before writing a detailed outline.

CLIFFHANGER. A suspenseful ending; frequently jeopardy or raised stakes at the act break and end of the season.

CLOSURE. In episodic drama, a story that is complete (arrives at its goal or conclusion) at the end of the hour.

COLD OPENING. See **TEASER**.

CONTINUING CAST. Main characters that return each week and "drive" the core stories in the series.

CREATIVE CONSULTANT. An experienced writer-producer who may oversee, rewrite or write episodes, but might not be a full-time member of the staff.

DAILIES. Unedited scenes screened after each day of production.

DEVELOPMENT. The process of bringing a project from concept to production; also the period when a writer works with producers to refine a script through all revision steps.

DESCRIPTION. The actions, images and sounds on screen, excluding dialogue. See **ACTION**.

DIALOGUE. Everything the characters say that may include expressions (e.g., sighs) and pauses as well as words.

DRAMEDY. A hybrid of drama and comedy.

ELEMENT. Significant talent, such as a producer, director or actors that may be attached to a project to enhance its clout.

EPISODE. In dramatic television, a one hour increment of the season; that week's group of stories. Also an installment of a continuing storyline.

EXECUTIVE PRODUCER. The top writer-producer on a TV series, often responsible for supervising both creative and business aspects of the show, overseeing the cast, crew and writing staff. See also **SHOWRUNNER**.

EXT. Abbreviation for Exterior, used in **SLUG LINES**.

FIRST DRAFT. A script written by the writer before responding to notes from a producer. All **SPEC SCRIPTS** and all drafts before submission are "first drafts," no matter how many times the writer has privately made revisions.

FORMAT. 1. A proposal for a series that may include characterizations, genre, **SPRINGBOARDS** for stories, and suggestions for episodes or a **PILOT**. 2. The structure of a story, which may involve a **FRANCHISE**. 3. The printed style of a script, usually set by screenwriting software.

FRANCHISE. Storytelling categories that generate dramatic situations, such as medical, legal, or detective work. Successful series may also franchise their **FORMAT**, as in *CSI*.

FREELANCE WRITER. A writer who is not on staff and receives an assignment for an episode.

GREENLIGHT. Approval for a script to proceed to production.

GUEST CAST. Actors not in the continuing cast who may appear in a limited number of episodes.

HIATUS. The break between seasons when the entire staff is on vacation.

HOOK. An early action or situation that grabs an audience's attention; also an opening of a pitch.

IN THE CAN. An episode that's ready to air.

INT. Abbreviation for Interior, used in slug lines.

LEGS. A series with legs is capable of generating numerous stories for episodes.

LOCKED. When a producer has approved the final version of an outline or script, it is locked.

LOG LINE. A one-sentence summary of a story; occasionally might be two or three sentences. It quickly conveys the **PREMISE** and the dramatic **ARC** or **PLOT**.

LONG NARRATIVE. Stories that have the depth and range to continue for years, especially in serials.

MANAGER. Similar to **AGENT**, except that managers are not licensed and may represent their clients in areas beyond immediate assignments. Managers typically charge 15%, compared with a 10% commission for agents.

M.B.A. Minimum Basic Agreement, the agreement between the Writers Guild of America and signatories (production entities) that specifies minimum pay, health and pension, and other contractual issues.

MOBISODES. Episodes available on mobile devices such as cell phones. These are usually short but might be bits of series.

OUTLINE. A list of every scene that will appear in the script, in order, beginning with number 1 in each act. Each outline "beat" is like a log line for that scene. However, some shows use outlines that are less specific. An outline is the first paid step in development. Also called **STEP OUTLINE**. See **BEAT SHEET**.

OVERNIGHTS. Quick national ratings that give a preliminary account of how many people watched a show.

PACKAGE. A commitment from actors or a director to **ATTACH** themselves to a show in the effort to make a network or cable deal; also all of the **ELEMENTS** needed to move a **FORMAT** (proposal) forward, which may include a pilot script and **SHOWRUNNER**. Some packaging agencies want to represent all **ABOVE-THE-LINE** personnel.

PICK-UP. A decision by a network or cable outlet to air (or renew) a series.

PILOT. Prototype for a series; usually the first episode.

PITCH. Telling a story to a potential buyer; a sales presentation.

PLOT. The dramatic structure of a story; how a story is executed from premise to resolution.

PLOT POINT. A strong "reversal," or turning point in the story. Plot points may coincide with **CLIFFHANGERS** and **ACT BREAKS**.

POLISH. A minor revision in a script, usually tightening scenes and refining dialogue, or cutting a shooting draft for production.

PREMISE. The inciting question or problem at the beginning; answers "what if?" or "why?"

PREMISE PILOT. Propels a series by placing the main character in a new situation or beginning a quest from which future stories will spring.

PREMIUM CABLE. Television channels available to subscribers for a fee such as HBO and Showtime. They operate without commercial breaks.

PROCEDURALS. Clue-driven series that solve puzzles or mysteries and close at the end of each episode. Examples include *CSI* and *House*.

PRODUCER. Most TV producers are writers whose titles have improved because of experience and credits. Producers may supervise and rewrite other writers. This differs from a line producer who is responsible for physical production.

PRODUCTION. Actually shooting the show, when cameras roll. Sometimes a series described as "in production" includes both preproduction (writing, casting, set-building), and postproduction (editing, music, effects).

PROLOGUE. See **TEASER**.

PROTAGONIST. The character who drives the action and makes key dramatic decisions; the person the audience roots for.

RESIDUALS. Additional payments to writers and other talent when a show reruns.

REWRITE. A significant revision of a script that may include re-structuring and creating new characters and scenes.

SCENE. The smallest dramatic building block, usually a step of the action, or a beat, with complete dramatic structure. In production, it is sometimes defined as the action in a single time and place.

SCENE HEADING. See **SLUG LINE.**

SEASON. A television season encompasses the months a show airs. Though the traditional network season runs September to May, cable and other outlets have different schedules.

SECOND DRAFT. A script that has been rewritten after receiving notes from a producer.

SERIAL. A series whose stories continue across many episodes in which the main cast develops over time.

SHOOTING SCRIPT. The final draft which goes into production.

SHORT ORDER. A **PICK-UP** that commits to airing less than a full season, sometimes only a few episodes of a new show.

SHOWRUNNER. The top **EXECUTIVE PRODUCER** in charge of a series, the one who determines the course of a show and supervises all aspects.

SLUG LINE. Some screenwriting software uses the term **SCENE HEADING.** In a script, **INT.** or **EXT.** is followed by the location of a scene, and time.

SPEC SCRIPT. A speculated screenplay written as a sample or in the hope of being sold. Beginners may write a spec of an existing series to demonstrate their skill.

SPRINGBOARD. A situation in a show that provokes action; aspects of a **FRANCHISE** that provide premises for episodes. Example: In a medical drama, the arrival of a new patient creates a springboard for a story.

STAFF WRITER. The first rung in the ladder of a writing staff, usually a beginner; also called "baby writer."

STEP DEAL. A writing contract which provides "cut offs" after each step of writing. For example, if a writer's outline doesn't work for the show, he may be cut off, not hired to proceed to the first draft.

STORY EDITOR. A member of a series writing staff above **STAFF WRITER** and below **PRODUCER** who writes and rewrites episodes.

SUPERVISING PRODUCER. A high-level writer-producer who may run the writing room.

SYNDICATION. The system of selling television series as packages to groups of stations and foreign markets after a network run is complete, usually requiring at least 88 episodes. A lucrative process that follows a show's first-run broadcast.

TEASER. Also called **PROLOGUE** and **COLD OPENING.** Dramatic material before titles that may or may not be related to the story in the episode which follows, but often does provide a **HOOK** or inciting incident.

TELEPLAY. Screenplay written for television.

TRADES. Daily or weekly newspapers that cover the entertainment industry, mainly *Variety* and *The Hollywood Reporter*.

TREATMENT. A narrative of the film, technically the entire script in prose without dialogue, but often abridged to a short summary.

WEBISODES. Episodes made for Web or Internet distribution. They may be auxiliary episodes of existing shows or original productions.

WRITERS GUILD OF AMERICA. The professional union that represents screenwriters. It has two branches, West (in Los Angeles) and East (in New York City), as well as affiliates in other countries.

About the Author

Pamela Douglas is an award-winning screenwriter with numerous credits in television drama. She was honored with the Humanitas Prize for *Between Mother and Daughter* (CBS), an hour drama that was also nominated for a Writers Guild Award.

She received an Emmy nomination and an NAACP Image Award for writing *Different Worlds,* an hour drama on CBS. Twice, her shows won awards from American Women in Radio and Television — her original drama, *Sexual Considerations,* and her episode of the series *A Year in the Life* (NBC).

As a developer, she wrote the pilot, bible and 13 episodes of the acclaimed PBS series *Ghostwriter.* Additional series credits include *Star Trek: The Next Generation, Frank's Place, Paradise, Trapper John, M.D.,* and many others.

She has been a member of the Board of Directors of the Writers Guild of America.

At the University of Southern California, she is a tenured professor in the School of Cinematic Arts, where she teaches screenwriting.

Ms. Douglas is available for consulting and seminars. Further information and excerpts from previous editions of this book are on her website:

www.PamDouglasBooks.com

or contact: *pamdouglaswords@aol.com.*

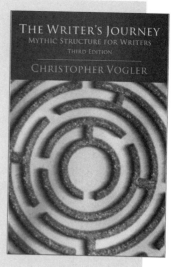

SAVE THE CAT!®
THE LAST BOOK ON SCREENWRITING YOU'LL EVER NEED!

BLAKE SNYDER

BEST SELLER

He's made millions of dollars selling screenplays to Hollywood and now screenwriter Blake Snyder tells all. "Save the Cat!®" is just one of Snyder's many ironclad rules for making your ideas more marketable and your script more satisfying — and saleable, including:
- The four elements of every winning logline.
- The seven immutable laws of screenplay physics.
- The 10 genres and why they're important to your movie.
- Why your Hero must serve your idea.
- Mastering the Beats.
- Mastering the Board to create the Perfect Beast.
- How to get back on track with ironclad and proven rules for script repair.

This ultimate insider's guide reveals the secrets that none dare admit, told by a show biz veteran who's proven that you can sell your script if you can save the cat.

"Imagine what would happen in a town where more writers approached screenwriting the way Blake suggests? My weekend read would dramatically improve, both in sellable/producible content and in discovering new writers who understand the craft of storytelling and can be hired on assignment for ideas we already have in house."
> – From the Foreword by Sheila Hanahan Taylor, Vice President, Development at Zide/Perry Entertainment, whose films include *American Pie, Cats and Dogs, Final Destination*

"One of the most comprehensive and insightful how-to's out there. Save the Cat!® is a must-read for both the novice and the professional screenwriter."
> – Todd Black, Producer, *The Pursuit of Happyness, The Weather Man, S.W.A.T, Alex and Emma, Antwone Fisher*

"Want to know how to be a successful writer in Hollywood? The answers are here. Blake Snyder has written an insider's book that's informative — and funny, too."
> – David Hoberman, Producer, *The Shaggy Dog* (2005), *Raising Helen, Walking Tall, Bringing Down the House, Monk* (TV)

BLAKE SNYDER, besides selling million-dollar scripts to both Disney and Spielberg, was one of Hollywood's most successful spec screenwriters. Blake's vision continues on *www.blakesnyder.com*.

$19.95 · 216 PAGES · ORDER NUMBER 34RLS · ISBN: 9781932907001

MASTER SHOTS
100 ADVANCED CAMERA TECHNIQUES TO GET AN EXPENSIVE LOOK ON YOUR LOW BUDGET MOVIE

CHRISTOPHER KENWORTHY

Master Shots gives filmmakers the techniques they need to execute complex, original shots on any budget. By using powerful master shots and well-executed moves, directors can develop a strong style and stand out from the crowd. Most low-budget movies look low-budget, because the director is forced to compromise at the last minute. *Master Shots* gives you so many powerful techniques that you'll be able to respond, even under pressure, and create knock-out shots. Even when the clock is ticking and the light is fading, the techniques in this book can rescue your film, and make every shot look like it cost a fortune.

Each technique is illustrated with samples from great feature films and computer-generated diagrams for absolute clarity.

Use the secrets of the master directors to give your film the look and feel of a multi-million-dollar movie. The set-ups, moves and methods of the greats are there for the taking, whatever your budget.

"Master Shots *gives every filmmaker out there the blow-by-blow setup required to pull off even the most difficult of setups found from indies to the big Hollywood blockbusters. It's like getting all of the magician's tricks in one book."*
— Devin Watson, Producer, *The Cursed*

"Though one needs to choose any addition to a film book library carefully, what with the current plethora of volumes on cinema, Master Shots *is an essential addition to any worthwhile collection."*
— Scott Essman, Publisher, *Directed By* Magazine

"Christopher Kenworthy's book gives you a basic, no holds barred, no shot forgotten look at how films are made from the camera point of view. For anyone with a desire to understand how film is constructed — this book is for you."
— Matthew Terry, Screenwriter/Director, Columnist
www.hollywoodlitsales.com

Since 2000, CHRISTOPHER KENWORTHY has written, produced, and directed drama and comedy programs, along with many hours of commercial video, tv pilots, music videos, experimental projects, and short films. He's also produced and directed over 300 visual FX shots. In 2006 he directed the web-based Australian UFO Wave, which attracted many millions of viewers. Upcoming films for Kenworthy include *The Sickness* (2009) and *Glimpse* (2011).

$24.95 · 240 PAGES · ORDER NUMBER 91RLS · ISBN: 9781932907513

STORY LINE
FINDING GOLD IN YOUR LIFE STORY

JEN GRISANTI

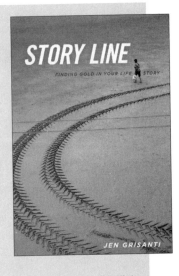

Story Line: Finding Gold in Your Life Story is a practical and spiritual guide to drawing upon your own story and fictionalizing it into your writing. As a Story Consultant and former VP of Current Programs at CBS/Paramount, most of the author's work with writers has focused on creating standout scripts by elevating story. The secret to telling strong story is digging deep inside yourself and utilizing your own life experiences and emotions to connect with the audience. As a television executive, the author asked writers about their personal stories and found that many writers had powerful life experiences, yet had surprisingly never drawn upon these for the sake of their writing because these experiences seemed to hit a little too close to home. This book is about jumping over that hurdle. The goal is not to write a straight autobiographical story which rarely transfers well. Rather, the intention is to dig deep into your well of experience, examine what you have inside, and use it to strengthen your writing. By doing so, you will be able to sell your scripts, find representation, be hired, and win writing competitions.

"Jen Grisanti has spent her entire professional life around writers and writing. Her new book is nothing less than an instruction manual, written from her unique perspective as a creative executive, that seeks to teach neophyte writers how to access their own experiences as fuel for their television and motion picture scripts. It aspires to be for writers what 'the Method' is for actors."

— Glenn Gordon Caron, writer/creator, *Moonlighting, Clean and Sober, Picture Perfect, Love Affair, Medium*

"Jen Grisanti gets to the heart of what makes us want to be storytellers in the first place — to share something of ourselves and touch the spirits of others in the process. Her book is a powerful and compassionate guide to discovering and developing stories that will enable us to connect — with an audience and with each other."

— Diane Drake, writer, *What Women Want, Only You*

JEN GRISANTI is a story consultant, independent producer, and the writing instructor for NBC's Writers on the Verge. She was a television executive for 12 years at top studios. She started her career in television and rose through the ranks of Current Programs at Spelling Television Inc. where Aaron Spelling was her mentor for 12 years.

$26.95 · 250 PAGES · ORDER NUMBER 156RLS · ISBN 13: 9781932907896

THE SCRIPT-SELLNG GAME - 2ND ED.
A HOLLYWOOD INSIDER'S LOOK AT GETTING YOUR SCRIPT SOLD AND PRODUCED

KATHIE FONG YONEDA

The Script-Selling Game is about what they never taught you in film school. This is a look at screenwriting from the other side of the desk — from a buyer who wants to give writers the guidance and advice that will help them to not only elevate their craft but to also provide them with the down-in-the-trenches information of what is expected of them in the script selling marketplace.

It's like having a mentor in the business who answers your questions and provides you with not only valuable information, but real-life examples on how to maneuver your way through the Hollywood labyrinth. While the first edition focused mostly on film and television movies, the second edition includes a new chapter on animation and another on utilizing the Internet to market yourself and find new opportunities, plus an expansive section on submitting for television and cable.

"I've been writing screenplays for over 20 years. I thought I knew it all — until I read The Script-Selling Game. *The information in Kathie Fong Yoneda's fluid and fun book really enlightened me. It's an invaluable resource for any serious screenwriter."*

> — Michael Ajakwe Jr., Emmy-winning TV producer, *Talk Soup*; Executive Director of Los Angeles Web Series Festival (LAWEBFEST); and creator/ writer/director of *Who...* and *Africabby* (AjakweTV.com)

"Kathie Fong Yoneda knows the business of show from every angle and she generously shares her truly comprehensive knowledge — her chapter on the Web and new media is what people need to know! She speaks with the authority of one who's been there, done that, and gone on to put it all down on paper. A true insider's view."

> — Ellen Sandler, former co-executive producer of *Everybody Loves Raymond* and author of *The TV Writer's Workbook*

KATHIE FONG YONEDA has worked in film and television for more than 30 years. She has held executive positions at Disney, Touchstone, Disney TV Animation, Paramount Pictures Television, and Island Pictures, specializing in development and story analysis of both live-action and animation projects. Kathie is an internationally known seminar leader on screenwriting and development and has conducted workshops in France, Germany, Austria, Spain, Ireland, Great Britain, Australia, Indonesia, Thailand, Singapore, and throughout the U.S. and Canada.

$19.95 · 248 PAGES · ORDER NUMBER 161RLS · ISBN 13: 9781932907919

THE COFFEE BREAK SCREENWRITER
WRITING YOUR SCRIPT TEN MINUTES AT A TIME

PILAR ALESSANDRA

BEST SELLER

At last, leading Hollywood screenwriting instructor Pilar Alessandra shows everyone who's ever wanted to write a screenplay how to do it — without quitting their jobs or leaving their families. Packed with over sixty 10-minute writing tools, *The Coffee Break Screenwriter* keeps it focused and keeps it simple. Now, writers can make real progress on their scripts with only ten minutes of stolen time.

The writer receives guidance and tips at every stage of the often intimidating writing process with a relaxed, "ten minutes at a time" method that focuses the writer and pushes him or her forward. At each step, writers are encouraged to "Take Ten" and tackle an element of their scripts using the templates and tools provided. "What You've Accomplished" sections help writers review their progress. And "Ten Minute Lectures" distill and demystify old-school theory, allowing the writer to unblock and keep writing.

"I had a 'first-draft paperweight' on my desk for months. With Pilar's help, my scripts have transformed from desk clutter into calling cards. I've been hired by Warner Bros., signed with ICM, and am a new member of the WGA. I can honestly say that I wouldn't be in the position I am today if it weren't for Pilar."

> — Bill Birch, writer of *Shazam*, Warner Bros.

"Pilar's techniques not only fine-tune your draft but serve as lessons that stick with you and make you a better writer overall. I highly recommend her if you want to take your writing to the next level!"

> — Monica Macer, staff writer *Prison Break* and *Lost*; former creative executive
> Disney Studios

PILAR ALESSANDRA is the director of the Los Angeles writing program "On the Page," which has helped thousands of screenwriters write and develop their feature and television scripts. She's worked as Senior Story Analyst for DreamWorks and Radar Pictures and has trained writers at ABC/Disney, MTV/Nickelodeon, the National Screen Institute, the Los Angeles Film School, The UCLA Writers Program, and more. Her students and clients have sold to Disney, DreamWorks, Warner Brothers, and Sony and have won prestigious competitions such as the Austin Film Festival Screenplay Competition and the Nicholl Fellowship. See her website at *www.onthepage.tv*

$24.95 · 280 PAGES · ORDER NUMBER 149RLS · ISBN 13: 9781932907803

THE MYTH OF MWP

In a dark time, a light bringer came along, leading the curious and the frustrated to clarity and empowerment. It took the well-guarded secrets out of the hands of the few and made them available to all. It spread a spirit of openness and creative freedom, and built a storehouse of knowledge dedicated to the betterment of the arts.

The essence of the Michael Wiese Productions (MWP) is empowering people who have the burning desire to express themselves creatively. We help them realize their dreams by putting the tools in their hands. We demystify the sometimes secretive worlds of screenwriting, directing, acting, producing, film financing, and other media crafts.

By doing so, we hope to bring forth a realization of 'conscious media' which we define as being positively charged, emphasizing hope and affirming positive values like trust, cooperation, self-empowerment, freedom, and love. Grounded in the deep roots of myth, it aims to be healing both for those who make the art and those who encounter it. It hopes to be transformative for people, opening doors to new possibilities and pulling back veils to reveal hidden worlds.

MWP has built a storehouse of knowledge unequaled in the world, for no other publisher has so many titles on the media arts. Please visit www.mwp.com where you will find many free resources and a 25% discount on our books. Sign up and become part of the wider creative community!

Onward and upward,

Michael Wiese
Publisher/Filmmaker